Shame and Sexuality

The experience of shame is a profound, painful and universal emotion with lasting effects on many aspects of public life and human culture. Rooted in childhood experience, linked to sexuality and the cultural norms that regulate the body and its pleasures, shame is uniquely human. *Shame and Sexuality* explores elements of shame in human psychology and the cultures of art, film, photography and textiles.

This volume is divided into two distinct sections allowing the reader to compare and contrast the psychoanalytic and the cultural writings. Part I, Psychoanalysis, provides a psychoanalytic approach to shame, using clinical examples to explore the function of unconscious fantasies, the shame shield in child sexual abuse, and the puzzling manner in which shame attaches itself to sexuality. Part II, Visual Culture, is illustrated throughout with textual analysis; contributors explore shame and sexuality in art history, politics and contemporary visual culture, including the gendering of shame, shame and abjection, and the relationship between shame and shamelessness as a strategy of resistance.

Claire Pajaczkowska and Ivan Ward bring together debates within and between the discourses of psychoanalysis and visual culture, generating new avenues of enquiry for scholars of culture, theory and psychoanalysis.

Claire Pajaczkowska is Reader in Psychoanalysis and Visual Culture at the School of Arts and Education, Middlesex University, London.

Ivan Ward is Director of Learning at the Freud Museum, London.

Shame and Sexuality

Psychoanalysis and visual culture

Edited by Claire Pajaczkowska
and Ivan Ward

Routledge
Taylor & Francis Group

LONDON AND NEW YORK

First published 2008
by Routledge
27 Church Road, Hove, East Sussex BN3 2FA

Simultaneously published in the USA and Canada
by Routledge
270 Madison Ave, New York, NY 10016

Routledge is an imprint of the Taylor & Francis Group, an Informa business

Typeset in Times by
RefineCatch Limited, Bungay, Suffolk
Printed and bound in Great Britain by
TJ International Ltd, Padstow, Cornwall
Paperback cover design by Design Deluxe

British Library Cataloguing in Publication Data
A catalogue record for this book is available from the British Library

Library of Congress Cataloging-in-Publication Data
Shame and sexuality : psychoanalysis and visual culture / edited by
Claire Pajaczkowska and Ivan Ward.
        p. cm.
    Includes bibliographical references and index.
        ISBN 978–0–415–42011–2 (hardback) – ISBN 978–0–415–42012–9 (pbk.)
1. Shame. 2. Sex. 3. Psychoanalysis. 4. Arts. I. Pajaczkowska, Claire.
II. Ward, Ivan.
        BF575.S45S49 2008
        152.4′.4 – dc22

                                                                    2007027952

ISBN: 978–0–415–42011–2 (hbk)
ISBN: 978–0–415–42012–9 (pbk)

Contents

Notes on contributors

Pennina Barnett teaches Critical Studies in the Visual Arts Department at Goldsmiths, University of London, and writes on contemporary visual culture. She was co-founder and co-editor of *Textile: The Journal of Cloth and Culture*, international peer review journal (Berg Publishers, Oxford, UK), and recently co-edited a special issue on String (with Claire Pajaczkowska). She is writing a book about cloth as a multidimensional metaphor for subjectivity, materiality, process and language. Her research is also concerned with postcolonial theory and themes of exile, memory and loss, and she has written extensively on the work of artist Chohreh Feyzdjou.

Suzannah Biernoff is a senior lecturer in the School of History of Art, Film and Visual Media at Birkbeck, University of London, with research interests in war and visual culture, histories of emotion and perception, and representations of embodiment. Her recent publications include *Sight and Embodiment in the Middle Ages* (Palgrave, 2002), and 'Carnal Relations: Embodied Sight in Merleau-Ponty, Roger Bacon and St Francis' (*Journal of Visual Culture*, April 2005). She is currently working on a book on the visual culture of First World War Britain. Focusing in particular on representations and perceptions of injury, disfigurement and death, her work connects with methodological debates in the history of medicine and new military history, and offers a new perspective on the relationship between war, propaganda and censorship.

Donald Campbell is a training analyst, past President of the British Psychoanalytical Society, and former Secretary General of the International Psychoanalytical Association. He worked for 30 years at the Portman Clinic, a National Health Service outpatient facility offering psychoanalytic psychotherapy for children, adolescents and adults who are delinquent, or violent, or suffer from a perversion. He has written extensively on the subjects of violence, suicide, child sexual abuse, perversion and adolescence.

Ranjana Khanna is an associate professor in the Department of English and

Margaret Taylor Smith Director of Women's Studies at Duke University. She teaches and conducts research in the areas of psychoanalytic, postcolonial, and feminist theory and literature. She is the author of *Dark Continents: Psychoanalysis and Colonialism* (Duke University Press, 2003), and *Algeria Cuts: Women and Representation, 1830 to the Present* (Stanford University Press, 2007).

Amna Malik lectures in Art History and Theory at the Slade School of Fine Art, London. Her research is on 'diaspora' in artistic practices and the relationship between art, cultural politics and psychoanalysis. Publications include 'Patterning Memory: Ellen Gallagher's "Icthyosaurus" at the Freud Museum', *Wasafari* (2006) and 'Surface Tension, Reconsidering Horizontality Through the Practices of Contemporary Iranian Diaspora Artists' in J. Harris (ed.) *Identity Theft*, Liverpool University Press (2007).

Phil Mollon PhD is a psychoanalyst (Institute of Psychoanalysis), psychotherapist (Tavistock Society) and clinical psychologist. His writings have included the clinical areas of trauma, narcissism, shame, the work of Heinz Kohut, and the interface between psychoanalysis and innovative therapies such as EMDR and Thought Field Therapy. He is head of psychology and psychotherapy services for an NHS service in Hertfordshire. Publications include *Multiple Selves, Multiple Voices: Working with Trauma, Violation and Dissociation* (1996), *Shame and Jealousy: The Hidden Turmoils* (2002) and *Remembering Trauma: A Psychotherapist's Guide to Memory and Illusion* (paperback 2002).

Claire Pajaczkowska is Reader in Psychoanalysis and Visual Culture at Middlesex University's School of Arts and Education and Director of Programmes in the History of Art and Design. Publications include *Feminist Visual Culture* (ed. 2000) and *Perversion* (2000). Her recent research as Leverhulme Research Fellow is on the sublime and sublimation in popular culture. Recent essays include 'On Humming: Marion Milner's Contribution to British Psychoanalysis' in *Winnicottian Perspectives in Psychoanalysis* ed L. Caldwell (2007), 'Thread of Attachment' in *String* a special issue of: *Textile: The Journal of Cloth and Culture* (Berg 2007), 'Urban Memory/Suburban Oblivion' in *Memory and the Modern City* ed. M. Crinson (2005).

Malcolm Pines is a former consultant psychotherapist at the Tavistock Clinic, and the Maudsley, St George's and Cassel Hospitals. A past President of the International Association of Group Psychotherapy and a Founder Member of the Institute of Group Analysis, London, he is Editor of the International Library of Group Analysis and former Editor of the journal *Group Analysis*. His collected papers have been published as *Circular Reflections* (Jessica Kingsley Publications) and he is the author of many papers on psychoanalysis and group analysis.

Griselda Pollock is Professor of Social and Critical Histories of Art and Director of CentreCATH at the University of Leeds. Author of works on international feminist cultural theory and visual analysis, she is currently working on trauma and cultural memory, psychoanalysis and aesthetics and the concentrationary imaginary in culture. Recent books include *Psychoanalysis and the Image* (2004), *Museums after Modernism* (2007) and *Encountering Eva Hesse* (2006). Forthcoming are *Encounters in the Virtual Feminist Museum* (Routledge) and *Theatre of Memory: Charlotte Salomon and Allothanatography* (Yale).

Ana-María Rizzuto, MD is an Argentina-born psychoanalyst in private practice in Brookline, MA, USA. She is a Training and Supervising Analyst at The Psychoanalytic Institute of New England, East (PINE) and was a Clinical Professor in Psychiatry at Tufts University Medical School until 1991. Dr Rizzuto is the author of *The Birth of the Living God: A Psychoanalytic Study* (1979), and *Why did Freud Reject God: A Psychodynamic Interpretation* (1998). She co-authored with W.W. Meissner and Dan H. Buie *The Dynamics of Human Aggression: Theoretical Foundations and Clinical Applications* (2004), and is the author of numerous articles on language in psychoanalysis, aggression, the clinical situation, psychodynamics of religion, and other subjects.

Penny Siopis is Associate Professor in Fine Arts at Wits University, Johannesburg, and one of the most influential artists working in South Africa today. Her career, spanning 30 years, includes her ironical 'history' paintings of the 1980s that critiqued apartheid through questions of race and gender representation in public history, and installations and films that explore personal memory in the post-apartheid era. Siopis' explorations of the psychology of shame in her exhibition at the Freud Museum in 2005 engaged global concerns and reflected her broader interest in 'a poetics of vulnerability'.

Ivan Ward is the Director of Education at the Freud Museum and manager of the Public Programme of talks and conferences. He has written on psychoanalysis and social theory, including essays on race and racism, 'ecological madness' and 'adolescent fantasies and the horror film genre'. Publications include *The Presentation of Case Material in Clinical Discourse* (ed. 1997), *The Psychology of Nursery Education* (ed. 1998), *Introducing Psychoanalysis* (2000), *Phobia* (2001) and *Castration* (2003), the latter two published in the Ideas in Psychoanalysis Series of which he is series editor.

Clifford B. Yorke, who died in June 2007, was a psychiatrist and psychoanalyst with children and adults, and a training analyst of the British Psychoanalytical Society. For many years he worked closely with Anna Freud at the Hampstead Clinic, first as psychiatrist in charge and then as her successor as co-director of the clinic from 1977 to 1987. He took a major part in the clinic's research and in his later years took an active interest in the developing links between psychoanalysis and neuroscience. Hugely respected among his colleagues, his published works include some 60 professional papers and three books including (with Stanley Wiseberg and Thomasa Freeman) *Development and Psychopathology: Studies in Psychoanalytic Psychiatry* (1989).

Note on references

In bibliographic references S.E. refers to *The Standard Edition of the Complete Psychological Works of Sigmund Freud*, translated from the German under the General Editorship of James Strachey, Volumes 1–24, London: Hogarth Press 1953–1973.

Introduction

Shame, sexuality and visual culture

Claire Pajaczkowska and Ivan Ward

It is a century since Sigmund Freud wrote the *Three Essays on the Theory of Sexuality* and it is still the most difficult of his works to assimilate. Starting from an investigation of the perversions, Freud describes the infantile elements of sexuality that coalesce into various adult forms, and the amnesia that suppresses awareness of the emotions and fantasies that are attached to these bodily sensations. In the developing mosaic of sexuality as Freud conceives it, shame has a pivotal role, acting as a counterweight to sexual expression and, in Freud's hydraulic/electrical metaphor, directing inchoate sexual currents into particular channels or paths. He suggests, at times, that shame is an innate human reaction to infantile sexual drives, as if the infantile drives, left unmoderated, threaten to overwhelm the subject or fragment its fragile sense of cohesion. Like anxiety, to which it has been compared, shame offers a foretaste of the psychic catastrophe that may lie in wait unless the instincts are 'tamed' (Freud 1937).

Of particular interest to the present volume, Freud argues that shame has an especially close relationship to scopophilia – visual pleasure – which is object related from the beginning. Thus shame, the most painfully isolating of emotions, announces the presence of another, the person who shames us and the person before whom we are ashamed, and as such it is one of the earliest of human social feelings. Darwin identified blushing as 'the most peculiar and the most human of all expressions' (Darwin 1872: 309) and noted that 'under a keen sense of shame there is a strong desire for concealment' (p. 320) Unlike disgust and morality, with which it is often coupled in Freud's book, shame exists in this double register of self-consciousness-with-others. This would suggest that shame is of considerable significance and interest to both visual culture and psychoanalysis, and yet the literature of shame is small. The chapters here survey this little-explored terrain and reflect on the meaning of shame and sexuality in both discourses, post-Freud.

The chapters on visual culture by Griselda Pollock, Penny Siopis, Amna Malik, Pennina Barnett, Ranjana Khanna, Suzannah Biernoff and Claire Pajaczkowska were written specifically for this project, as were the psycho-analytic essays by Phil Mollon and Donald Campbell. The chapters by

Clifford Yorke, Ana María Rizzuto and Malcolm Pines have been selected from three different professional journals as key writings on the psycho-analysis of shame. The psychoanalytic essays use material from clinical prac-tice in their exploration of shame and provide a paradigm that includes developments in the theory of pre-Oedipal subjectivity and narcissism. Else-where, Mervin Glasser has suggested that 'primitive anxieties concerned with the obliteration of both object and self, usually reached only after many years of analysis, show us that what is regarded as the distinctive feature of narcis-sistic disorders, namely shame, is part of a defensive structure concerned with the exclusion from consciousness and action of extreme violence and intoler-able guilt' (Glasser 1992: 502). Over time the affect of shame can be resolved into more elementary energies and processes that are inferred from the words spoken and fantasies revealed in analysis. Using the hard-won resources of clinical practice the psychoanalytic essays can add considerably to the anal-ytic methods currently employed in academic, scholarly research into cul-ture.[1] Conversely, the study of visual culture may enable psychoanalysts to reconsider the significance of the part played by sight, visual fantasy and iconic representation in the earliest phases of the construction of the self, and the wider significance of shame in everyday life. We encourage readers to make their own connections between the psychoanalytic and cultural discourses. The effect of an appropriate psychoanalytic interpretation, like the effect of a great work of culture, can be profound and liberating, reaching through to experiences that have remained unvoiced and inarticulate. It is in order to give recognition to the powerful effects of shame that have remained unacknow-ledged in our culture and psyche that we offer these essays to the reader.

The confluence of shame, sexuality and vision may be said to lie at the heart of the psychoanalytic project. When Sophocles wrote:

> Marriages accursed
> That gave us birth and, having borne us, gave
> The same seed in return, that since have made
> Fathers and sons and brothers all in one,
> Incestuous brood of mothers, wives, and brides,
> A deed most shameful among all mankind.[2]

he wrote of the complexity of human sexuality as it is expressed in the nexus of family relationships. The shameful 'deed' is the fulfilment of Oedipal fan-tasies that threaten to dissolve differences between generations and to fuse ties of consanguinity with those of sexual desire. Sight is implicated even before the deed itself. It might be said that the blind seer Tiresias, the Delphic oracle who foretold the Oedipal crimes of parricide and incest, embodies the monstrous destiny of the hero who blinds himself when, with the perspec-tive of hindsight, he 'sees' his deeds. This project offers an opportunity to reconsider the Oedipal and pre-Oedipal dynamics of shame and sexuality and to investigate how traces of infantile sexuality and affective life manifest themselves in visual culture. We are not aiming for an homogeneous approach; differences within and between the discourses of psychoanalysis and visual culture are here maintained in order to encourage dialogue and discover if it is through knowledge of the 'other' that we can fulfil the injunction of the Delphic oracle: Know Thyself.

Shame and abjection

It is not an object, not even a coherent object of study. Shame, which is the greater part of the experience of abjection, begins precisely where words fail us and where the difference between self and not-self ceases to exist (Kristeva 1982). Abjection is, as psychoanalyst Julia Kristeva suggests, the place at which the origins of self are found in the act of differing from 'mother', so that anything that threatens to revoke or dissolve that difference invokes abjection. In the loss of difference there is the visceral, somatic state that eludes symbolization and, therefore, language. Shame is implicated in the first self-conscious experience and the first experience of self-consciousness, since it is through the mirroring look of the mother, and the equally necessary aversion of her gaze, that the nascent self is brought into being. The result is a lifelong dependence on the regard, and more especially the depreciation, of others.

It is in differing from its environment that the self first becomes an object of consciousness, expressed as a fantasy of being a visible object, located in spatial terms, 'out there'. Because it is experienced at the threshold of self and not-self, of object and abject, shame is of especial interest to us. We can be overwhelmed with shame and self-consciousness if we are scrutinized too closely, or if we are ignored. Given its psychological origins in the earliest stages of human development shame retains something of the all-pervading, indistinct quality of those primitive states of mind. The state of being ashamed is one that is experienced as without boundaries, it seems eternal, endless and global. It seems to pervade all the self and, since it appears to arrive from without, brings with it an experience of an 'elsewhere', a space of otherness from which one is visible, exposed and thus acutely helpless. This experience of shame is one which, Donald Campbell suggests, is circumvented by the erection of a 'shame shield', a barrier between the fragile self and the shaming intrusiveness of the outside world. Shame is experienced when our competence and effectiveness in the external world breaks down, and with the dissolution of this boundary between external and internal worlds we are threatened with the dissolution of other important differences. There are the boundaries between masculine and feminine, between self and other, between the inner world and outer reality which threaten to dissolve, leaving the self exposed to the psychotic anxiety beneath.

Malcolm Pines explores the differences between shame and guilt. Unlike guilt, directed at an internal object, the agony of shame is one that exists throughout the whole exterior surface of the self, giving meaning to the descriptions of shame as being 'flayed alive', and to the physical symptoms of blushing, of wanting to hide and turning away or averting one's gaze. Denial, the common defence, casts shame into oblivion, invisibility, and often projects it on to an 'other', who is then punished for bearing this stigma or mark of shamefulness. This characteristic of shame as located at the visible interface between an 'interior' self and an 'outside' makes it significant to visual culture. The proliferation of named and 'authorized' differences that arise within the visible threshold between self and its others, and the complex interaction between the visible differences of sex, gender, race and culture are analysed here by Griselda Pollock, Suzannah Biernoff, Penny Siopis, Amna Malik, Pennina Barnett and Ranjana Khanna. The concept of the gaze as an unconscious structure that informs the logic of visual culture has generated a distinctive approach to understanding contemporary visual artefacts and their uses, and the essays collected here acknowledge this work. Some extend it to investigate the sexual imagination of the history of empire and power, bringing new psychoanalytic horizons and theoretical formulations to the topic.

When we describe abjection as that which lies beyond and before words, we invoke the world of verbal language, words in syntax: thought, spoken or written. Because of its agency in the formation of the earliest, preverbal representations of the self, shame refers us to a relationship to representation based on iconic signs and visual, spatial logic that precedes the word and its syntactic language of time and grammatical subject. The world of iconic representation, which shares some of the structures of 'primary process thinking', is one in which the difference between matter and meaning has not yet been securely established for the subject. When matter merges into meaning the propriety of language is contaminated with its elemental 'stuff'. When meaning dissolves into matter the feared loss of boundary precipitates the subject into a vertiginous slide downwards towards the degradation of indifference.

When our symbolic borders are dissolved or transgressed the violence done to our sense of order threatens us with debasement. In her well-known study *Purity and Danger* (1965), anthropologist Mary Douglas describes this transgression of symbolic borders as our experience of 'contamination', and defines the objectification of this feeling as 'dirt'. The many anxieties that are produced by the fear of contamination by dirt give rise to complex rituals and taboos, the observance and repetition of which are believed to have magical powers of cleansing, cure, salvation or restoration of symbolic boundaries. Referring to Mary Douglas's work, Julia Kristeva concludes: 'The function of these religious rituals is to ward off the subject's fear of his very own identity sinking irretrievably into the mother' (Kristeva 1982: 64).

Working in America, psychoanalyst Ana-María Rizzuto presents her analysis and treatment of the unconscious sense of shame as it appeared in dream, transference and unconscious fantasy of a 'borderline' male patient. This painstaking investigation into the psychic specificity of fantasy offers scholars of culture an opportunity to reconsider the nature of the relationship between the experience of shame and its manifestations in symptomatic and encoded forms. The investigation into the specificity of visual, iconic signification, and the inquiry into the spatial relationships of proximity and distance generated by iconic representation, is one that characterizes many of the essays in this volume.

Shame and the ideal ego

Clifford Yorke notes that shame becomes inflected, through developmental stages, with the meanings that the ego attaches to bodily functions and mental contents. The disgust that Freud notes as the inhibiting counterpoint to oral appetite will also become part of the shame complex as it is transformed by anal, phallic and genital stages of development. Auto-erotic and narcissistic aspects of shame will be supplemented by determinants from the two-person and three-person relationship, with language, social convention, ritual obligations and rules of etiquette providing additional opportunities for development and complexity. In the aptly titled *Many Faces of Shame* psychiatrist and editor Donald Nathanson writes: 'The mature emotion shame evolves from a myriad life experiences, different for each developing child, summating eventually to form the particular kind of shame experience characteristic for each adult' (1987: 23).

Despite significant differences in the respective theories of pre-Oedipal development, psychoanalysts seem to agree that shame differs from guilt. If guilt corresponds to an attack upon the ego by the superego, with its compacted network of abstract moral dichotomies – good and bad, right and wrong, correct and incorrect, true and false – shame is more often spoken of as a failure of the ego to reach a narcissistic ideal. The prototype of this is an infantile attempt at mastery or communication (with the mother, say) that falls short of its intended goal, leaving the subject feeling humiliated, bereft and overwhelmed by a sense of inadequacy. Soon the approval and disapproval of authority figures are brought into the equation, and the determinants of shame become progressively internalized. One historical example of the difference between shame and guilt is to be found in the account given by psychoanalyst Martin Wangh of the Nazi war trials, in which Eichmann was being tried for the part he played in the Third Reich. Day after day, in 1960, Eichmann listened to lists of the atrocities he committed, without displaying any signs of interest or discomfort. However, when told that he had failed to comply with courtroom etiquette by not standing when the judge entered the room he became visibly distressed, blushed, stammered and was embarrassed to have been seen as breaching codes of deference to authority. Wangh identifies this absence of an active superego or moral sense, which is replaced by an exaggerated ideal ego or sense of propriety, as an indication of a regressed psychopathology (Wangh 1964).

Reflecting on the burden of shame suffered by survivors of persecution, Bruno Bettelheim and Primo Levi write of not having had the courage to speak, to bear witness (Agamben 1999). Beneath the ethics of justice and morality there is the 'grey zone' described by Primo Levi in which it is difficult to distinguish guilt from shame. If the shame of the survivor circulates around the idea of having 'taken the place of another, or one who did not survive' this seems to bear out the hypothesis that shame is experienced in relation to a pre-Oedipal relationship such as that of the unconscious aggression between siblings rather than the Oedipal guilt that accompanies unconscious parricidal fantasies. Eichmann killed hundreds of thousands, but he never managed, in fantasy, to kill the one that mattered. Rather, the victims of his crimes might better be seen as sacrifices to the still-living father, who occupied the place of the ego ideal.

The blind spot, the vanishing point and the stain

The metaphor of *scotoma* as the psychic 'blind spot' derives its meaning from Freud's theory of fetishism, which proposes that fetishism is both a sexual act and system of 'knowledge' and belief predicated on the unconscious logic of syntax: 'I know, but nevertheless . . .'; a disavowal which implies knowledge of the very thing disavowed. What is denied in fetishism is the infantile observation of mother's sexual difference, an observation that leads to the 'unbelievable' idea of castration as the cause of such difference and loss of the illusion of infantile omnipotence. 'Eventually all children must accept the fact that they will never possess both genders and will forever be only half of the sexual constellation,' says Joyce McDougall, a circumstance she describes as 'a scandalous affront to infantile megalomania' (1995: xiv). For his own part, Freud identified a schism that sets in the ego; conflicting ego functions of observation and belief cause the self to deny evidence of sight and data of observation and to maintain faith in the illusion. Where sensory data perceives reality, the evidence of the senses is denied and the belief that preceded investigation is restored, defensively, in the construction of a fetish or fetishistic ritual. The restored belief nevertheless betrays signs of the very trauma that led to its return, and scotoma, the vision denied, develops in the form of a perverse logic that denies reality in the service of self-preservation. If castration comes to represent the ultimate humiliation, the scotoma is the blindness to the self that enables the subject to disavow the experience of shame. At the same time, in the play of acknowledgement and denial, it becomes the stain or spot that must be excised. Shame is then a stain on the immaculate self, a stain which makes the experience of self-consciousness one of an introversion of the gaze.[3] Here we think also of Julia Kristeva's contention, in the *Revolution of Poetic Language* (1984), that modernist textuality is a revelation of the repressed semiotic 'chora' of feminine-maternal embodiment which classic realism occludes in order to create the perfect illusion of transparency. The stain, spot or macula betrays the illusion of Immaculate Conception.

Shame, as the emotion of self-knowledge, becomes particularly significant in the art of the Renaissance, the historical birth of the 'modern' human subject within the western episteme. It is at this time that we find visual evidence of a perspectival geometry that allows painters to create, simultaneously, an illusion of three dimensionality within the frame, and an optical vanishing point that infers the position of a potential spectator before the frame. The spectator is an embodied and unified subject, for whose gaze the painting's composition is organized. The polytheistic culture of classical antiquity is recovered through the optical logic of monotheistic, Mediaeval Christianity and the art of the Renaissance shows the long process of integrating these two traditions, as two parts of the subject. The imaginary omniscience offered by Renaissance iconography is accompanied by an invisible spectator for whom the world is organized as meaningful and optically three-dimensional. This optical logic becomes distorted with Baroque and Mannerist perspectives, such as in the tortuous and seductive *contraposto* figures in Counter Reformation composition. However, the Renaissance perspective continues to be the basis of the art of western Europe until the Modernisms of the early twentieth century assert a challenge to the Renaissance concept of the human subject. Might post-Renaissance European realism, with its optical organization of meaning conferring mastery and immobility on the spectator, be a defence against shame or against activities that might lead to shame if they were allowed to be expressed? What libidinal forces are 'tamed' in the construction of the new aesthetic ideal?[4]

As Modernist art began to explore the power of culture to uphold and to dissolve the boundaries between external and internal reality, between self and other, subject and text, masculine and feminine, image and language, matter and thought, the twentieth century brought an accelerated awareness of history to the western episteme. Freud's theory is central to this twentieth-century transformation of the concept of the subject. With the first and most explicit description of the mind as dynamically structured through conscious and unconscious systems of thought, the Freudian revolution initiated a seismic shock more powerful than the Copernican or Darwinian revolutions, to which Freud compared it, because it spoke directly to the consciousness of every human subject. Whereas the heliocentric theory of the universe might be considered a matter for astronomers or theologians, and the Darwinian theory of evolution could be thought of as the concern of biologists and palaeontologists, the insights of psychoanalysis – articulated first, let us remember, in a book about dreams – threatened to remove every hiding place and to reveal to all the 'secrets' of the soul. The significance of shame is an unavoidable effect of Freud's stratified conception of the mind and his radical adoption of the maxim that the child is father to the adult:

> A child's play is determined by wishes: in point of fact by a single wish –
> one that helps in his upbringing – the wish to be big and grown up. He is
> always playing at being 'grown up', and in his games he imitates what he
> knows about the lives of his elders. He has no reason to conceal this wish.
> With the adult, the case is different. On the one hand, he knows that he
> is expected not to go on playing or phantasying any longer, but to act in
> the real world; on the other hand, some of the wishes which give rise to
> his phantasies are of a kind which it is essential to conceal. Thus he is
> ashamed of his phantasies as being childish and as being unpermissible.
> (Freud 1908: 146)

That sexuality became the icon of the shameful hidden unconscious alerts us to its visibility and its availability to fantasy; the exponential growth of pornography through the privatized world of the internet can be a surprise to no one and, indeed, could have constituted the entire subject matter of this book. That the theory of infantile sexuality remains unassimilated after a century of dissemination alerts us to the more difficult, more obscure and unknown reality of our earliest emotional relationships and states of infancy.

European traditions of painting have evolved an optical logic of imaginary mastery, and have developed a culture of modernist, avant-garde, authorial primacy. Other arts, such as the textile arts, have retained their 'other' status, embodying the tactile and the corporeal, and challenging the logic of optics with an emphasis on the 'haptic gaze'. Pennina Barnett has explored the significance of the differences between the optical and the haptic in relation to cultures of masculinity and femininity. Whereas the logic of the gaze implies that there can be a difference, and even an opposition, between active and passive forms of experience, the logic of touch refutes this opposition, as touching is always, simultaneously, being touched by. This reversibility of active and passive experience refers us to earliest relationships between infant and mother, and seems to have a neurological substrate; when sight is deployed from close up there is an activation of the neurone receptors for touch, which accounts for the almost 'synaesthesic' experience of textiles. The significance of textile, touch and smell as offering a solution to the paradox of 'proximity to' and 'control over' is evident in adult fetishism and children's 'transitional objects' (Winnicott 1953).

In her essay on the 'stain' in the work of a number of textile artists, Pennina Barnett explores the variety of meanings imbricated in the relation of cloth to corporeal experience. Her analysis of a text by Verdi Yehuda shows how the folktale of the Goose Girl who receives, from her mother, a handkerchief with three spots of blood, is a narrative form of consciousness of shame at loss of infantile omnipotence and entry into a world of 'adult' sexual difference.

Cloth absorbs moisture in a way that condenses tears and blood. Tears of grief at loss and maternal separation with blood that is the icon of the wounds in which the physical barrier that demarcates the body's inside from its outside is breached. Blood made symbolically visible as stain also bears the meaning of menstrual blood, the indication of menarche and another Oedipal separation of mother and daughter as they are united in adult womanhood. The shameful stains and shameful pains of loss are both revealed and revoked in the relationship of the artist to her work. Textile artists, Barnett notes, have used techniques of staining, blotting, tearing and mending in ways that suggest the importance of shame, hiding and revealing, in our relation to the haptic and to touch.

Man's averted gaze and woman's covered body

Images of the gendering of shame are fascinating and revealing. Masaccio shows us the gender dimorphism of Renaissance Europe in which man is the bearer of the gaze and woman is its object. When the ego ideal makes its appearance in the form of God's presence the human couple becomes aware of their nakedness and ashamed. But the shame is attributed differently to each of them. He hides his eyes and she hides her breasts and pubic hair. This difference corresponds to another, more archaic difference in the etymology of the words for shame in all Indo-European languages. Within the antithetical concept that fuses shame and honour, there are two ways in which shame is described. The first is active and unambiguous, usually associated with uninflected 'bad' states. The second is the allied concepts relating to modesty and humility, as virtues deriving from the raw experience of shame in the former sense. The 'raw' meaning of shame is attributed to masculinity and agency whereas the cultural version of shame that has become acculturated is attributed to femininity and passivity. Seeing is the agency of shaming, whereas being seen is the condition for modesty or being seen as shameful.

Another example of gender difference is made by a character in Salman Rushdie's *Shame* (1995). Brought up in social isolation, the hero Omar Khayyam is forbidden by his three 'mothers' to feel shame – an emotion he has never experienced – when he is finally allowed out into the world. ' "What does it feel like?" he asked – and his mothers, seeing his bewilderment, essayed explanations. . . . "It makes women feel like to cry and die," said Chhunni-ma, "but men, it makes them go wild" ' (Rushdie 1995: 39) The example of so-called 'honour killings' shows just how wild men can go and for how little provocation. In a recent case in the UK a woman left her abusive husband, chosen by the family, and was murdered by her father and uncle. One might speculate that, whatever the role of cultural obligations and tradition, it is the shame of other men seeing the perpetrator unable to control 'his' women which motivates such actions. The shame, in other words, of being seen as impotent and emasculated.

Donald Campbell further theorizes this gender dichotomy in his concept of the 'shame shield' as a sense that protects the autonomy of the subject in relation to the body and the psyche simultaneously. In his chapter, Campbell traces the consequences of the violent destruction of the innate sense of shame and propriety caused by the anal rape of a boy by a man. As an adolescent, the victim of abuse himself becomes an abuser. Perpetration of sexual abuse is understood as a projective defence which shows us the need to be rid of shame through reversing the position of helpless passivity into active agency. Included in the meanings of the shame of the victim is the idea that he has been feminized by being made to take on the passive role in sex, by being penetrated.

In the dyadic logic of the gaze, meanings of difference and of objects in the world may take on attributes provided by the different libidinal stages of ego development. The oral gaze may engulf, swallow, ingest and devour, or may spit out and ostracize. The anal gaze may constrict in an optical sphincter of visual control or may abandon the object, which is surrendered to dark oblivion. The phallic gaze of Medusa may turn its object to 'stone'; as bearer of sexual control and of castration anxiety, the phallic gaze has received much attention in film theory (Metz 1982; Mulvey 1982). It is Yorke who reminds us that phallic narcissism, like all libidinal deployments, is an *infantile* predicament. Art historians may find it useful to consider the power of the psychic dynamics of exhibiting, hiding, seeing, possessing and knowing as elements in the fission and fusion of visual culture. Do we detect in the prestigious cultures of display an inversion of the shame-filled desire for obscurity?

Turning again to Masaccio we ask why it is that, at the moment of shaming, it is the man who sees himself seeing and the woman who sees herself being seen? The differences between the sexes that are rather schematically defined in modern European cultures are, in one sense, expressions of the difference between the active and passive aims of the instincts as described by Freud, rather than being attributable to man and woman as such. So scopophilia and exhibitionism are liable to be characteristics of any male or female subject. Equally, for both sexes, shame can be violently projected into the other in order to avoid the painful affect itself and to restore the sense of 'honour' and psychic integrity. The perennial excuse of the rapist that the woman tempted him 'leads to the notion of the woman making a sexual attack upon the man' (Flugel 1924: 184), and makes *her* the perpetrator of the shameful deed and the bearer of shame. In contrast, a structure of gazes that replaces the gaze of shaming ostracism, the narcissistic gaze of the seer seeing himself seeing, or the inverted gaze that takes the form of the omniscient eye of God, is the embodied look of subjective reciprocity. The question of how 'respect' can enter the dyadic logic of the gaze to turn it into a space of intersubjective dialogue is now an important part of the political and cultural agenda.

Sex as shameful

It is not difficult to see why genitality, the supposedly 'healthy' reproductive sexual activity of what Foucault calls the 'Malthussian Couple' (Foucault 1981) which is idealized as the antithesis of the perverse, will still carry the meaning and experience of the infantile universe. British psychoanalyst Phillip Mollon advances a hypothesis that it is sexuality, with its biological impera- tive, that threatens to dissolve the symbolic boundaries of culture and thus disturb the order of social structure, which is why sex is experienced as fright- ening and shameful. Mollon's hypothesis is that sexuality has been lost in contemporary psychoanalytic interest in the infantile processes of depend- ence, attachment and separation. The question of how trauma becomes sexu- alized in perversions is one that interests him. Like Stoller (1975) he suggests the libidinization of traumatic failures of self-esteem is achieved through fantasy.

The supposed insignificance of the infantile is belied by its indomitable reappearance in all aspects of adulthood. But it is especially, annoyingly and inappropriately present as 'love's trance', in that most 'adult' of deeds, sex (Sappho, cited in Longinus c. 213–273 AD). In colloquial euphemism the term 'adult', indeed, is coterminous with sex, and because 'adult' is here a euphem- ism, it denotes, with the unerring accuracy of the unconscious, the shameful- ness of repressed, infantile need. The paradox of perversion is that each of its 'deeds' is actually a communication seeking a non-sexual, adult, parental response. The imaginary autonomy of the pervert, like the infant, is depend- ent on the 'facilitating environment' that sustains it, and it is earlier failures in this environment that the perverse acts communicate in their strange iconic language of hiding and revealing. Lest we imagine that perverse sexuality is somehow of a different kind to 'normal' sexual activity, Freud reminds us that 'this disposition to perversions of every kind is a general and funda- mental human characteristic' (Freud 1905: 191). Writing in an age when women's fashion and the fetishization of women's bodies was at its height (or at least no less than it is today), he further reminds us that 'a certain degree of fetishism is . . . habitually present in normal love' (Freud 1905: 154). Specific sexualities and fantasies emerge into consciousness and are banished from it according to the tides of cultural convention and social style, yet there are always aspects of residual infantile sensualities that will trouble adult sexual acts. Not everyone will empathize with Freud's fear that his readers would find the idea of sharing one's spouse's toothbrush repellent, but all readers one hundred years later can understand very well the unruly emergence of irrational fears and delights within the most straightforward of carnal acts. With Freud we wonder what it is that sexuality is doing in infancy and what it is that infancy is doing in adulthood.

Might it be the case in part, as Mollon suggests, that it is in its biological centrality to our lives that sex is intrinsically shameful? It is interesting to compare this analysis with the theory of the shamefulness of sex being derived from its infantile origins. In both cases there is a substratum of biological dependence and infantile helplessness that becomes a source of humiliation in the course of 'growing up'. Whether biological or infantile, each source, nevertheless, insults the ego with its insistence on 'another story' which the ego is impotent to influence or control. We are, as Freud contended, no longer masters in our own house (Freud 1917: 143).

Loss as shameful

> To fresh defeats we still must move, and the final defeat of grief.
>
> (Auden 1940)

It was John Bowlby who noted that premature separation of infant from mother gives rise, in adulthood, to feelings of shame (1980). One might conjecture that it is the intensified activation of the scopic drive, aiming to find the missing object and failing to do so, that reactivates the sense of shame. That shame is one of the states endured in the process of mourning is not as well known as the recognition of guilt and rage, and this relative obscurity of the liminal state of shame can generate painful conflicts. All losses are likely to bring us back to an encounter with the earliest losses, disappointments and trauma of separation that Winnicott calls the 'disillusionment' of the infant by the mother, and the 'healthy and beneficial tragedy' that follows the Oedipus complex. Experiences of loss, loss of love, abandonment and betrayal are inevitable vicissitudes of psychic development and leave a residue of shame-proneness in the minds of everyone, which can be mobilized in the consumption of visual culture. Since John Berger's groundbreaking *Ways of Seeing* (1972) it has become a truism to say that advertisements play on a sense of failure and inadequacy in their audience. Shame is attached to our inadequate bodies, personal hygiene, social status, possessions and much else that taps into infantile scenarios of humiliation and disappointment, and it is the task of the advertisement to mobilize unconscious shame and offer the prospect, through purchase, of achieving the ideal. The purchase may be sanctioned (sanctified one might say) by an appeal to the narcissism which psychoanalysts have identified as the primary defence against shame: 'Because you're worth it'. In religious discourse it is the hypothesis of 'sin' that explains abandonment by and separation from God's loving embrace; but for the infant scarcely old enough for conceptual thinking it may simply be a diffuse experience of being 'bad' and at fault. With early experiences of separation and loss the child internalizes the rage that he is unable to direct at the loved parents on whom he is dependent, while a transposed relationship to a supernatural authority may unleash the criticism that has been withheld. St Augustine's *Confessions* may equally be called his *Accusations* (to his parents), yet in the shame-filled stories of his youthful transgressions he never once allows himself a complaint to his Almighty judge 'Oh Lord, why didst *thou* abandon me?' The genesis of shame in the relations of love, fear and dependence between a *small* child and *big* adults determines its course, its effects and its forms of representation. Freud showed that for a young child, criticism from parental figures is the equivalent of 'loss of love', so that sensitivity to criticism in adult life, to which we are all prone to some degree, may be one of the painful indications of debilitating shame. If the effects of the castration complex are profound and incalculable (Ward 2003), it is also the regressive powers of loss that reactivate shame in later life. The two currents meld together in the puzzling way in which 'a sense of sin' is attached to the ordinary experience of masturbation, which is hardly ever a topic of dinner-table conversation.

Loss, persecution and confusion are the sequelae of another uncanny pre-Oedipal experience. For Freud and Klein, the fantasies of the 'combined parent figure' and the 'primal scene' are unavoidable and traumatic developmental moments, which leave their mark as an ineluctable residue of shame. Few people, even as adults, can tolerate the thought of their parents' sexuality and the strange impossible act which engendered them. In contrast to the viewer of Renaissance painting, placed in his position of specular omniscience, the spectator to the primal scene is thrown into confusion about where to place himself and what it means. Intensely emotional and exciting, the bewildered onlooker is drawn into it and repelled at the same time, caught in the grip of a forbidden fascination. With parents transformed into monsters and infantile urges made flesh and visible, the primal scene, one might say, has 'everything', including the exclusion and abandonment that evokes shame and its cognate emotions. Psychoanalysts since Freud have investigated the cataclysmic emotional import of the primal scene and traced its symbolic representation in adult life and artistic practice (McDougall 1995); Freud used the drawings of his Russian patient, the Wolfman, as evidence.

The almost triadic structure of the primal scene shatters any illusion of 'oneness' and generates an inevitable *nostalgia* for the lost paradise of an earlier dyadic relationship with the mother. The pleasures of this fantasy of fusion, in-difference, and 'oceanic' synaesthesia are well known, but the fears, anxieties and dangers it can trigger are less well understood. It can be experienced in later life as a threat to the imaginary, scopic control exercised by the ego, and the loss of control may be defended against with violence. This violence may in fact be a defence against the experience of shame, and the humiliating reminders of infantile longing and dependence. What was once the pleasurable experience of being at one with the mother becomes represented in later life as a fear of being suffocated, constricted or devoured by the surrogates who have taken her place. Since shame, unlike guilt, is rooted to pre-Oedipal experience, the scale of the threat cannot easily be measured; but shame threatens a more total annihilation of self, and therefore more global defences. Character traits and emotions such as spite, envy, haughtiness, narcissism, masochism and rage may be built up on the basis of defensive manoeuvres against shame, attempting to obliterate, avoid, project or internalize the mental pain it entails. The defence may take the form of a violent and ruthless obliteration of the object or, more often, the 'witness' to the shameful experience. An averted gaze may signify that someone has been obliterated in fantasy.[5]

Loss of ideals may also lead to shame and can underlie forms of visual representation. Parents let us down not only because the expectations of the child are unrealistic, but because the parent has privileges to which the child is not entitled and is, therefore, always open to the charge of hypocrisy and betrayal. Ideals are derived from these early relations to parental figures and it is the shattering of illusions about them which rebounds on the subject in a devastating way. If the 'other' shames us with his shaming gaze, it is one of the paradoxes of shame that it is also the other's shame which infects us. Such was Freud's experience as a nine-year-old child when his father, regarded as a hero, told the tale of his cowardice in the face of an anti-Semite who knocked his new fur hat into the mud. Freud's experience is memorable because it is written in *The Interpretation of Dreams*, but each of us has a similar tale in which the father is shown to have feet of clay, to be a hypocrite or even, as the anguished adolescent often accuses, to be 'full of shit'. In adult life, Freud's dream of his dead father as the iconic hero Garibaldi masked the more disturbing association of the intestinal blockage from which his father had died (Freud 1900: 425). Malcolm Pines references these accounts to argue that, as a Jew in an anti-Semitic culture, Freud was particularly sensitive to shame in his own life.

Children are shamed by the inevitable failures of their parents and, seeking relief from the burden, they look for occasions to denigrate them. A further turn of the screw is accomplished when the parents' shame is transmitted unconsciously to the child. An adult is ashamed of his secret fantasies and unconsciously ashamed of his unconscious fantasies, but he may also be the bearer of somebody else's shame. Most often it is the shame of a parent or parental couple, unconsciously transmitted and, according to the analysts who have most investigated this metapsychology of secrets, 'encrypted' in a secret part of the psyche where it exists as a 'phantom', passed from generation to generation, replicating its effects (Abraham and Torok 1994). 'The presence of the phantom indicates the effects, on the descendents, of something that had inflicted narcissistic injury or even catastrophe on the parent' (Abraham 1975: 174). The feeling of rotting inside may be one effect of this burden of another person's shame (Abraham and Torok 1975: 146).

'Shame is a revolutionary feeling'

As a complex social emotion, shame has been identified as a product of the 'hidden injuries of class', or of a 'matriphobic' culture, or as a determining element in the guilt of the victim. Che Guevara, for example, was reputed to

have claimed that: 'At the risk of sounding ridiculous, it must be acknowledged that shame is a revolutionary feeling.' The unease shame generates can
signal a discontent with civilization that directs our attention outwards to
external wrongs. Is shame a necessary component of the social sense, as guilt
is to a moral sense?

Historian at the University of London's Slade School of Art, Amna Malik,
cites American artist Kara Walker who, as a young woman, was exasperated
by being desirable insofar as she represented racial and sexualized otherness
to her suitors. She saw herself being seen by the shameless, sexual and predatory curiosity of the racial and sexual other. Through such rites, fantasy and
sexual desire are reduced to the two-dimensional world of the power relationships depicted in Walker's monochrome silhouettes. All three-dimensionality
has gone, and there is, in the place of mutual intercourse, these scenarios of
apparent refinement and ridiculous debasement. The genteel art of découpage
that was popularized during the early nineteenth century as a form of pre-
photographic portraiture is in Walker's work reunited with the shadow world
of that century's sordid, open secret: the slave trade that shored up European
colonialism. The perversion of respect that was the basis and legacy of slavery
is given form here. Respect is withheld – denied – and shame is forced on to
the victim. Deadly serious and wildly playful, Walker's icons, suggests Malik,
are the shadow play of the other story of nineteenth-century white narcissism
and its reverberations today.

The difference between body and mind can come to take on the meaning
of the difference between feminine and masculine, or the difference between
racial or ethnic type. The way in which ethnic difference is traced through the
body and through corporeal identity makes it a powerful locus of shame. If
racial difference, either real or imaginary, is found on the body and its surfaces or visible aspects, these visible differences become stigmata that are
targeted by the aggression that imaginary difference generates. Freud's expression 'the narcissism of minor differences' is well chosen (1918: 199).

South African artist Penny Siopis uses the country's recent history to
explore the shame created by a social sense of implication in apartheid. Placing
her work in the Freud Museum generates questions of relating political, social
practices to the 'private' practice of psychoanalysis. Her installation in Freud's
former home at 20 Maresfield Gardens, London included taped interviews
with prominent South Africans invited to reflect on their experiences of the
end of apartheid. The voices of people recalling intense feelings of guilt and
shame, set in the context of Freud's consulting room, brought the meaning of
shame into focus at the interface between individual and social worlds of
public and private selves.

Feminist literary theorist Ranjana Khanna analyses the meaning of the
veil in the history of Orientalism and colonialism, examining the work of a
number of contemporary women artists who have foregrounded the question
of shame in their works. Her discussion of shame as a bodily or psychological

state leads her to investigate psychoanalytic theories of affect and to reflect on ethics and morality as a borderline between public and private experience. She considers the symbolic attributes of clothing and nakedness, the inter-woven notions of honour and pride, and the veil as a specific yet polyvalent use of fabric's capacity to cover and reveal. This enables her to avoid any simplifications of either political or cultural interpretations of the use of veil and hijab, and to reflect on the interface between seen and unseen aspects of the boundaries between Islam and Judeo Christian culture.

Shamelessness and spectacle

Contemporary culture, claims Situationist Guy Debord, has become a civil-ization of the image, of spectacle (Debord 1967). In a world in which events are relayed through the media of instantaneous and visible communication, the word whose meaning depends on the deferred gratification of syntactic closure cannot secure attention. The word retains its gravity by means of the distance and separation that the Symbolic order imposes on the subject, while the image seems to exist as a disembodied eye of fantasy. For example, visual culture has played a central part in the 'war on terror'. The incidents aimed at bringing terror into the western culture of spectatorship, such as the passen-ger planes flown into the World Trade Centre, were designed to be seen 'tele-visually' in order to be understood. Visual culture was their form if not their content or cause. Similarly, in the reportage of this war, images such as photographs and cartoons have become articulation points at which the vio-lence of inchoate rage becomes visible in iconic form. The confusion between ethics and shaming that arose in the incidents that proliferated over the photographing of ritual humiliation of political prisoners at Abu Ghraib raises questions that illuminate the relationship between vision, occlusion, hiding and shame. The military technology of the stealth bomber deployed against Iraq was noted for two distinctive visual characteristics: first, the form of its mass was designed to be imperceptible to radar; second, its replacement of a windscreen by a digital display screen enabled pilots to navigate and to deploy missiles without entering into any optical relationship to a perceived external reality. Rationalized as a technological and design 'evolution', the unconscious relationship of aggression, violence and vision is nevertheless writ large within the optical logic of this and many other examples of military design and architecture. That there is an integral link between shame, narcis-sism, violence and sight is obvious if only in the ubiquity of the many forms of denial and spectacular shamelessness that circulate in contemporary visual mass media. Contemporary news presents many stories of killers whose acts of violence are performed for 'the public eye', as if to be within the public eye invites hope of being sheltered from the severity of the harsh gaze of the superego. Where shamelessness is an attempt to re-create the unashamed pleasures of childhood, it also, like shame-fuelled violence, creates a gross distortion of ethical codes. The aim of shamelessness 'in the public eye' is to generate both speechlessness and attention. The shame of Oedipal wishes can be so deeply destabilizing that it is covered over, as it were, by a regression to shamelessness and exhibitionism.

Discussing First World War medical illustrations of facial injury, historian of visual culture at Middlesex University, Suzannah Biernoff, offers an analysis of the emotional meanings attributed to heroism and nationalism in wartime Britain through an examination of masculine and feminine identification with depictions of the wounded male body. Her analysis of the photographic embodiment of abstract idealizations (of valour and redemptive sacrifice, for instance) hinges on the culture's ambivalent deployment of disgust and the defensive avoidance of shame. The wounded body bearing the sign of its sacrifice took on a talismanic quality; but this simple iconography broke down in the case of serious facial injuries when shame and disgust were less easily overcome.

Smell, sight and sociable babies

In his essay 'Strong Smells and Polite Society' Adrian Stokes (1961) noted that our admiration for refined sensibility and good taste in art is not so very different from our carnal appetites for whatever is good to eat. The idealization of the former is in direct ratio to its proximity to the baser and more shameful or 'disgusting' senses of smell and taste. The sense of smell, for adults, is all the more uncanny and shameful since it cannot be brought under voluntary control. Like breathing, it refers us to a body boundary that we cannot help but breach. In no other sense organ is our vulnerability to aperture so extreme. Even the receptive ears can become oblivious to noises that we have 'turned away' from. In sleep we can stop hearing sounds from the outside world, but the smell of smoke will often awaken the sleeper involuntarily, while fragrant herbs, flowers and incense can reach the limbic brain long after words, sight and even touch have vanished.

Although smell remains the first sociable sense, its primacy in infancy is rapidly overtaken and reorganized in relation to the sense of sight. Research into the neurology of perception has revealed new facts about the earliest organization of sight, hearing, smell, taste, touch and other senses, and inaugurated a new era of infant observation enriched by information gleaned from the apparatus of scientific research (Stern 2004). Video recordings of infants' gazes show transformations that take place within fractions of a second, not visible to the naked eye, and allow us to understand that the communication between mother and infant takes place in an uncanny time and space, both familiar to us and yet utterly different from our adult world. The evolution of mind from brain has resulted in a semi-autonomous development of a self in relationship to what Winnicott, rather unsentimentally, terms the 'facilitating environment'.[6] Neurologists trace the development of the brain in infancy and note the sequences through which cross-modal integration takes place; we are shown that the crucial human evolutionary advantage of hand to eye co-ordination occurs through a specific pattern of actions that organize neurological structures in the brain. Remember the infant game of grasping and dropping a toy that Freud described in his grandson's play as the 'fort-da' game, in which language begins to symbolize presence and absence in the mind (Freud 1920: 15). Neuroscience affirms the significance of this 'apprenticeship' to language through the body's movement, and psychoanalysts have understood the baby's game of clasping and releasing as the early prefiguration of being able to 'grasp' a concept. Neuroscience also shows the close relationship of optical and tactile senses on the level of neuronal structure. As touch and smell precede sight in the mind's capacity for orientation, perception and attachment, the proximity of these senses is never fully separated; so, for example, as described above, when an object is seen close up the neurone receptors of touch are activated, which recalls the less differentiated sensory regime of early infancy and can generate some uncanny experiences of loss of distance control and separation.

Vision, emotion and the world of images and objects coalesce and interact with each other. There are missed objects at each phase or dimension of development, and each developmental transition entails the negotiation of profound losses and abjection. Connected both to the body and to fantasy, sight and shame accrue meaning through all phases in which the gaze is, sequentially, implicated. Some of these meanings are explored in this book, revealing the fragility of the world we grasp in visual representation and the infantile emotion which underlies our understanding. As you will see in the following chapters, 'shame' has proven to be a promising avenue to explore, inviting us to decipher some of the most troubling and obscure aspects of human subjectivity and its effects on visual culture.

Notes

1 The way that academic use of psychoanalytic theory has tended to remain limited to the Lacanian, philosophical paradigm over the last 30 years has resulted in the paucity of writing on affect, body and infantile sexuality. These are elements that are central to an adequate understanding of shame and visual experience.
2 Sophocles, *Oedipus Rex*, cited in Longinus *On the Sublime* 213–273 AD, trans. G. M. A. Grube (Indianapolis, Hackett, 1991).
3 Norman Bryson offers us a different, Lacanian concept of stain and scotoma: 'Between retina and world is inserted a screen of signs, a screen consisting of all the multiple discourses on vision built into the social arena. The screen casts a shadow, sometimes Lacan calls it a scotoma, sometimes a stain.'
4 Freud includes 'the claims of aesthetic and moral ideals' as one of the 'dams' that 'impede the course of the sexual instinct' in development (Freud 1905: 177).
5 You 'cut someone dead' by averting the gaze.
6 D. Winnicott, *The Maturational Processes and the Facilitating Environment*, London: Hogarth, 1965.

References

Abraham, N. (1975) 'Notes on the phantom: A complement to Freud's meta-psychology', in N. Abraham and M. Torok *The Shell and the Kernel*, N. Rand (ed. and trans.), Chicago and London: University of Chicago Press, 1994.

Abraham, N. and Torok, M. (1975) ' "The lost object – me": notes on endocryptic identification', in N. Abraham and M. Torok *The Shell and the Kernel*, N. Rand (ed. and trans.), Chicago and London: University of Chicago Press, 1994.

Abraham, N. and Torok, M. (1994) *The Shell and the Kernel*, N. Rand (ed. and trans.), Chicago and London: University of Chicago Press.

Agamben, G. (1999) *Remnants of Auschwitz*, New York: Zone Books.

Auden, W. H. (1940) 'In Memory of Sigmund Freud', in *Horizon* edited by Cyril Connolly.

Berger, J. (1972) *Ways of Seeing*, Harmondsworth: Penguin.

Bowlby, John (1980) *Attachment and Loss, Vol. Three: Loss, Sadness and Depression*, Harmondsworth: Penguin.

Darwin, C. (1872) *The Expression of the Emotions in Man and Animals*, Chicago and London: University of Chicago Press (1965). Also online at http://www.darwin-literature.com/The_Expression_Of_The_Emotions_In_Man_And_Animals/13.html

Debord, G. (1967) *La Société du Spectacle*, Paris: Bouchet/Chastel.

Douglas, M. (1966) *Purity and Danger*, London: Routledge.

Flugel, J. C. (1924) 'Polyphallic symbolism and the castration complex', *International Journal of Psychoanalysis* 4: 155–196.

Foucault, M. (1981) *History of Sexuality*, Vol. 1, Harmondsworth: Penguin.

Freud, S. (1900) *The Interpretation of Dreams*, S.E. 4, 5.

—— (1905) *Three Essays on the Theory of Sexuality*, S.E. 7.

—— (1908) 'Creative writers and daydreaming', S.E. 9: 141–153.

—— (1917) 'A difficulty in the path of psychoanalysis', S.E. 17: 135–144.

—— (1918) 'The taboo of virginity', S.E. 17: 191–208.

—— (1920) 'Beyond the pleasure principle', S.E. 18: 1–64.

—— (1937) 'Analysis terminable and interminable', S.E. 23: 209–253.

Glasser, M. (1992) 'Problems in the psychoanalysis of certain narcissistic disorders, *International Journal of Psycho-Analysis* 73: 493–503.

Kristeva, J. (1982) *Powers of Horror: An Essay in Abjection*, trans. L. Roudiez, New York: Columbia University Press.

—— (1984) *Revolution in Poetic Language*, trans. M. Waller, New York: Columbia University Press.

Longinus (c. 213–273 AD) *On the Sublime*, trans. G.M.A. Grube, Indianapolis: Hackett, 1991.

McDougall, J. (1995) *The Many Faces of Eros*, London: Free Association Books.

Metz, C. (1982) *The Imaginary Signifier*, trans. B. Brewster, London: Macmillan.

Mulvey, L. (1982) *Visual and Other Pleasures*, London: Macmillan.

Nathanson, D. L. (1987) 'A timetable for shame', in D. Nathanson (ed.) *The Many Faces of Shame*, New York: Guilford Press.

Rushdie, S. (1995) *Shame*, London: Vintage.

Stern, D. (2004) *The First Relationship: Infant and Mother*, Boston: Harvard University Press.

Stokes, A. (1961) 'Strong smells and polite society', in A. Stokes *A Game that must be Lost: Collected Papers by Adrian Stokes*, ed. E. Rhode, Cheadle Hulme: Carcanet Press, 1973.

Stoller, R. J. (1975) *Perversion: The Erotic Form of Hatred*, New York: Pantheon.

Wangh, M. (1964) 'National socialism and the genocide of the Jews—a psychoanalytic study of a historical event', *International Journal of Psycho-Analysis*, 45: 386–395.

Ward, I. (2003) *Castration*, Cambridge: Icon Books.

Winnicott D. (1953) 'Transitional objects and transitional phenomena', *International Journal of Psychoanalysis* 34: 89–97.

Part I

Psychoanalysis

Chapter 1

The inherent shame of sexuality

Phil Mollon

Despite a seemingly sexually liberated culture, sexuality is still disturbing and puzzling. Freud's original emphasis on the importance of sexuality has largely been lost in much contemporary psychoanalysis, displaced by a focus on 'attachment'. However, his intuition that sexuality and civilization are in some sense in conflict may have profound implications, throwing light on the nature and function of our linguistic culture and the fetishistic nature of human sexuality. Sexuality, it is argued here, is the paradigmatic object of shame and repression, tending to incorporate all else that is repressed and in opposition to the quasi-linguistic structure of culture. Human beings may tend to long for experience that is unmediated by the linguistic – and this is the promise and the terror of sexuality.

Why is sexuality shameful? Consider a quotation from a person suffering from Tourette's syndrome – a neurobiologically based condition displaying a compulsion to utter obscenities. Its significance will become apparent as my argument unfolds.

> 'See, FUCK MY FUCKING FUCKING FUCKING CUNT, FUCK, FUCK, FUCK, FUCK, FUCK, I finished tenth year of high school FUCK MY FUCKING CUNT and the new year started, the eleventh, and I went to school, and I was in school ten minutes when one of the teachers that knew me FUCK
> MY FUCKING CUNT and was teaching at the school when I was there before. . . .' (and so it goes on)
> (from a paper by Martindale 1977, quoted in Rancour-Laferriere
> 1985: 226)

Why is such speech, with the intrusion of the crudely sexual, so disturbing – embarrassing – shameful (especially when heard rather than read)?

I propose the following thesis. Sexuality is frightening for human beings, because its biological imperative threatens the symbolic nature of our socio-cultural world and personal identity. The development of the symbolic socio-cultural world may actually have depended upon the repression of sexuality (leading to displacement of signification and the creation of symbols – as in dreams and our communicative language). Because sexuality is threatening and frightening, it is repressed or banished from discourse (even in our supposedly sexually liberated society) and is referred to only indirectly. Sexuality, like the body, is clothed. Because sexuality is the fundamental object of repression, it tends to incorporate whatever else is repressed – so that a person's most shameful and unexpressed needs and narcissistic injuries tend to become sexualized. One hundred years after the publication of Freud's *Three Essays on Sexuality*, much of psychoanalysis has lost touch with the importance of sexuality. Freud said:

> I can only repeat over and over again – for I never find it otherwise – that sexuality is the key to the problem of the psychoneuroses and of the neuroses in general. No one who disdains the key will ever be able to unlock the door.
>
> (Freud 1905: 115)

Ironically, psychoanalysts today do not talk about sex very much – preferring instead to focus on issues of attachment, dependence, fears of abandonment, aggression and envy.

Shame is associated with the desires and other aspects of self that are not allowed access to shared discourse. The objects of shame are driven from the group, the tribe, the conversation. This barring from discourse is not necessarily the same as repression, which prevents mental contents from finding access to the language of consciousness. The object of shame may be conscious (allowed access to private internal discourse) and yet denied entry to the social realm of shared discourse.

We are all prone to shame and embarrassment – the potential is ever-present whenever people are gathered together, since misperception, misunderstanding and failures of empathy are always possible when human beings interact. Shame arises in the gaps and failures in human communication, in the misconnection of expectation that one has of another (Mollon 2002). Every situation of embarrassment is one involving disrupted expectations that one person has of another. Embarrassment is an immediate shock reaction experienced at the moment of disrupted presentation of self in a social situation – shame is the close associate of embarrassment, but may be a more enduring, and sometimes lethal, pain arising from the memory of the scene of embarrassment.

This response of shame and embarrassment to failures of communication and expectation is very basic and hard wired in the human brain. It is displayed even by preverbal infants, as demonstrated in the 'still face' experiments (Tronick *et al.* 1978) when mothers were asked to make eye contact with their babies but avoid smiling or being facially responsive – the infants became distressed and averted their gaze in a manner that seemed a precursor of adult shame (Broucek 1991).

However, some are more shame-prone than others. For example, a successful lawyer always feared that his outward persona, with high social status, would be discovered to be a sham and he would be revealed to be 'a disgusting pile of muck'. His childhood relationship with his mother had been such that he felt he could win her love and approval only if he were compliant and hid any trace of potential rebellion or other characteristics that might evoke her formidable scorn and condemnation. He became adept at presenting himself in a favourable light to her and to others – inwardly harbouring mounting rage, at her and all the others whom he placed in the same position of needing to be pleased or placated, and at himself for his chronic inauthenticity. His achievements and professional acclaim gave him fleeting gratification but no real satisfaction, being associated with contempt for both self and others. I have called this kind of situation 'psychic murder syndrome' (Mollon 2002), using a metaphor of a Stepford Child, derived from the film in which the menfolk of a small American town systematically kill off their actual wives and have them replaced by robotic replicas that are perfectly compliant with their desires. In psychic murder syndrome the child feels that his or her actual self is unwanted, a faecal self to be disposed of – the disgusting pile of muck – and to be replaced by a self compliant with mother's desires. Erikson (1950) linked struggles over shame and autonomy with the anal stage of Freud's psychosexual scheme – and, indeed, the child may come to feel that those parts of the self that do not meet mother's approval are only fit for disposal down the toilet. This is part of the basis of the 'false self' described by Winnicott (1960).

Some of the areas of self most likely to be foreclosed from social discourse are those of sexuality – and indeed sexuality has always been deeply associated with shame. In the German language, the genital region is called *die Scham*, the pubic mound *Schamberg*, and pubic hair *Schamhaare*, and the labia *Schamlippen* (shame lips). For some reason, the 'private parts' are universally regarded as private and not for public display or reference. Why is this?

One patient, Jeanette, reported, with tremendous embarrassment, how she had learned to masturbate and give herself an orgasm at the age of seven and had indulged regularly in this over the subsequent years, but always feeling some sense of shame afterwards. Her turning to her own body for pleasurable stimulation had been given impetus partly by her feelings of loneliness and lack of emotional stimulation – her lone parent mother tending to be preoccupied and often intoxicated. One day, whilst at school aged 14, Jeanette had experienced a sudden 'realization' of the nature of her sexual activities and was overwhelmed with intense feelings of shame and a terror that others would know her secret. She had rushed home and tried to tell her mother, who failed to respond in an empathic manner but instead reacted with anxiety and disapproval. Subsequently Jeanette developed a disabling social anxiety, which turned out to be based on the fear that the word 'masturbation' would crop up in conversation and that she would go red. Naturally her anxiety about blushing and this being seen tended to bring about the very effect she feared whenever a conversation turned to sexual matters. Jeanette's adult feelings of shame centred not only on her childhood masturbation, which she regarded as excessive, but also on her view of herself as having an abnormal interest in sex. Discussion of her sexuality in psychotherapy led to a rapid diminution in her feelings of shame and associated anxiety.

Parents often do interfere with the child's autonomy in relation to its exploration of the body's sexuality. Amsterdam and Levitt (1980) suggest that a common source of painful embarrassed self-consciousness is the negative reaction of a parent who looks anxiously or disapprovingly when the child is engaged in genital exploration or play. They argue that the mother's disapproval of the child's autoerotic exploration may be one of the first narcissistic injuries experienced by the child. Amsterdam and Levitt point out that, in contrast to the 'gleam in the mother's eye' which Kohut (1971) emphasized as a foundation of the child's sense of self, mothers in our culture do not normally beam whilst their infants play with themselves. They argue that in this way the child's dream of his or her own perfection is destroyed and the source of pleasure – his or her own bodily sensations – now produce shame. Exploration of sexuality has led the child out of the Garden of Eden. One might say that at such a moment the child learns that not all experiences and desires are admissible to shared or social discourse. A division occurs within the self – between what can be admitted to discourse and what cannot – and the latter is associated with shame. Freud wrote of something similar in his paper 'On the Sexual Theories of Children' (1908), in connection with the child's suspicion of the spurious explanations given by grown-ups of where babies come from:

> With this, however, the child experiences the first occasion for a 'psychical conflict', in that views for which he feels an instinctual kind of preference, but which are not 'right' in the eyes of the grown-ups, come into opposition with other views, which are supported by the authority of the grown-ups without being acceptable to him himself.
>
> (Freud 1908: 214)

Sexuality is the paradigmatic quality to be banished from discourse. It is, I suggest, inherently disturbing to the child (Bollas 2000) – partly because the child cannot make sense of it. There is something inherently mysterious about sexuality – dimly recognized yet not understood by the child. Consider the phantasy of the primal scene, the actual or imagined intercourse of the parents in the eyes or mind of the child. The child is fascinated by, and excluded from, a scene that he or she does not understand. If she enquires, she will not receive a reply that satisfies. The child may be aware of bodily excitements that are experienced as both pleasurable and puzzling. These do not easily find a way into conversations with parents, or indeed with other children. In our contemporary society, children rarely observe animals mating, or giving birth. Thus the question 'Where do babies come from?' is not easily answered in a way that satisfies the child. The great puzzle of sexuality, with its attendant curiosity – the state of not knowing – is itself experienced as shameful.

We might contrast this with another pleasurable bodily activity – eating – which is public and social. The child knows about eating – there is no mystery to it – the child sees adults eating and knows that it is essentially the same activity that he or she engages in every day. Eating and desires to eat can be referred to publicly and explicitly without shame. This remains the case for adults. If a man were to go up to a woman and say 'Hello would you like to fuck?', this would usually not be a very successful means of initiating intimacy (there may be exceptions) – whereas 'Hello would you like to have dinner with me?' is much more likely to result in a favourable response. Although this is obvious enough in terms of our cultural experience and expectations, I suggest that the *reason* for this contrast between oral and genital activities is not immediately obvious. Why is the oral desire more socially acceptable and validated? There is no embarrassment in saying 'I'm really hungry – I'm dying to eat something!' – whereas one would normally need to have established a degree of intimacy with a person in order to say 'I really want to fuck you!'

Activities and desires associated with the bottom and the genitals undergo repression insofar as they are banished from language, either in part or completely. Freud emphasized the factor of the human erect posture – and what he called the 'organic repression' of smell and sexuality:

> With the assumption of an erect posture by man and with the depreciation of his sense of smell, it was not only his anal erotism which threatened to fall a victim to organic repression, but the whole of his sexuality; so that since this, the sexual function has been accompanied by a repugnance which cannot further be accounted for, and which prevents its complete satisfaction and forces it away from the sexual aim into sublimations and libidinal displacements. . . . Thus we should find that the deepest root of the sexual repression which advances along with civilization is the organic defence of the new form of life achieved with man's erect gait against his earlier animal existence.
>
> (Freud 1930: 106)

Note Freud's phrase regarding the repugnance that 'cannot further be accounted for', suggesting that he was aware of the puzzling nature of the repression of sexuality. In the *Three Essays*, he emphasized that the dams which restrict the flow of sexuality – 'disgust, feelings of shame and the claims of aesthetic and moral ideals' – are essentially 'organically determined' (1905: 177). Freud also makes a number of references in his letters to Fliess to the role of smell in the 'organic' repression of sexuality. Thus in letter 55, dated 1897, he writes:

> The principal sense in animals (for sexual as well as other purposes) is that of smell, which has lost that position in human beings. So long as smell (or taste) is dominant, hair, faeces and the whole surface of the body – and blood as well – have a sexually exciting effect.
>
> (Freud 1886–1899: 241)

Then in letter 75, also dated 1897, he writes of:

> the changed part played by sensations of smell: upright carriage adopted, nose raised from the ground, at the same time a number of formerly interesting sensations attached to the earth become repulsive – by a process still unknown to me.
>
> (Freud 1886–1899: 268)

He reasons that if the normally abandoned sexual zones persist, then perversion results. Moreover, he argues that the normal process of repression provides:

> the affective basis for a multitude of intellectual processes of development, such as morality, shame etc. Thus the whole of this arises at the expense of extinct (potential) sexuality. From this we can see that, with the successive waves of a child's development, he is overlaid with piety, shame, and such things, and how the non-occurrence of this extinction of the sexual zones can produce moral insanity.
>
> (Freud 1886–1899: 270)

Similarly, in his 1909 paper on the Rat Man and his obsessional neurosis, Freud comments:

> By his own account, when he was a child, he had recognized every one by their smell, like a dog; and even when he was grown up he was more susceptible to sensations of smell than most people. . . . And here I should like to raise the general question whether the atrophy of the sense of smell (which was an inevitable result of man's assumption of an erect posture) and the consequent organic repression of his pleasure in smell may not have had a considerable share in the origin of his susceptibility to nervous disease. This would afford us some explanation of why, with the advance of civilization, it is precisely the sexual life that must fall a

victim to repression. For we have long known the intimate connection in the animal organization between the sexual instinct and the function of the olfactory organ.

(Freud 1909: 247–248)

It seems clear from these quotes that Freud felt there is something peculiar and distinctive about the relationship between sexuality and repression – a relationship that is nevertheless somewhat obscure. Note also Freud's implication in the above quote that in some way the development of human civilization has depended upon repression of sexuality.

Although there are many references to sexuality in our culture, these are to large extent allusions – images that are suggestive rather than explicit. Banishment from language is an important aspect of repression in the Freudian perspective. The repressed re-emerges in displaced and disguised form, in dreams, in parapraxes, and in its cultural images. Even in our sexually liberal culture, a woman will not go to a nightclub and wave her naked bottom at a man and request intercourse, but she may dress and dance in a way that is suggestive and evocative of nakedness and the promise of intercourse. Places established for explicit sexual expression, such as fetish clubs, are not characterized by complete nudity but are for the display of fetishistic clothing and fetishistic activity. Human sexuality is inherently fetishistic – metonymic (part stands for the whole), and metaphoric (one thing stands for another) – the perfumed breast cleavage stands in place of the pungent bottom. It may well be the repression of direct sexuality that has helped to drive the development of general human culture. In the *Three Essays*, Freud comments:

Historians of civilization appear to be at one in assuming that powerful components are acquired for every kind of cultural achievement by this diversion of sexual instinctual forces from sexual aims and their direction to new ones – a process which deserves the name of 'sublimation'.

(Freud 1905: 178)

The displacement from direct sexual satisfaction means that much more work has to be put into the processes leading up to mating. Perhaps we cannot undo the repression of sexuality because this has been selected by evolution – the diversion of energy and activity away from direct and immediate intercourse with biologically ready mates facilitates the development of culture and complex society.

The babble of sexual discourses, during our own and other cultural periods, displays not direct sexuality but its repression and displacement into linguistic forms. It may even be that the repression of sexuality has played a crucial part in the origins of language and all the quasi-linguistic dimensions of culture. Repression means that direct sexual communication must be displaced – so that one thing stands for another. This is language – a word always stands for something else. In place of a direct display of the genitals and an overt invitation to intercourse, there is a hint, an allusion – a 'phallic symbol', a glimpse of flesh that suggests more. The traditional sexist adverts, in which an attractive and scantily clad woman sits on top of a car, or licks a stick of chocolate, are able to play on the phallic attributes of such images precisely because human sexuality and language are like that. Fundamentally, language and culture are all displaced sexuality. This is perhaps why those who have an investment in the maintenance of societies tend to feel threatened by the emergence of very overt sexuality and sexual acts – direct sexual expression is antithetical to culture and the human society that rests upon culture. The sexually derived nature of language is also suggested by the way in which adolescents, and those whose culture is less refined, will liberally pepper their discourse with language that has a direct sexual reference. It is as if the more degenerate the culture, the more sexualized the language becomes, with less and less displacement from direct sexual reference.

Tourette's syndrome is interesting, with its dramatic intrusion into language of the forbidden sexual. It has been reported that during sexual arousal the Tourette symptoms abate (Martindale 1977). It is as if there is some inherent tension between language and sexuality.

Sexual freedom is frequently seen as undermining of cultural achievements. Thus, religions and ideological political groups may condemn sexual liberty, whilst those wishing to overthrow established culture will invoke sexual freedom. Breakdown of culture and society always leads to rape, especially during periods of war, when Eros appears hijacked by Thanatos, in a terrifying slide towards entropy. Sexual abuse of children is rightly seen as a threat to culture and civilization – an attack on the necessary period of latency and its associated sublimation of libido, since the excessively and prematurely sexually energized child cannot manage his or her excitements and terrors and cannot learn.

Adam and Eve tell the story. The fig leaf is representative of culture. The birth of culture began with the shame of sexuality and the emergence of a linguistic covering. Instead of direct sexual display and action, human beings began to use sounds and images that were in place of sex – that alluded to sex but were not in themselves sex. This was the birth of language.

The birth of language and culture also meant that human beings had not only a physical body but also a linguistic self – a self constructed out of the available images and roles to be found or given in the cultural marketplace. When we are born, we are given a sound, a word, and told that this is who we are. Later we build on to this first linguistic identity many other images and roles that culture provides – and then we believe we are this false self. All human selves are false selves – the linguistic clothing that hides our essential emptiness (Mollon 2001, 2002).

Our physical clothes not only keep us warm and protected but also have a linguistic function, signalling status and position in the cultural marketplace.

In torture, part of the humiliation is to strip the person of their clothes, their physical and linguistic covering – and their linguistic identity. The person is reduced to a biological process. To shame someone is to render them invalid – not partaking of group life and not admitted to human discourse.

We feel shame if found linguistically naked, without a semiotic covering, just as we do without our physical clothes – if we are seen outside the role and identity that is recognized by others, caught with our linguistic pants down. Shame is associated with whatever is outside the discourse, whatever cannot be spoken of. Socially phobic, or socially incompetent people may experience their whole self as shameful – particularly since they may quite literally not find access to the discourse. Consider, for example, the plight of the silent member of a therapy group – the longer he or she is silent, the more profound the shame and the more difficult it becomes to enter the discourse.

Shame is associated with aspects of self that cannot be communicated – and it is found whenever some new aspect of self begins to emerge in psychoanalysis. New and hitherto unknown aspects of self emerge from behind the linguistic covering, revealing that 'I' am not as you think. This is a sensitive area of psychoanalytic work that is often overlooked. For people who have been particularly captivated by the image of them that is held in the mind of the other – the mother's image of her child – the 'true' self, beyond the attributed image, is felt to be shameful (Mollon 1993). He or she will be in the grip of a chronic conflict between wishes to present an authentic self and feeling that this must be forever banished. Private sexual desires are particularly subject to shame. A rather shame-prone man was caught by his wife looking at pornography on the internet. His ensuing reaction of catastrophic shame was such that he felt he must do away with his whole self, and made a serious suicide attempt.

Extreme states of toxic shame and humiliation can trigger psychosis. This extreme shame is experienced as a violent expulsion from the symbolic order – a state of being driven out of the human group in its totality – one's name expunged. The symbolic self, constructed from the relevant words, roles and identities available in the family and wider social world, is dissolved – resulting in a fateful psychotic break and the emergence of hallucinations – these being degenerate disintegration products (Kohut 1977) of the collapse of the symbolic self.

Psychoanalysis works to reduce shame by drawing more and more of the analysand's self into the spoken symbolic realm. To do so successfully requires the analyst to be maximally sensitive to shame and appropriately tactful. Unless this is the case, the danger is that the shame-laden parts of the self will remain ever more deeply repressed, sealed over by an identification with the analyst's values and perspectives. If the patient suspects that the analyst will view his or her sexual desires and fantasies as 'perverse' these are less likely to be disclosed than if the analyst manages to convey an interested and non-judgemental attitude towards the rich spectrum of human sexuality.

However, the symbolic is to do with separation – words are not the things in themselves, but are signs pointing to those things. The entry more fully into the symbolic is thus akin to entry into Klein's depressive position, where the separateness of the caregiver or other object of love is appreciated and tolerated. The symbolic order means separation from the fantasy of union with the mother. By contrast, sex offers the promise of union with an other's body – thus inherently placing itself outside of the symbolic discourse. Sex is thus maximally appealing and at the same time full of potential dread, in its signification of death and loss of the symbolic self. A schizophrenic woman talked to me of her utter terror at the idea of sexual intimacy – she feared that in sexual union she would become completely lost in, and confused with, the other person. The conflict between intense sexual desire and intense terror is, of course, a key factor in many forms of so-called perversions.

Another intriguing feature of sexuality is the way in which it strangely incorporates the deepest wounds to the self in the desires and fantasies that it generates in its name. Robert Stoller (e.g. 1976, 1986), amongst others, demonstrated very clearly how sexuality cleverly transforms the greatest wounds to the developing self – for example, the threats of castration, feminization (of the male) or denial of autonomy – into the most crucial foci of sexual excitement. Why does sexuality do this? It seems to me that what sexuality does is to take all that is banished from the realm of language – all of what in childhood could not be spoken of, the areas of experience that are rendered dumb and invalid – and weave these into fantasy and desire. Sexuality is akin to Freud's 'navel' of the dream (1900: 525) – it is the hole in the symbolic, tantalizing, seductive, gathering all that is banished and repudiated from the symbolic self.

I will now speculate a little more as to why sexuality is inherently terrifying for human beings – how it threatens, if approached in too direct and unmediated a manner, a descent out of the symbolic world and loss of all bearings in the socially constructed world. Kirshner, writes eloquently and with clarity about the meanings of Lacan's perception of the human dilemma. I will quote him:

> For Lacan . . . subjective experience is dependent entirely on language. For him the capacity to use symbols, including identifying pronouns, and the ability to employ proper names is what makes us human. This is what he means when he repeats in many ways that the subject is an effect of the signifier. There is thus a break from the biological real created by the symbolic order, which in a way captures and restructures the organic basis of life. The body, for example, is conceptualized and organized by labels and categories that stand in the way of any unmediated experience of its reality. . . . Our experience is always filtered through language and the spread of meanings through associations. . . . On the other hand, the symbolic order always falls short of totally capturing lived experience,

inevitably excluding a part of the real in which we are rooted. This insufficiency is attributable to the very nature of symbols, which are structured around missing or absent objects. . . . For Lacan, the inability of the symbolic to totally encompass its referents or to represent fully what has been lost creates a constant gradient of desire, a perpetual reaching out for the pure reality beyond representation.

(Kirshner 2004: 104–105)

This rather clear account of Lacan gives a glimpse of the dilemma for the human species – that having evolved a linguistic cultural world, substituting a linguistic self for a more immediate sensory experience of the world, we may long for what is missing, unknowable and indefinable, tantalizingly beyond the boundary of language, and yet if we merge too closely with this lost something (the *objet petit a*), we risk dissolving our linguistic self. Here is Kirshner again:

Jouissance refers basically to the full satisfaction that we unconsciously pursue. Because such satisfaction is by the nature of our symbolic existence impossible, attempts to approach it breach the boundary of the symbolic and the limits of the pleasure principle, which is constrained by what we can 'enjoy' . . . in the world of symbolic reality. Jouissance is therefore 'beyond the pleasure principle' . . . it has a deadly aspect in that it operates without regard for the welfare of the subject, including her personal meanings, pleasures, and symbolic identity, and when approached is accompanied by pain and distress.

(Kirshner 2004: 106)

It seems to me that raw and naked sexuality, with its biological imperative, is fundamentally what draws us towards this terrifying jouissance – and this is why we have to dress up sexuality with so many fig leaves, clothing it with layers of signifiers. I believe Freud was right to regard sexuality as fundamental to the problems of the mind in relation to the body – and I also believe that we tend to be horrified by forms of sexuality that are generally considered perverse precisely because they remind us of our universal dread of jouissance, of the sexuality that lies beyond the symbolic, behind the fig leaf.

References

Amsterdam, B. and Levitt, M. (1980) 'Consciousness of self and painful self-consciousness, *Psychoanalytic Study of the Child* 35: 67–83.
Bollas, C. (2000) *Hysteria*, London: Routledge.
Broucek, F. (1991) *Shame and the Self*, New York: Guilford Press.
Erikson, E. H. (1950) *Childhood and Society*, New York: Norton.
Freud, S. (1892–1899) 'Extracts from the Fliess papers', S.E. 1: 175–280.

—— (1900) *The Interpretation of Dreams*, S.E. 4, 5.

—— (1905) *Three Essays on the Theory of Sexuality*, S.E. 7: 125–243.

—— (1908) 'On the sexual theories of children', S.E. 4: 207–226.

—— (1909) 'Notes upon a case of obsessional neurosis', S.E. 10: 152–318.

—— (1930) *Civilization and its Discontents*, S.E. 21: 59–145.

Kirshner, L.A. (2004) *Having A Life: Self Pathology after Lacan*, New York: Analytic Press.

Kohut, H. (1971) *The Analysis of the Self*, New York: International Universities Press.

—— (1977) *The Restoration of the Self*, New York: International Universities Press.

Martindale, C. (1977) 'Syntactic and semantic correlates of verbal tics in Giles de La Tourettes Syndrome: A quantitative case study', *Brain and Language* 4: 231–247.

Mollon, P. (1993) *The Fragile Self: The Structure of Narcissistic Disturbance*, London: Whurr.

—— (2001) *Releasing the Self: The Healing Legacy of Heinz Kohut*, London: Whurr.

—— (2002) *Shame and Jealousy*, London: Karnac.

Rancour-Laferriere, D. (1985) *Signs of the Flesh: An Essay on the Origin of Hominid Sexuality*, Bloomington: Indiana University Press.

Stoller, R.J. (1976) *Perversion: The Erotic Form of Hatred*, Hassocks: Harvester Press.

—— (1986) *Sexual Excitement: Dynamics of Erotic Life*, London: Karnac.

Tronick, E., Adamson, L., Wise, S. and Brazelton, T. (1978) 'The infant's response to entrapment between contradictory messages in face-to-face interaction', *Journal of Child Psychiatry* 17: 1–13.

Winnicott, D.W. (1960) 'Ego distortion in terms of true and false self,' in D. W. Winnicott *The Maturational Processes and the Facilitating Environment*, London: Hogarth, 1979.

Chapter 2

A psychoanalytic approach to the understanding of shame[1]

Clifford B. Yorke

In 1909, Freud recalled with approval one of Nietzsche's aphorisms:

> I have done that, says my memory. I could not have done that, says my pride, and remains inexorable. Finally, my memory yields.
>
> (Freud 1909: 184)

The reference is to pride. Pride is the obverse of shame, but the point is a powerful one if thought of in terms of the regulation of self-esteem. The *fear of shame* is a forceful motivator of human behaviour.

Distinctions are not always clearly drawn between shame, disgust and guilt as affective regulators of personal conduct. Freud sometimes lumped these motivational forces together but, in a letter to Fliess (27 September 1898) he presents a potted case history that will serve present purposes well:

> I have started on a new case. He is a young man of twenty-five who can scarcely walk owing to stiffness of the legs, spasms, tremors etc. . . . The accompanying anxiety makes him cling to his mother's apron strings, like the baby that lies hidden behind. The death of his brother and the death of his father in a psychosis precipitated the onset of his condition, which has been present since he was fourteen.
>
> He feels ashamed in front of anyone who sees him walking in this way and he regards that as natural. His model is a tabetic[2] uncle, with whom he already identified himself at the age of thirteen on account of the accepted aetiology (leading a dissolute life). Incidentally, he is a regular bear in physique.
>
> Please observe that the shame is merely appended to the symptoms and must relate to their precipitating factors. He volunteered himself that his uncle was in fact not the least ashamed of his gait. The connection between his shame and his gait was a rational one many years ago, when he had gonorrhoea which was naturally noticeable in his gait (gonorrhoeal arthritis), and even some years earlier, too when constant (aimless) erections interfered with his walking. Besides this, the cause of his shame

lay deeper. He told me that last year, when they were living on the (river) Wien, which suddenly began to rise, he was seized with a terrible fear that the water would come into his bedroom – that is to say, his room would be flooded, and during the night. Please notice the ambiguity of the experience: I knew he had wetted his bed when he was a child. Five minutes later he told me of his own accord that while he was at school he still regularly wetted his bed and that his mother had threatened that she would come and tell the masters and all the other boys about it. He had felt tremendous anxiety. So that is where the shame belongs.

(Freud 1898: 275)

The whole passage is richly informative and illustrates a number of points to be underlined in this presentation.

In the interest of brevity I will not review the expanding literature on shame. It has been a topic of interest at the Anna Freud Centre since the Index Group, under the Chairmanship of Joseph Sandler, first studied it.[3] Reflections on their discussions and on the published literature suggest that an analytic approach to shame should start from the following position.

Shame is a powerful and painful affect. It may be sudden in its onset and reach overwhelming proportions. The experience may be global, obliterating all other feelings and thoughts (see Spero 1984). Shameful experiences are not easily forgotten, and when recalled the affect itself may be strongly re-experienced. It carries with it a strong sense of exposure (or fear of exposure), of bodily or psychological nakedness, in which innermost secrets that are felt to be the mental equivalent of body contents are bared to view. The feeling of exposure is linked with the fact that shame always has an external as well as an internal referent. It is doubtful if it is ever completely internalized. There is always an awareness of an observer, a possible observer, a former observer, or a fantasized observer. The observer is always experienced, in some form or other, as disapproving or condemnatory. The fact that one can feel deeply ashamed even when alone does not run counter to this view.

The awareness of an observer partly reflects a link between shame, pride, exhibitionism-voyeurism and the defences against it that underlie the need to hide. This calls for elaboration in developmental terms of oral, urethral, anal and phallic exhibitionism. The links with looking were emphasized by Freud (1905) when he said that small children were essentially without shame and enjoy exposing their bodies. Only later did the counterpart – the wish to see other people's genitals – appear when a sense of shame had already started to develop. Freud's comments on dreams of being naked and their relation to looking, hiding and shame, and the links he made between scopophilia and shame, are important in this connection (Freud 1900, 1905).

In the child, shame is often induced and sometimes maintained by parents, siblings, peers and teachers. From the parents' side, it is often couched in terms of 'What will the neighbours say?', which is a major social derivative of the shame experience and may contribute in due course to a shaming super-ego. These social derivatives underline the fact that the cultural component in, and enforcement, reinforcement and maintenance of shame varies from land to land and from place to place even within the same country.

Shame differs from 'negative affects' other than guilt in that it is a major regulator not only of social conduct and personal relationships, but even at times of thinking itself. One can be ashamed of one's thoughts or be afraid to have them – a tendency that may be strongly reinforced by religious belief and culture (and include the notion that God is watching and knows exactly what one is thinking).

Shame differs from guilt, which is also a major regulator, in material respects (see, for example, Piers and Singer 1953; Sandler *et al.* 1963; Levin 1967; Pines 1987). Clinically, the difference between the two is striking: it has been rightly said that guilt brings material into analysis while shame keeps it out, a fact exemplified in cases to be discussed. Conceptually, distinctions have proved less easy to draw. The problem has to be considered in terms of the growth of the superego complex, with the moves from outer to inner approval or condemnation, and the changing contributions of love and hate to its unfolding. Sandler *et al.* (1963), extending the work of the Index Group on the *representational world* (Sandler and Rosenblatt 1962), discussed shame in terms of the awareness of a discrepancy between the ideal self (the self-I-want-to-be) and the perceived self.

In our coming deliberations, we need to be mindful that while shame is a normal affect its excessive and repeated experience can border on, or indeed amount to, pathology. Where it is missing altogether there is pathology of some import. But the topic of *shamelessness* is a complex one. There is little doubt that it can have reactive or defensive functions, or be part of serious developmental pathology.

Developmental considerations

It may be helpful to approach a developmental understanding of shame by considering *disgust*, because this powerful affect helps to bring about the internal rejection of hitherto pleasurable activities. It strikingly exemplifies an early link between affective experience and defensive measures. In the experi-ence of disgust, the subject attempts to place the offending object *outside* the body, as expressed in his physical or psychological revulsion. The object 'stinks', but it does not belong to him: rather, he sees it as if he were thinking: 'I wouldn't like to have *that* inside me!' But, in shame, it cannot be denied that what offends is *inside* the mind or the body; but it is *outside*, too – hence the unpleasant feeling of exposure (Spero 1984).

Does this help to place the roots of shame developmentally, in time? The first thing to decide, if this view of the *localizations* of shame and disgust is correct, is which comes first. The attempt to place the disgusting object *outside* the body does not do away with the fact that the attempt *is* an attempt, motivated by the intense dislike of locating the object inside oneself. To this extent the *defensive* organization of disgust (reaction formation) is psychically *internal*, and when the manoeuvre of externalization fails to work, or cannot be sustained, the disgust of something within oneself is quite overt. But if, unlike disgust, shame occurs on the *border* between self-awareness and object-awareness, and follows the beginning of internalization of the external and shaming parental attitudes, then it must precede disgust in terms of the *localization* of its origins.

Spero places the affect of shame in the second year of life: certainly, it develops in the context of the 'anal organization', and we have to examine that organization more extensively in considering how and when shame and disgust appear.

When Freud (1917) talked about the 'pre-genital organization' he did not refer to instinctual drives alone but to a totality of developing mental life. The term *anal organization*, likewise, carries this wider sense. The use of a body zone to characterize a childhood epoch simply underlines the fact that the ego (in the sense of 'the self') is, to quote Freud (1923: 2–27), 'first and foremost a body-ego', i.e. a 'body-self'.

The key to our understanding of this phase is *sphincter control* and its *mental equivalent*. It is this control that marks a major forward movement in object relationships. It establishes self-boundaries. Because there is a growing and clearer awareness of what is *inside* and *outside* the body, mental representations of the body-self are laid down and distinguished from representations of the environment, of objects.

Abraham (1921, 1924) distinguished two stages of the anal phase in which the expulsive, destructive one is followed by the holding, retentive phase of sphincter control. It is in this second stage of the anal organization that bodily experiences come to be represented by thoughts, and that the beginning and rapid growth of body- and object-representations permit a burgeoning understanding of their relationships to each other. The growing capacity for self/object discrimination sets the stage for the child to understand and question parental wishes, expectations and interdictions. Freud (1917) had already pointed out that the ability to hold on to or let go faeces enables the child to decide, for the very first time, between self and object love. He can 'sacrifice' his faeces to the object of his love, or can retain them auto-erotically.

These developments go side by side with an increasing awareness of, and control over, the body musculature. The child's physical motility and his growing capacity to put physical distance between himself and his mother has its psychic counterpart in *thought*. Thoughts can be offered or retained, played with, shifted around. Like the faeces themselves, thoughts can be valued or despised, idealized or derogated – a polarity that influences giving on the one hand and retentiveness on the other.[4] This phase brings with it a measure of secrecy and fear of thoughts being known.

As Shengold (1985) puts it, this freedom to move around (both physically and psychically) is linked with a 'developmentally determined and environmentally enforced' struggle over who will control the child's anal and urethral sphincters (cf. Freud 1917). It is during these developments that the internalization of the dictates of the parents (as perceived by the child) begins. There is a change in the quality of the child's internal picture of himself, his objects, and the relationship between them.

Robert Fliess (1956) discussed the unconscious involvement of the anal sphincter in the mastery of 'regressive and archaic affect' – that is, the primitive feeling that is characteristic of infantile life and dichotomized in bliss and murderous rage. This mastery is tenuous in young children: we see it give way in the temper tantrum. It is during the anal phase that 'archaic affect' becomes increasingly differentiated and refined and lays the foundation for what, if all goes well, becomes the rich variety of affect available in later life.

These forward moves are accompanied by an increasing elaboration and sophistication of the defences. Just as the earlier and more primitive mechanisms of externalization and projection are psychical reflections of orality – of spitting out and taking in or incorporating cannibalistically – so with the expanding anal organization a basis is laid for the forerunners of repression and those mechanisms that involve a repressive component. There is an important intermediate stage when the mechanisms of isolation and undoing enter the child's defensive armamentarium for the first time.[5] But in general the anal phase starts to play a vital part in the construction of a hierarchy of defences and lays the ground for the later, massive infantile amnesia that is the hallmark of the repression barrier.

The anal organization presides over the power of both *devaluation* and *idealization*. The parents' punitive and restrictive attitudes are experienced and internalized side by side with their tolerance, acceptance and encouragement. These steps are strongly influenced by anal ambivalence, linked with the way toilet training is achieved through both love and fear of the parents. All this is enormously intensified by the fact that the stools can be seen either as 'pure gold', to be retained or parted with as a gift, or as noxious dirt to be derogated and despised. The experiences of the 'good' and the 'bad' during the oral organization are necessary forerunners of all this. The anal organization structuralizes, internally, this sense of 'goodness' and 'badness', and therefore embraces the setting up of precursors of the superego and ego-ideal. (See Ferenczi, 1925: 267; Freud 1940: 195; Kennedy and Yorke 1982; Shengold 1985: 54.)

It remains to clarify Shengold's use of the term *anal-narcissistic defence* before developing the present argument. He refers to those near-somatic, body-self defences developed by children during the anal phase. These act as 'a kind of emotional and sensory closeable door that serves to control the largely murderous and cannibalistic primal affects derived from the destructive and from the perverse sexual drives of early life' (1988: 24). The 'door' operates along the lines of the body-self in its control of the anal sphincter and its close psychological derivatives.[6]

Can we usefully understand, in the light of all these considerations, shame as involving a *regressive* breakdown of anal defensiveness? Certainly, the sense of nakedness that accompanies shame suggests a breakdown of a barrier between self and other. It is as though one's physical and psychological clothes have been stripped away. To put the matter in this way is to extend the concept beyond the anal barrier itself, central though this is as a nodal point of development. There is a rupture, or partial dissolution, of those parts of the body schema that have a high instinctual investment, including the defining surface of the skin. It includes those erotogenic zones that acquire fresh and changing importance of greater centrality as development proceeds. Those parts of the body that border the junctions of skin and mucous membrane, that are in repeated contact with others or with other parts of one's own body, all that is erotogenic whether intrinsically or by displacement – all these body areas have a high degree of investment that may be fostered or interfered with in the context of growing awareness of self and object relations.

What gives the *sphincters* such importance is their special link between inside and outside and their role in the expulsion and retention of urine, faeces and other body content. Here we are truly on a borderline, since the body products concerned retain their inner and outer referents. And since urinary control is normally attained before bowel control, its link with shame might be expected to start there.

Freud (1908), discussing the sexual theories of children, says that, once they become aware that the father inserts his penis into the mother, their ignorance of the vagina leads them to believe that 'if the baby grows in the mother's body and is then removed from it, this can only happen along the one possible pathway – the anal aperture. *The baby must be evacuated like a piece of excrement, like a stool.*' A later theory of birth – through the umbilicus – *is* expressed aloud and easily remembered: such theories 'no longer contain anything objectionable'. By then children have 'completely forgotten that in earlier years they believed in another theory of birth, which is now obstructed by the repression of the anal sexual components that has meanwhile occurred. At that time a motion was something that could be talked about in the nursery without shame. The child was still not so distant from his constitutional coprophilic inclinations. There was nothing degrading about coming into the world like a heap of faeces, which had not yet been condemned by feelings of *disgust*' (Freud 1908: 219; my italics). The cloacal theory – which after all coincided with the reality of birth in so many animals – was a very natural one at the time and *common to both sexes*.

Before referring to gender difference in the evolution of the sense of shame, it seems important to re-emphasize that the anal organization and the way it develops is strongly influenced by the oral organization that precedes it, and neither the origins of shame nor of disgust can be considered without reference to that earlier phase. After all, taking into the body and spitting out are characteristic of this stage even if body boundaries are at best only primitively defined. But the sense of 'good' and 'bad', originating from the pleasure/pain principle, is an important forerunner for the judgements and bodily dealings of the anal phase. And distaste, and perhaps what has been inelegantly called dis-smell, begin but do not end with the oral organization.

What has been said about the early roots of the shame experience would not in itself point to obvious gender distinctions. Subsequent development is a different matter, with the appearance of penis envy in girls and the vicissitudes and variants, and differing courses in boys and girls, of the phallic organization, castration anxiety and the Oedipal conflict itself. In 1905, in *The Three Essays*, Freud speaks of the role of shame and disgust in the inhibition of sexuality, and thought this took place earlier in little girls than in boys. Whatever the truth of the matter, the cloacal concept of the genitals may, in girls, be anatomically reinforced, may have a strong bearing on the close tie with shame, and has been the subject of repeated comments in the literature.

The cardinal distinction drawn some years ago by Edgcumbe and Burgner (1975) between the phallic-narcissistic and the phallic-Oedipal phase is very helpful for present purposes. For it is in the phallic-narcissistic phase that exhibitionism, for instance, takes on a new dimension. As the authors put it, the pride that was once expressed in terms of 'look at what I can produce' is replaced in this phase by 'look at what I am', and there is a shift of emphasis to the whole body rather than body contents. That shift can only come about as the body-ego, the body-self representation, becomes more fully structuralized along with a greater awareness of the differences between the sexes. The boy's pride is centred on his possession of a penis, which becomes the focus of his bodily concerns. The girl develops envy of that organ, but finds compensatory fantasies to deal with it: for example, that a penis is merely hidden inside her; or that one day a penis will grow, sprout and become visible; or the whole body is experienced as itself a penis, though this is something that contributes in both sexes to the narcissistic character of this phase. But it does have a special part to play in female narcissism.

To look at all this in terms of penis envy alone is to see but a part of the problem, though a very important part at that. Helene Deutsch (1930) drew attention to the fact that when, perhaps for constitutional reasons, there is a shift from activity towards passivity, the girl lacks an organ with which that receptivity can be expressed. And this, in Deutsch's view, is an important forerunner of penis envy, because the boy has something quite conspicuous for which he can see some future use in a way that the girl cannot. She has to deal with a more primitive awareness. The entire matter is complicated by other factors. For example, we are well aware of the painful feeling that results from the child's awareness of physical inferiority to the parents. The boy cannot have a penis as big as the father's, and although the little girl may want babies, have fantasies of babies, and play with babies, she cannot as yet match the mother and give birth to one. And the boy too envies the woman's capacity and the girl's future ability to mother a child. If a child sees, believes, or fantasizes that a sister or brother possesses something or can do something that he or she cannot, and believes this is something that should already have been attained, grounds for shame may be felt to exist. And if these grounds are conspicuous in bodily terms, they are not confined to them. A child who cannot write, for example, but can see his peers able to write very well, feels ashamed of himself in that regard. When such an awareness dawns, it is not so very far from a regressive experience, from an awareness or feeling that one has fallen behind, if not fallen back.

The forerunners of shame

Mother–toddler observations

Extensive observations in our mother–toddler group, where the children's ages range from 16 to 27 months, have failed to identity unequivocally the earliest roots of shame. It was difficult to know whether a particular piece of behaviour was a source, expression or result of shame. Typical observations record the pleasure in direct gratification of instinctual needs, in messy play with water, in aggression and assertiveness. But we have observed pre-stages of a disgust reaction. One two-year-old stopped in his tracks as he noticed a piece of plasticine, brown in colour, lying on the table. He looked long and hard at it, but didn't attempt to touch it.

By and large, toddlers show little concern about wetting accidents. This would be in line with the view that outer proscriptions, prohibitions, and disapproval have to begin to be internalized before shame can be experienced. *It is not enough for bladder control itself to be established and relapses to occur.* A little girl whose bladder control had been very satisfactory for some time showed surprise, but no distress, when she made a large puddle in the middle of the floor, causing some commotion when she did so. Even the concerted efforts of the adults to mop up appeared to elicit no embarrassment or self-consciousness.

Parental concern and shame in regard to a child's behaviour are another matter. Some mothers easily felt shown up by their children's behaviour, especially if the child insisted on gratifying needs that the mother felt ought to have been outgrown. Amelia, 23 months old, wanted her dummy: the mother told her she did not have it with her, although she whispered to the observer that it was in her pocket. When Amelia started to search for it, the mother pushed her away, and told the observer she herself had used a dummy until the age of 13. It seems that those aspects of a child's behaviour that a parent finds difficult to tolerate are those she or he are most heavily defended against internally.

Many of our mother–toddler group observations certainly show the *mother's* shame, with the feeling of exposure, of the regressive actions on the part of the child, and her identification with that child in the shaming behaviour. *From the mother's point of view*, the shame is both internal and external, bordering on both and including them in the identificatory process. This might be one use of the term *projective identification*. Certainly, in such instances, the mother experiences the shame long before the child does. From the child's point of view, the awareness of external disapproval long precedes shame itself and where bowel and bladder control is concerned this will initially begin with 'sphincter morality' (Ferenczi 1925). The parental attitudes are a formative part of the social sources of shame that are forever retained after internal sources have become established.

There is a story from the wartime Hampstead Nurseries often told at the Clinic and recorded elsewhere (Kennedy and Yorke 1982). One of the children, Brigid, who had difficulty in acquiring bladder control, reached a turning point when she was able to announce, with affect *bordering on pride*, 'No more wee-wee on the floor: Mummy doesn't like it; Nurse doesn't like it; Brigid doesn't like it.'

Nursery school observations

Nursery school observations were more rewarding and I have selected just three examples. The first, *Julie* (2:5), one of the youngest children in the nursery, went to the toilet and returned to snack with pants and knickers round her ankles. The two oldest children (4:5) put their hands over their mouths and gasped, giggled and whispered to each other. No other children present at the time took any notice of Julie.

In the second, the nursery children were preparing for the paddling pool. *Ruby* (2:6) was in her knickers and a T-shirt when a teacher told her that if she didn't get ready she wouldn't get her turn. In the middle of the circle of children Ruby took off her clothes and, standing naked, put her knickers between her legs. Mohammed laughed at her, pointed and said loudly, 'Look at her!' Julie (now 4:0) said to her, disgustedly, 'You're rude!' Ruby was unfazed, stood there for several minutes, then put her suit on.

Lastly, *Carrol* (4:10) showed the observer some lipstick and called it 'poison'. A little later she ran towards her and with shrieks of laughter tried to smear the lipstick over the observer's skirt. She had to be restrained; she stopped but went on laughing and ran away. Shortly afterwards she called to the observer and asked her to join her. She did so. Carrol began to sing to her in a taunting and denigrating tone, 'Jill (the observer) is a cry-baby. Jill doesn't know anything. Jill picks her nose.' She sang this repeatedly, eventually ending with a chorus of 'Shame on you'. Another observer recalled that other children *pretended* to try to smear Jill with *chocolate*.

In these examples the link between shame, wetting, being dirty and defences and defensive manoeuvres against them need little comment. The children's demonstrations of how regressive actions *appropriate to a younger child but sometimes a cause of shame in an older one* (being a cry-baby, being more ignorant – sexually ignorant? – than one ought to be) likewise need little comment. Other examples showed that the fear that one might not be able to carry out a particular task – especially one that is easily accomplished by one's peers – and make a fool of oneself, can become a source of shame or prompt defences against it.

Pathological shame: a clinical vignette

Arlo began analysis when he was ten years old on account of his refusal to go to school. This followed a bout of diarrhoea and a severe reprimand for using the staff toilet. Over the months his fear of messing and his anxiety about using the toilet, particularly at school, had steadily increased.

Arlo's family moved to England some years before due to his father's work as a diplomat. They settled well, although Arlo found his school academically demanding and he lagged behind his peers. However, he was popular, since he fitted in well with the athletic milieu of an English boys' private school.

Arlo was fond of his sister, some years his senior. His relationship with his older brother Jeff was problematic and significant. For some years Jeff repeatedly teased and bullied him, behaved as if disgusted and called him 'smelly', so that Arlo lost all self-confidence in Jeff's presence. His mother was unable to control Jeff's vicious behaviour, and his father, who travelled a great deal, was often unavailable to help him.

Arlo's development was uneven. While confident in some respects, in others he was ridden with anxiety. This anxiety, coupled with the impact of a well-intentioned but overly intrusive mother, especially in matters of bodily care, contributed to delays in his development.

In the analysis Arlo's passivity and feelings of helplessness were pervasive. He was afraid his analyst would share his poor opinion of himself. He was fearfully overwhelmed by his violent and omnipotent fantasies which were intensified by Jeff's attacks on him. Slow to talk at first, he gradually gained confidence in his therapist and was able to discuss some of his school difficulties and, later, the fear and guilt about his sexualized aggression – he was excited by the danger he felt his aggression aroused. But he was unable to discuss directly his fear of toilets and of messing. In this way he kept his shame out of analysis. As analytic work proceeded he was once more able to attend school regularly, but still avoided using the toilet.

Arlo felt bad, stupid and humiliated by his academic failures. With further analysis there were improvements in his self-esteem, but three sessions that followed a period of resistance cast some light on his sense of shame. In the first of these he was tracing pictures from a comic book with no particular content. He often did this when he felt vulnerable and feared exposure. He found himself tracing Bananaman, a boy who, when he ate bananas, turned into a super-hero, 'clumsy and a bit stupid, but helps people'. He worked with absorption, excluding the analyst. When she asked what happened to Bananaman, Arlo pushed the book towards her and said, curtly, 'You can read the story.' Bananaman was chasing criminals, at the same time wondering what his portrait in the Hall of Fame would look like if he were caught in certain poses. Arlo traced two portraits of Bananaman, one with his pants down round his ankles, and another in which he was filthy and covered with dirt. With eyes cast down and a simple 'um', Arlo agreed with the comment about his worries and the bind he was in, not knowing what to do.

The next day Arlo quickly finished the picture. He allowed his analyst to see it when she asked, then let her know how exposed he felt as he quickly grabbed it out of her hand and hid it in a book. The analyst talked about Bananaman's worries about having his pants down and everyone seeing. Arlo agreed with his usual 'ums', avoiding eye contact, that it was frightening to be exposed and that his picture could be called 'The Hall of Shame'. He traced two stern-looking teachers and listened as the analyst took up Bananaman's fear that others would think as badly of him as he did of himself.

In the next session Arlo quietly continued his drawing. He traced, between the two teachers, pictures of children from various stories. The first a fat boy taken from a page entitled 'Things You Shouldn't Mention'. The second was a frightened-looking girl with children sitting in a row at school and the words 'Keep Silent'. The analyst wondered why they were silent, but Arlo couldn't remember. In the third, two boys were entangled in a fight. The analyst talked of the teachers who kept a close eye on the children and wondered if the children had something they wanted to talk about but were too afraid and ashamed to do so. Perhaps they also worried that the teachers would be angry and ashamed of them. As she was speaking, Arlo confirmed the interpretation by quickly and competently sketching the boy freehand. He looked at his analyst, read aloud from the story he had previously told her, and remembered why the children kept silent: whatever they said, the teacher made fun of them and put them down.

A regressive rupture of 'sphincter defensiveness': Maria

Maria was in analysis from the age of 17. Her symptoms of anorexia nervosa followed a sexual assault when she was thirteen and a half. She had been accosted by a man in a park. He approached her from behind, knocked her to the ground and forced her to masturbate him. (He wanted her to gratify him by fellatio but did not try to enforce this.) When he asked her if she was a virgin, she failed to comprehend and kept repeating 'Who? Who?' She arrived at home in a state of shock.

At the start of the analysis she was unable to talk about the assault, which was surrounded by an intense aura of secrecy and shame. She felt free association allowed her to avoid the subject. When she *did* bring herself to mention it she cried, emphasizing the secret between herself and her mother. When talking of the *unexpectedness of the attack* Maria brought two early associations. These occurred to her when she emphasized *again* that the man had approached her from behind and added that, although he did not force fellatio, he had held her head. She recalled childhood scenes when her head was held over the toilet whenever she was sick. (Unlike many anorexics, Maria never vomited.) She strongly retained the smell of the man. She remembered a childhood game where father played a Red Indian who crept up on her from behind and tickled her. She liked the game only if she was expecting it. She emphasized that the assailant had put his hand over her mouth and threatened to hurt her if she made any sound. She was disgusted by what happened and felt dirtied when his semen spurted over her. But her compliance, which already had the status of a character trait, although augmented by fear and shock, was such that she asked the man 'Am I doing it right?' when she was rubbing his penis, and kissed him on the cheek when he asked her, deeply despising her actions.

Maria's story illustrates a number of points. Although both the *oral* and *phallic* organizations are deeply involved in her symptoms as well as in the trauma, the element of invasion, of *being forced from behind*, both physically and psychically, is striking and plays an important part in the sense of outrage. Furthermore, she experiences *disgust* when messed up by semen, and *shame* when she recalls the compliance. The disgust is linked with the body product and is itself a defence (a reaction formation); while the shame is the mental counterpart of what was experienced as a forcible physical intrusion. It is in effect a loss of psychological sphincter control, against which, at the time, Maria felt she had no defence. The psychological 'doors' (Shengold) were irresistibly opened with the physical intrusion; shame overwhelmed Maria as a reversion occurred along the hierarchical line of the defence organization with no possibility of arrest at 'defensive anality'. This regressive shift was compounded by a partial reversion along the developmental line of thinking, and expressed in a loss of comprehension that led to Maria's bewildered answer to the assailant's questions. Even after the capacity to think was restored, she continued to feel spoiled and damaged so that *castration anxiety was reinforced by the continued memory and mental re-experience of the traumatic and narcissistic breakthrough*. The subsequent attempts to re-establish control, and its re-emergence in the anorexia, is a remarkable story told at length elsewhere (Cohen 1977).

Shamelessness and shame-readiness

Something should be said about shamelessness. A child who is repeatedly humiliated over his inability to spell or to read may react with disruptive behaviour that sometimes appears outrageously shameless. But the shamelessness may be a reaction against shame; and it may be asked whether such responses are reinforced in cultures where shaming is prevalent. Although shameless disruption at school is not to be identified with exhibitionism, it may involve an exhibitionistic gratification, a way of separating from the parents, and a way of maintaining self-esteem. We have to acknowledge too that conspicuously 'outrageous' dressing with a counter-shaming bravado (analogous to counter-phobia) serves to deny shame, may be a way of shaming the parents, and meets with the social support of peers who adopt a similar style of 'counter-cultural' behaviour.

Defensive 'shamelessness' is illustrated by an extract from an interim report of John, who started analysis when he was nine and a half. His level of schoolwork nowhere reflected his outstanding potential. He failed all his tests, cried a great deal and was repeatedly lost in daydreams. (He was particularly upset by his failures in maths, at which he badly wanted to do well.) He brought his concern about these failures fairly quickly into his treatment; but for a very long time a profound sense of shame prevented his talking about his sexual activities.

John repeatedly longed for a magic solution to his difficulties without expending any effort himself, and his passivity was interpreted on many occasions. When he came back from a successful fishing holiday, his analyst told him he wanted learning to come to him just as easily as the fish had come to his rod. He said in response, 'I could catch a decimal-dogfish, a multiplication-mullet, a subtraction-swordfish – and an addition-angler.' Masturbation themes came into treatment early when John discovered that there were lots of things the analyst didn't find disgusting. To test, seduce or excite her, he introduced a 'shit-shop' – a construction he and his friend Sam were secretly making at school. The contents were 'kit-crap, Hambogeys' etc. Later he added a special ear-wax drink and reassuringly told his analyst not to worry: they had penis pudding as well. He wanted to have his lunches at school to gain more time to work on the shop.

When Sam was away for a while, John appeared somewhat dispirited and found school particularly wretched. One day he arrived for his session in a state of excitement and announced, 'You'll be pleased to hear, shit-shop's on the road again!' It was then that it became clear how much of his school misery had been caused by Sam's absence.

He complained that the French teacher bored him. He suddenly recalled that when he had moved from the big house, mother had made him throw away an elephant toy. He was troubled about clearing his room because his sister Susan left him no space for sorting things out. He agonized over what to give up. The drawings took up the themes of anal retention and loss, and when the analyst let a pie drop out of the window (he was learning to do 'pi' graphs in maths) he looked at her long and thoughtfully and said, with a conspiratorial smile, 'I see,' then asked, 'Do you know what a bum is? It's an American word for tramp.' He paused and added, 'Sam looked it up in the dictionary and it says buttocks.'

John was desperately afraid that if he didn't comply with Sam's wishes and join in his games, Sam would find a substitute. He saw himself as help-lessly manipulated, denying he had any choice in this mutual excitement. He blamed Sam for a detention, saying it was his fault for 'messing about' in class. But he couldn't remember the date of the punishment, and this caused him further misery. He became more and more distressed in his struggle to deal with the threatening presence of Sam. In one session he said, after some hesitation, 'If I tell you things I don't mind telling you, will it be easier for me to tell you things I do mind telling you?' Eventually he said, 'We show each other. I don't want to, but Sam tempts me.' He couldn't concentrate in class because of it, and if the teachers found out and told their parents there'd be terrible trouble. He didn't think shit-shop was disgusting but a boy in class had sucked off Sam and that was disgusting and silly. John said he'd never entered a competition to see who could expose himself the most. But he did take his penis out. 'If you get it on the desk you get 10 points. If you show all you get 100, but that's just about impossible.'

In discussion, the analyst expressed her view that it was the *fear of losing Sam* that eventually enabled John to force himself to overcome the shame sufficiently to bring the masturbatory material. It is worth adding that this material was kept out of the analysis for fully 18 months during a period when John's father left the home and John was ashamed of his mother's promiscuity. There was evidence that Sam, for all his closeness to John in age, was looked up to as a juvenile father figure.

Shamelessness is not always defensive. There are some people who never express, or even experience, shame, guilt, remorse, regret or, indeed, self-criticism of any kind. This seems to point to primary developmental deficits. Such cases are not confined to delinquents: indeed, delinquents may carry a heavy burden of shame. This is true of some forms of petty pilfering and may have precipitated the recent suicide in London of a public figure caught and convicted of such an offence.[7]

An example may be of interest. A woman recently consulted a psychiatrist about her inability to stop herself passing dud cheques, but she had to over-come her considerable sense of shame before she could tell him about it. She could not explain her action, but could simply say of it that she could only leave home in the morning if she had a full wallet. In this example, shame did not act as a deterrent. On the other hand, patients in analysis sometimes give up delinquent practices, not through a sense of guilt or because the under-lying unconscious motives have been analysed, but because they are unable to face the shame of telling the analyst about them – if, that is, they make conscious efforts to follow the basic rule.

We have to consider not only shamelessness but the undue readiness with which many people experience shame. In such cases shame may become sufficiently pronounced to interfere seriously with social functioning and social adaptation. Even the *thought* of a social occasion to come, especially one from which one cannot readily withdraw, or the memory of an occasion where, rightly or wrongly, one feels one has shown oneself up, can become a focus of self-torture and find itself allied to malign guilt.

Every clinician can observe the role of excessive and maladaptive shame in the widest variety of pathologies. One of our adult patients carried a *child's potty*, concealed together with toilet paper, in the back of his car, in case of an 'accident'; and he was careful to plan his route so that he passed as close as possible to public lavatories. The fear was lifelong, in spite of the fact that he had no recollection of any episode of faecal or urinary incontinence. Another patient who was beautiful, charming, gracious and employed as a beauty consultant feared vomiting, crying, loss of bladder or bowel control in front of others as if all these acts were on a par, and was anxious about talking or even listening in public because words had to enter or leave through bodily orifices – the ears and mouth. She was successful in her job and achieved promotion through counter-phobic measures, but shame or the fear of shame haunted her throughout her working day. And there are indeed many patients who are, almost literally, sick with shame at the very thought of vomiting in front of others.

The developmental factors that underlie a special proneness to shame need further study. They would include the nature and intensity of shaming parental and social influences, the recognition and awareness of physical and psychological disabilities and insufficiencies and – since the body may be said to have started it all – childhood illness felt to be of a shaming or 'disgusting' kind. But all this borders on the difficult but important issue of both shame and shamelessness as significant characterological traits – matters that cannot be pursued in a restricted presentation.

Concluding remarks

In concluding, it must again be emphasized that every developmental phase makes its contribution to those that have gone before. The cannibalistic pregenital organization contributes to the anal one and both have a bearing on the phallic and phallic-Oedipal organization. And what can easily be talked about in one phase of development may become, if only temporarily, a matter for concealment and secrecy in others. Latency boys will relish 'dirty talk', but it is unlikely that their enthusiasm for these social activities would readily spread to voluntary or involuntary loss of sphincter control.

Although in one phase the genitals have to be hidden, contests between latency (and some adolescent) boys to see who can pee the farthest become occasions for exhibitionistic pride. In John's case, this seems to go rather far, but every boy will recognize that in some degree this kind of competitiveness is well-nigh universal. And if elders are excluded from, and kept in ignorance of, these activities, the restriction may be less on account of shame than of fear of hierarchical disapproval. But none of these emphases on the sexual and aggressive roots of pride and shame should obscure the fact that their displacements, developments and transformations into skills and achievements, or into failures and successes of every kind, can just as readily retain major motivating affects that began with the body and moved into mental activities and social relationships.

If, in the shame experience, there is a reversion to a stage of development preceding the acquisition of sphincter control, there may be some concomitant loss of impairment of other functions established or developed during the stage of the anal organization. There is a loss of the sense of clear differentiation between self and object, with a blurring of distinctions between what is inside and what is outside the psychological self and bodily self. Side by side with the loss of the sense of control of anal and urethral sphincters, thought reverts to primitive ideation (exemplified in the case of Maria discussed above). Likewise, there is a reversion of affect to a comparatively undifferentiated and *negative* archaic state. The expectations of the ego ideal are massively betrayed as it stands on the border of self and other: there is a loss of clear distinctions between parental love and expectations and their internal personalization. The achievements of the rapprochement subphase go by the board. There is a massive and negative narcissistic invasion. There is a reversion of the defence organization, which now lies in tatters, with the reduction of the self to noxious and derogated dirt. There is a reversion of the superego to the border between inner and outer.

The question is sometimes asked: can shame operate at signal level? There seems to be general agreement that any affect can be 'sampled' so that its emergence is prevented or its intensity restricted by inhibition, externalization, projection, denial, avoidance or limitation of affect-arousing experiences. But it may perhaps be argued that the most effective defence against the full force of what is felt to be a shaming or shameful experience is the avoidance of social exposure. There are degrees of fear, and degrees of fear of shame, but once the affect itself fully develops it floods the psyche and at that point there is no possible defence against it. The psychic gateway has been breached.

Notes

1 This is a shortened version of a paper (Yorke 1990) based on the work of a study group at the Anna Freud Centre and written in collaboration with its members: Tessa Balogh, Pauline Cohen, Jenny Davids, Audrey Gavshon, Moira

McCutcheon, Duncan McLean, Jill Miller and Janet Szydlo. First published in the *Sigmund Freud House Bulletin* 1990, vol. 14/2, and reprinted with permission of the Anna Freud Centre. A longer version of this article appeared in *The Psychoanalytic Study of the Child*, vol. 45.

2 Tabes is a neurological disorder arising from syphilitic infection.

3 Editors' note: the Index Project at the Anna Freud Centre was devised by Dorothy Burlingham as a way of classifying and organizing case-specific analytic material to make it (a) available to more than one therapist for research and reference; (b) to facilitate comparison between different cases; (c) to stimulate and open up new lines of research.

4 Nothing appears to illustrate more clearly the borderland, during this phase, between mind and body, and the regression towards it, than the obsessive compulsive attempts to wash away the thought of dirt (Anna Freud 1966) and/or 'dirty thoughts' by repeatedly washing the hands (cf. Yorke *et al.* 1975, 1989; Yorke and Burgner 1980).

5 Isolation is an early way of controlling and restricting affect, and divorcing it from mental content, and undoing a way of negating and contradicting direct impulses and wishes that can come to be expressed as readily in contradictory thoughts as it is, initially, expressed in contradictory actions. The undue persistence of either, or a regressive reactivation of them, can lead to or characterize pathology.

6 Shengold (1985) adds that the specific anal defence mechanisms enable the child to master those inner and violent forces that threaten to overreach his capacity. This defensive complex may be brought into regressive operation in subsequent psychic danger situations in a return to narcissistic safety. It is a valuable protective device that reduces unpleasure and pain, avoids excessive stimulation, and restricts and avoids 'conflict-ridden feelings associated with object ties. If the defence goes too far. . . . everything that evokes value and meaning can become undifferentiated stuff, and turn to excretable shit'.

7 No account is taken here of shamelessness in relation to delinquent perversion, a matter studied by Dr Duncan McLean and discussed elsewhere.

References

Abraham, K. (1921) 'Contribution to the theory of the anal character', in K. Abraham *Selected Papers on Psychoanalysis*, London: Hogarth Press, 1945.

—— (1924) 'A short study of the development of the libido, viewed in the light of mental disorders', in K. Abraham *Selected Papers on Psychoanalysis*, London: Hogarth Press, 1945.

Cohen, P. (1977) 'The beginning of change from relentless pursuit of thinness', case conference, Anna Freud Centre.

Deutsch, H. (1930) 'The significance of masochism in the mental life of women', in R. Fliess (ed.) *The Psychoanalytic Reader*, New York: International Universities Press, 1950, pp. 223–236.

Edgcumbe, R. and Burgner, M. (1975) 'The phallic-narcissistic phase', *Psychoanalytical Study of the Child* 30: 161–180.

Ferenczi, S. (1925) 'Psycho-analysis of sexual habits', in S. Ferenczi *Further Contributions to the Theory and Technique Psychoanalysis*, London: Hogarth Press, 1953.

Fliess, R. (1956) *Erogeneity and Libido*, New York: International Universities Press.

Freud, A. (1966) 'Obsessional neurosis', *International Journal of Psychoanalysis* 47: 116–122.

Freud, S. (1898) Letter 97, S.E. 1: 275–276.
—— (1900) *The Interpretation of Dreams*, S.E. 4, 5.
—— (1905) *Three Essays on the Theory of Sexuality*, S.E. 7: 125–243.
—— (1908) 'On the sexual theories of children', S.E. 9: 205–226.
—— (1909) 'Notes upon a case of obsessional neurosis', S.E. 10: 3–149.
—— (1917) 'On transformations of instincts as exemplified in anal erotism', S.E. 17: 125–133.
—— (1923) 'The Ego and the id', S.E. 19: 3–59.
—— (1940) 'An outline of psychoanalysis', S.E. 23: 141–207.
Kennedy, H. and Yorke, C. (1982) 'Steps from outer to inner conflict viewed as super-ego precursors', *Psychoanalytical Study of the Child* 37: 221–228.
Levin, S. (1967) 'Some metapsychological considerations and the differentiation between shame and guilt', *International Journal of Psychoanalysis* 48: 267–276.
Piers, G. and Singer, M. (1953) *Shame and Guilt*, Springfield, IL: Charles C. Thomas.
Pines, M. (1987) 'Shame – what psychoanalysis does and does not say', *Group Analysis* 20: 16–31. The present volume Chapter 6.
Sandler, J., Holder, A. and Meers, D. (1963) 'The ego ideal and the ideal self', *Psychoanalytical Study of the Child* 18: 139–158.
Sandler, J. and Rosenblatt, B. (1962) 'The concept of the representational world', *Psychoanalytical Study of the Child* 17: 128–158.
Shengold, L. (1985) 'Defensive anality and anal narcissism', *International Journal of Psychoanalysis* 66: 47–73.
—— (1988) *Halo in the Sky*, New York: Guilford Press.
Spero, M. H. (1984) 'Shame: An object-relational formulation', *Psychoanalytical Study of the Child* 39: 259–282.
Yorke, C. (1990) 'The development and functioning of the sense of shame', *Psychoanalytical Study of the Child* 45: 377–409.
Yorke, C. and Burgner, M. (1980) 'A developmental approach to the assessment of obsessional phenomena in children', *Dialogue: Journal of Psychoanalytical Perspectives* 4: 35–47.
Yorke, C., Putzel, R. and Schacht, L. (1975) 'Some problems of diagnosis in children presenting with obsessional symptomatology', in *Studies in Child Psycho-analysis*, New Haven and London: Yale University Press.
Yorke, C., Wiseberg, S. and Freeman, T. (1989) *Development and Psychopathology*, New Haven and London: Yale University Press.

Chapter 3

Shame in psychoanalysis

The function of unconscious fantasies[1]

Ana-María Rizzuto

Shame, and its counterpart pride, cannot be understood from the point of view of only one component of psychoanalytic theory. In this chapter I suggest that the conceptualization of shame in the clinical situation may gain clarity by linking the emergence of shame to unconscious fantasies. The concept of unconscious fantasy allows in its broad latitude for the understanding of experienced shame as the result of conflict affecting the sense of self and narcissistic self-evaluation in the presence of a significant object. It also permits the inclusion of drive and defence as component dynamic elements in the concrete experience of shame. Conflict between ego, ego-ideal and super-ego may appear either in the content of the fantasy or in its potential to elicit shame.

To discuss the connections between shame and unconscious fantasy I have divided the chapter into four sections: phenomenology of shame, conceptualization of unconscious fantasy, a case illustration, and clinical and theoretical conclusions.

The phenomenology of shame

Shame is ubiquitous in human experience, and a prevailing theme in child rearing, acculturation, literature and religion. It is eternally present in the tuning of love relations and human communication.

The wish to hide to avoid exposure (Fenichel 1945; Lewis 1971; Wurmser 1981) is intrinsic to the experience of shame. Exposure of sexual organs, or the naked body, and feelings or thoughts about them evoke shameful feelings (Freud 1910). The same feelings arise from any loss of control, of bodily functions (Freud 1918), of impulses, of emotional restraint, of social poise (Jacobson 1964). These experiences have some relation to the sexual and aggressive drives. Failure to achieve goals (Morrison 1987) or to master tasks set up for the person, be it by the ego ideal (Piers and Singer 1953; Joffe and Sandler 1967), or by real circumstances, bring about shameful feelings. This aspect of shame appears most directly related to ego and superego functions. The subjective or objective perception of being weak, defective, abnormal, less than others in any respect, becomes a continuous source of shameful feelings about a defective sense of self. Being the target of excessive public attention, of ridicule, of unfavourable comparison to what was expected of the individual elicits intense feelings of shame and frequently rage and wishes for revengeful reparation. Being related to individuals who are found in shameful circumstances, poverty, jail, or demotion may bring shame by association. These experiences seem most directly related to the sense of self, of being oneself in relation to others.

Pride is the feeling on the other side of shame, frequently associated with feelings of joy, well-being and social expansiveness and a communicative disposition. It is related to the opposite of the previously described experiences: a sense of being a worthwhile, respected, successful, strong, deservedly well-liked person in charge of one's own life. Pride gives the body and the sense of self as much of an expansive feeling as shame moves them to shrink to their minimal size.

Shame is directly related to visual imagery. The eye is the prevailing organ of shameful exposure (Thrane 1979). To see oneself or to be seen by others in a shameful condition is an essential and invariable component of feeling ashamed. Other components are the way one sounds and smells to others as ways of revealing aspects of the sense of self. The eye, however, prevails. As I mentioned earlier, the eye of the object seems indispensable for the experience of shame. Even when patients say 'I see myself as . . .' the implication is that the inner vision is shared by others, whether actually present or internalized as part of the superego. The shame experience cannot occur without the 'presence' (Schafer 1968) of another person who 'sees' the ashamed individual. This critical component of the shame experience has a direct connection to actual and internalized object relations and, therefore, to the superego and the ego-ideal as they relate to the sense of self in the presence of the maternal eye and, later, to other people. Winnicott (1971) and Kohut (1971) attribute great significance to the mirroring function of the maternal eye in the formation of the sense of being oneself. There are two types of shame:

1   *Signal shame* (Fenichel 1945), like anxiety, alerts the individual to the possibility that external circumstances or private mentation may evoke the actual experience of shame as a fully developed painful affect. Signal shame serves a normal ego regulatory function of the person's sense of well being.
2   *Painful shame* appears when signal shame fails to modulate the impact of humiliating external circumstances or when psychic defences are unable to suppress or repress conflictual internal imagery or external behaviour unacceptable to the person's sense of self. Pathological shame is a persistent predisposition to painful shame.

The review of the literature on shame reveals the great significance attributed to early development and the adequate communicative function of the early objects (Kohut 1971; Basch 1976; Emde *et al.* 1976; Wurmser 1981; Lichtenberg 1983; Stern 1985; Demos 1986; Morrison 1987). There is, however, a remarkable omission. Nowhere is fantasy mentioned as an essential component of the experience of shame. In my opinion the predisposition to pathological shame requires the participation of unconscious fantasies. Freud, in his letter of 19 February 1899 to Fliess, presents a beautiful clinical observation intended to illustrate the connection between wish fulfilment and hysterical attacks. Freud looks at the formation of the symptom and its connection to fantasy but does not theorize, here or elsewhere, about the connection between shame and fantasy. He describes:

> our friend E. [who] turns red and sweats as soon as he sees one of a particular category of acquaintances. . . . He is ashamed . . . of a phantasy in which he figures as the deflowerer of every person he meets. He sweats as he deflowers, he works very hard at it. An echo of this meaning finds voice in him, like the resentment of someone defeated, every time he feels ashamed in front of someone: 'Now the silly goose thinks I am ashamed in front of her. If I had her in bed, she would see how little embarrassment I feel with her!' And the time at which he directed his wishes on to this phantasy has left its trace on *the psychical complex which releases the symptom.*
>
> (Freud 1950: 279, my italics)

The example could easily be used to comment on the main points of my chapter and clinical case.

Unconscious fantasy and the experience of shame

Unconscious fantasies are a critical component of our psychic life. No conscious or unconscious act, whether we are awake or dreaming, can be carried out outside the influence of unconscious fantasies. Arlow suggests:

> The persistent influence of the unconscious fantasy creates the mental set against which the data of perception are perceived, registered, interpreted, remembered, and responded to.
>
> (Arlow 1985: 526)

Unconscious fantasy formation begins in early childhood and continues throughout life. The individual keeps his or her sense of self and identity by reworking and transforming conscious and unconscious fantasies throughout a life course characterized by frequent external and internal changes. These fantasies are ego-regulated compromise formations aimed at providing a sense of safety, self-respect and identity in the presence of wishes and affects, in conflict with needed objects or with the demands of the superego, the ego-ideal, and the ideal self.

Unconscious fantasies are so crucial for the organization of mental life that 'even aspects of behaviour that are far removed from imaginative activity, and which appear at first glance to be governed solely by the demands of reality, emerge as emanations, as "derivatives" of unconscious fantasies' (Laplanche and Pontalis 1973). If such is the significance of fantasy and unconscious fantasy, how could shame have been studied so carefully without attending to the possible connections between them? I think that the answer is twofold:

1   *Theoretical*: the persistent association between shame and preverbal, early narcissistic experiences, always conceptualized as pre-structural pathology and therefore outside the realm – in classical theory – of true fantasy. The concept of unconscious fantasy requires the pre-existence of a conscious or preconscious fantasy, i.e. ego activity;

2   *Clinical*: shame prompts the patient to seek to hide, sometimes with obvious withdrawal, sometimes with the most subtle defences. The source of the shameful feeling is avoided as much as possible. The analyst may facilitate the hiding by accepting the feeling of shame as self-explanatory in the context in which it is presented. Transferential and countertransferential avoidance of shame may be at play in such acceptance.

Sandler and Sandler (1986a: 112) make the need for ego functions in fantasy formation very explicit: 'It is only when the ego participates in the organization of content into wish-fulfilling imaginative products that we should speak of fantasying or fantasy formation.' Forming the content of the fantasy requires the tripartite model: instinctual wish, superego demands and an ego capable of forming a fantasy as a compromise among conflicting agencies. Neither these structures nor shame as a conscious affect are present at the earliest levels of development when narcissistic preverbal trauma supposedly establishes a predisposition to pathological shame.

Present at the time are: (a) the biological programme for affect (Tomkins 1982, 1987) and (b) the reservoir of connected bodily memories of wish satisfaction and frustration provided by early objects. These include memories of affective communication and message responsiveness or of failures in those realms (Rizzuto 1988). Memories of bodily processes and communicative exchanges become building blocks the child can use when fantasy appears developmentally to form interpretive, defensive, and for the time, adaptive fantasies about 'scenes' (Freud 1916) between herself and the objects. The fantasies are motivated by wishes of many types. The fantasies, in turn, become themselves powerful motivating factors in psychic life. There is a period of most active fantasizing, around the age of three to five, in which narcissistic concerns connect to Oedipal issues ('Am I worth loving?'). The infantile amnesia takes over, and the fantasies, with their powerful capacity to evoke feelings, undergo repression. They now belong to the unconscious and the most powerful among them represent 'the memory content of an unsatisfied wish . . . The seduction fantasy becomes a wish to be seduced, one which remains capable of being aroused throughout the individual's life' (Sandler and Sandler 1986b: 179). The fantasies portray directly or indirectly interpersonal scenes (Freud 1916) capable of evoking specific affects or defensive actions against them.

Clinical practice does not seem, at first, to support my thesis that pathological shame can only be experienced with the participation of unconscious fantasies. Patients do talk about very early shameful feelings and withdraw into silences that to many analysts appear as proof of the analytic enactment of preverbal trauma. It is true that in analysis during periods of regression it is possible to observe how very early experiences are 'narrated' in somatic, motoric or early symbolic forms. The question is whether they are always 'proof' of early trauma. Preverbal presentations of early circumstances would seem to be compatible with findings and theorizing of analytic researchers in the field of child development about early modes of experiencing and communicating (Brinich 1981, 1982; Edgcumbe 1981, 1984; Stern 1985). The verbal function, to be used later as the essential medium of analytic work, appears relatively late in development in comparison with the much earlier dialogue of bodies and affects in the parent–child dyad. Spoken language appears when many sensory modes of mutual attunements have occurred in the communicative function of the 'conversation' between the child and the parents. This communication involves all the senses of the parent and child, and their concomitant pleasures and frustrations. A basic matrix of affective experience and modes of avoiding pain gets established before verbal language appears. These experiences connect, through feeding, the mother to the interior of the body, and, through skin contact and bodily ministrations, they link the mother to the surface of the body. The eye and the preverbal voice (sound, pitch and modulation) as part of play and of all types of interactions become critical means for affective communication and for ego and superego development. They seem to provide both parent and child with a feeling of contact with the infant as a total being.

In my view, these preverbal communicative interactions provide sensory, proprioceptive and visceral memories in a matrix of progressive formation of self- and object-representations coloured by two types of feelings: those evoked by bodily pleasure or displeasure and those derived from achieved or failed affective communication. The second type of feelings seem related to the later development of feelings of *painful shame* and the ego's defensive development of *signal shame*. Thus, I believe, remembered representations originating from moments of *failed affective communication*, whether they are related to drive satisfaction or not, are those utilized later in development in the formation of unconscious fantasies capable of evoking feelings of painful shame. They are related to self-representations of being exposed, defective, a failure, unable to exert self-control; in short, they are all images of an individual who is unappealing to the object, unable to excite it to respond in a particular manner and, as a result, narcissistically depleted.

I have suggested that the wish to speak and to reveal inner experience and its related affect 'requires as an indispensable condition enough experiences of achieved bodily communication during the first year and of verbal communication during the second and third years' (Rizzuto 1988: 383). Achieved bodily communication implies similar affect in both partners and complementarity of messages (p. 383). If the child smiles the mother smiles back (similar affect), interprets the wish of the child to play and responds in a playful manner (complementarity of messages). These experiences provide the cumulative 'ideoaffective organizations' (Tomkins 1982) that later mediate the affective experience. They are the building blocks of later fantasies, conscious and unconscious.

Painful shame results from: (a) the failure to elicit from another person, in reality or in imagined scenes, some similar affect or (b) the inability to obtain a complementary message. In ordinary life the unacknowledged friendly greeting elicits shame or its defence, narcissistic rage, or both. The wish to hide, to disappear, connects with the feeling of not having been noticed as a being deserving a complementary response. The sense of being a worthwhile being is challenged. These conditions obtain throughout life beyond the formative years. The self psychologists have described these experiences during early life with the less precise phrase 'failure of validation'.

The multitude of exchanges between mother and child leave behind remembered processes for the progressive formation and transformation of self- and object-representations (Rizzuto 1979). They include the type of experiences provided by the exchanges and their corresponding affects. Even from early life affects are mediated by an extraordinarily complex network of memories and representations, regulated by no less complex defensive operations. 'As a result of these psychic operations, all consciously experienced affects are the final common product of multiregulatory process. Unpleasurable affect emerges when the ego is able to tolerate it and deal with it (e.g. normal mourning) or when the defences fail and the affect becomes "ego dystonic" (Rizzuto 1988). *Normal shame* refers to the first instance, as when we feel ashamed of having committed some indiscretion but take ourselves with a pinch of salt. It relates to consciously identifiable experiences. *Pathological shame* refers to the unconscious connection between an actual or imaginary event and pre-existing beliefs and unconscious fantasies about one's own worth, defectiveness or unlovability. There is a disproportion between the event and the shame experienced, and an intolerance of the affect itself, as illustrated in Freud's clinical observation mentioned above.

The metaphors used by pathologically ashamed patients always refer to experiencing themselves in the presence of another, be it real, remembered, imaginary, or, simply, in front of a vague 'other' or 'they'. The ashamed person feels not seen or heard; believes herself repulsive in bodily appearance, foul smelling, monstrously horrifying; is convinced that his body is defective, puny, ridiculous, or contrariwise fears his power to destroy, to kill, to go out of control; claims to be totally empty inside, 'no one at home', 'nothing there', or assures the analyst he is 'full of shit', 'all dirty inside'. To these many metaphors with a bodily reference one may add those related to mental functions and feelings: being 'stupid', 'empty headed', 'unfeeling', 'full of hatred', and many others. These metaphors come with a powerful feeling of *conviction*, frequently with a wish to compel the analyst to join in and agree with the patient that she or he is 'nothing' but what they claim to be. Attention must be paid to the verb to be. All these metaphors belong to the area of being a certain type of person in the presence of another.

The metaphors are of great interest because they reveal an anatomy that, like the anatomy of the hysterics, does not coincide with the actual bodily anatomy. They seem to be metaphors organized around the affect evoked by a sensorial bodily experience (repulsively smelly) on the one hand, or a communicative experience on the other (being too stupid to understand mother's hints). These fantasies occur to all human beings but they become unconscious organizers of painful experience for patients suffering from a pathological disposition to feelings of shame; they may also form restricted pockets of pathological shame in any person.

The fantasies appear as organizers for past experiences that are telescoped (A. Freud 1951) into present-day self-referring metaphors. They have the function of memory, be it of actual events or of earlier psychic events, i.e. fantasies about, or interpretations of, actual events. Anna Freud suggests: 'The memory of a traumatic fall, a traumatic injury, may cover the whole series of smaller and bigger accidents which happened almost daily in a child's life. One traumatic prohibition or punishment, remembered or reconstructed, becomes the representative of hundreds of frustrations which had been imposed on the child' (1951: 157).

The verbalization of the shamed person's self-perception appears as a metaphor that 'fuses sense experience and thought in language' (Sharpe 1940: 155). Sharpe suggests that to do justice to the sources of metaphorical language 'our search when we listen to patients must be for the physical basis and experience from which metaphorical speech springs' (p. 156).

It is my understanding that the physical reality used for shame metaphors is not that of the body as a physical reality but as a mental construct of that physical reality as it was experienced in reality and in fantasy in the libidinal, aggressive and communicative experiences with the parental objects. The conscious or preconscious affect of those experiences colours the affect of the fantasies that go into the construction of affect-laden metaphoric body representations. The same representational constructs of past and present exchanges between parent and child modulate the later emergence of affect and are the essential and unavoidable referent for all the self-connoting words spoken between people (Rizzuto 1988).

It is my hypothesis that the body imagery used by the feelings of shame relates to childhood bodily representations akin to childish sexual theories. They represent constructions, imaginative representations of the interior of the body, of its surface, of its sensory qualities, and of the total body of the child, and the child itself, as it is felt it might have been perceived by the adult present at the time when the particular construction took place. The manner in which the child feels the adult sees him may relate to a correct perception of the parent or to the child's projections of his own fantasies and feelings. Frequently, both components blend into a single representational construction.

As soon as the capacity to fantasize appears, the subject becomes, as Freud said, 'the hero of the daydreams', of the conscious and unconscious fantasies. These fantasies are the construction of 'scenes' in relation to childhood wishes, 'scenes and events in which the subject's egotistic needs of ambition and power or his erotic wishes find satisfaction' (Freud 1916: 98). To Freud's list of wishes I may add wishes to make emotional contact, to be responded to with complementary messages, and to feel safe. The fantasies may represent the wish in a 'scene' of rejection, eliciting shame for having the wish. An example is the analysand's fantasized wish to sit on the analyst's lap, portraying the analyst as disgusted, rejecting the patient.

The scenes need not refer to a real or even a realizable event. Primal scenes, where shame and rejection are experienced, may result in constructions organized around causal explanations about being kept out of the parental bedroom: 'They exclude me because I am dirty, full of shit.' The fantasized explanation reveals the sense of self of the individual, as it is experienced at the moment of rejection. These interpretations persist preconsciously, requiring the active participation of complex defensive process to make them tolerable. Many of these fantasized explanations begin in early childhood, after the eighteenth month, when the emergence of secondary process, language, fantasy and self-awareness allows for the possibility of interpreting current events, bodily sensations and appetites.

Whether factual or imaginary, humiliating experiences may engender compensatory fantasies of triumph or revenge. The experience and the fantasies provide remembered self–other representations that facilitate the later conscious appearance of painful shame. The emergence of shame in the course of analysis and in life occurs in the context of the relation with the analyst or with people. The emergence of the feeling, as it happens with telescoped childhood memories, is the result of extraordinarily complex processes the nature of which cannot be ascertained without considering its genetic, structural, dynamic and transferential components organized as present shameful perceptions of something happening in the analytic moment itself. The present-day perceptions acquire their particular form and effect under the guiding power of unconscious fantasies. The unconscious fantasies are the result of repressed interpretive fantasies concocted by the child after frustration of wishes or of attempts to communicate with the parent. The unconscious fantasies focus on 'scenes' of being given satisfaction of libidinal and aggressive wishes; others relate to revengeful fantasies for inflicted injuries or to convictions about having been injured, mistreated, maimed or restricted in the use of power or in the fulfilment of ambitions; and others are derived from passive longings to be adequately responded to after having failed to obtain a desired response. Whether the source is libidinal or narcissistic, the fantasy always presents the subject as the hero (Freud 1916) of some interpersonal event. The manner in which the hero is portrayed in the present connects to nuclei of actual memories, and to the early and later interpretations of the events. Unconscious fantasies related to the memory of that specific portrayal of the child as the desiring and frustrated hero of an unresponded-to affective message are, in my opinion, the main source of the painful sting of shame.

I do not mean to say that repeated traumatic experiences of being shamed, rejected, slighted in childhood, or of having depressed, withdrawn, unresponsive parents are not directly related to a disposition to pathological feelings of shame. There is no doubt that such cumulative trauma leaves indelible marks in the child's psyche. The affect experienced in such moments of rejection and of failed communication is a critical component of the experience of shame in later life. What I mean to say is that the *meaning* of the shame experienced at the time depends on the nature of the interpretation and later reinterpretations the child provided for himself to explain why that particular event happened to him or her. If the fantasized interpretation cannot be worked through, it may become repressed as an unconscious fantasy. The wishes enmeshed in the unconscious fantasy give it its dynamic power, frequently manifested as complex derivatives to disguise them and avoid their potential exposure, which may evoke feelings of painful shame or may require defensive manoeuvres (signal shame) to ward them off.

In summary, shame is related to a self-evaluation (ego and superego) of being undeserving of a desired affective response. It concerns the narcissistic component of any experience or fantasy, be it pre-Oedipal, Oedipal or post-Oedipal. Behind the negative self-evaluation lurk the fears of the loss of the object and of loss of love.

These considerations have significant consequences for analytic technique. A face value acceptance of a feeling of shame as due to one or another cause, e.g. maternal rejection, may be simultaneously true and defensive. It may call attention to one of the participants of the 'scene', the humiliating mother, to cover up the deeper feeling, related to the earlier interpretation that the mother humiliated the child because the child was 'repulsive', undeserving of anything else. The acceptance of the first explanation leaves the patient alone with the shame about himself not being 'the right person'. At this point it is indispensable to introduce some of Freud's (1914) considerations about parental fantasies about their offspring:

> The child shall have a better time than his parents; he shall not be subject to the necessities which they have recognized as paramount in life . . . The child shall fulfil those wishful dreams of the parents which they never carried out – the boy shall become a great man and a hero in his father's place, and the girl shall marry a prince as a tardy compensation for her mother.
>
> (Freud 1914: 91)

The child's direct or indirect perception of these universal parental wishes, whatever new forms they acquire with changing times, makes the childhood experience, of necessity, a situation in which it is impossible to be 'the right person'.

To the ordinary childhood misery of being unable to satisfy parental dreams must be added the parent's tendency to curb or modify childhood behaviour with critical, shaming comments such as 'Don't be silly'. Childhood conscious and unconscious fantasies are called forth to modulate all these childhood sufferings. The failure of the interpretive, defensive or adaptational function of the fantasies to provide a tolerable self-representation brings about experienced shame, or calls for more obvious and conspicuous defences: acting out, phobias, panic attacks, avoidance, withdrawal, disavowal, or displayed narcissistic rage, or other less frequently used defences.

In conclusion, the traumatic effects of repeated childhood humiliations, the impossibility of fulfilling idealized parental wishes, the natural immaturity of the child, the inability of depressed or disturbed parents to respond to the child frequently enough with similar affect and complementary messages, and the unpredictable vissicitudes of life's insults are powerful realities constantly impinging on the child's and the adult's efforts to maintain acceptable or tolerable self-representations. These efforts are based in the constantly active elaborations of conscious and unconscious fantasies aimed at providing satisfaction of wishes and simultaneously a sense of well-being and self-respect. I cannot conceive of fulfilment of wishes in fantasy separate from the search for an accepted and acceptable sense of self. In the world of fantasy formation, narcissism and object love, fulfilment of libidinal and aggressive wishes are so deeply interwoven that one cannot attend to the satisfaction of wishes without considering the sense of self of the one who is obtaining the satisfaction.

Clinical example

I have selected as a clinical example a completed analysis with satisfactory resolution of the distressing symptoms that interfered with a young man's personal and professional life. The example presents Mr B, a man who experienced intense shame in his relations with people, and a need to humiliate the woman he loved. His symptoms were organized around pre-Oedipal and Oedipal unconscious fantasies about himself and his mother. The earliest fantasies portrayed scenes of locking admiring eyes in blissful union with a mother who was 'crazy' about him. The fantasy condensed memories of exciting moments of mutual admiration between mother and child and an exalted view of his excellence. A re-elaboration of the fantasy added his later conviction that he *could* seduce his mother, and the disavowed knowledge that he was a child. The unavoidable Oedipal failure prompted him to transform the fantasy into scenes in which his mother would *want* to seduce him. Finally, in early adolescence, he transformed the fantasy into the unconscious belief that if the perfect woman would *want* to make love to him it would prove that he was a man. This became the core unconscious fantasy of his adult life, the derivatives of which, the mental depiction of the perfect woman, constantly occupied his conscious fantasy life.

Overview of Mr B's case

Mr B was a 32-year-old single business executive who reluctantly came to analysis after making no progress in several brief psychotherapies. He wanted help for his inability to find 'the right woman for me'. He was in a pattern of falling in love, having a first great moment of love, and then devaluing the woman until she rejected him. He was very ashamed of his performance as a man and suffered intensely when he felt others did not see him as 'a real man' but as a wimp. He wanted 'them' to show him 'they' valued him but was afraid of the self-exposure involved in obtaining it through his own actions. He saw himself as a sad fellow always longing for the 'right woman' to want him and always feeling humiliated when women did not 'come to me'. He was an accomplished executive, who knew his senior and junior coworkers respected him but he could not feel that 'they' saw him as 'a man'. The shame about self-exposure inhibited him in presenting business reports, talking to his superiors, or exposing his work in any manner. He reacted with phobic avoidance whenever a situation required self-exposure. Mr B fantasized dreadful moments of humiliation if 'they' came to see him as he was, 'a softy'. His inhibiting shame enraged him with himself but no matter how determined he was he could not overcome it.

Mr B was the only child of a couple belonging to a very large, and, in his words, affectionate extended family. As a child and as an adolescent he was always secretly ashamed that his well-loved father was less accomplished than his cousins. The parents always laughed in retelling the story of how they had fallen 'head over heels' in love with each other and how they had remained in love. Mr B described them as affectionate with each other and with him as well as with the extended family. Mr B slept in the parental bedroom until he turned four years old. There were no major traumas, illnesses or problems in the household. Life was a quiet routine of work, family gatherings and outings.

Mr B was told he was a much wanted child, bright, precocious and handsome with 'curly hair' and bright eyes. He felt that everybody in the family 'was crazy about me' and that his parents 'admired' his good looks and gifts. His development was uneventful without any visible problems with the exception of some mild worries during toilet training. He was afraid of 'splashing all around the pot'. Otherwise, he 'did not make waves', but, in secret, since his early childhood, he felt angry and not properly appreciated.

He described his father as a mild, thoughtful, affectionate man who treated him as a younger pal, and who used long, patient explanations to guide the child through his growing up. The patient 'adored' his father and feared getting angry with him. Secretly, however, Mr B deeply resented the father's overt affection for the mother and attempted to create some conflict between them by seeking his father's help to release him from some of his mother's demands. He described his mother as devoted to them and to the house. Her overprotective attitude, he felt, did not permit him to become 'a man'. He saw her as an always well-groomed, physically attractive woman who enjoyed getting 'all dressed up' to wait for the father in the evening and welcomed him with 'hugs and kisses'. The patient felt great affection for her and great hatred that she did not 'really appreciate' him. He blamed her for his misery.

In prepuberty, soon after his first sexual explorations, he felt horrified by a classmate's report about intercourse, 'the guy puts his jack into the girl's crack', and by a nightmare: *He was caught in a cave, head in first. It was very smoky in the cave. A guy was running after him. He tried to run but his feet felt so heavy that he could not run.*

Mr B became 'a very sad adolescent' in frequent hassles with his parents, constantly blaming his mother for holding him back and 'not being able to be what I wanted to be' and 'not having what I wanted to have'. He could not pinpoint in his mournful complaints what it was she was doing to stop him. He spent his adolescent days studying, singing and listening to sad lonely songs. He identified with 'passive' men while masturbating and fantasizing about 'the perfect woman'. He felt too shy and inhibited to date. College, away from home, brought better days for him. He did not date much but fell in love and had a sexual relationship with a woman he loved very much who in the end rejected him. He admired and belittled her because she was not 'the perfect woman'. All other women would receive the same treatment. He was affectionate, caring and had no problem with intense sexual involvement. However, in his heart, and in his words, he always berated the woman with bitter complaints of 'not having the right posture', 'not being woman enough' for him, or other complaints about the woman as a person.

Mr B wanted to marry and to have the kind of affectionate family his parents and relatives had. He could not, however, restrain himself from demolishing with his criticism the woman he loved.

The analysis

Mr B was a perfect patient: he came at the appointed time, never missed an hour, paid promptly, and tried his best to participate in the process. He felt motivated by genuine suffering.

In the analysis he greeted the woman analyst with insinuating smiles, bodily displays, and searching seductive eyes. He insisted that he had to be seen as a special person while he avoided acknowledging that he needed to be loved. This defensive move seemed to be a form of signal anxiety. In his relation with a woman Mr B did not want 'to give in and love her because I feel that the right person is there but I can't move . . . I feel trapped'. He connected the feelings to his mother:

> It is hard to accept that *I need* her love. I try to push her away. Permitting her to love me means that *I* am not a man, but a mamma's boy (avoidance as signal shame).

These words reveal a paradoxical manner of experiencing affective communication. Similar affect and a complementary response on the woman's part did not bring him joy but great shame. The later unravelling of his unconscious fantasy made intelligible his conflictual avoidance of the love he wanted.

The first part of the analysis required dealing with his extreme fear of being criticized (signal shame) which interfered with his listening to the analyst's remarks:

> I feel hurt that I said something . . . I made an effort . . . I have a sense of shame . . . of humiliation. A bad child: I can't transgress boundaries; I am ashamed of myself. I am frightened of superiors, older people, family members . . . I can't compete with you. I have to submit. I am overpowered and embarrassed. I feel defeated in relation to you. I have a sulking feeling of a bad, hurt boy (painful pathological shame).

Mr B's words illustrate the pervasive pathological shame connected with an internal inhibition to achieve affective communication with people and to accept their complementary response. He constantly felt like a 'bad child', undeserving of such mutuality. Submission, he felt, was his only choice.

These most painful analytic moments were followed by many hours in which Mr B had vengeful fantasies of overpowering the woman analyst, moving into her house and bossing her around. He wanted her to feel the pain and humiliation of having to submit to his imperious orders. At the high point of his vengeful imaginary acts he would demand that she throw herself on the floor and he would make her his sexual toy: he would penetrate her anally, like 'a bitch', humiliating her as much as he felt humiliated. Soon after, he acted out opening forbidding doors in the analyst's office to peer with exhilaration into 'the private parts' of her office. Analytic investigation uncovered that he had peaked through the 'open crack' of his parents' bedroom door to watch his mother changing clothes.

The revengeful fantasies reveal the obverse of meaningful communication: he matched affect prompted by the perceived rejection of him with his perception of the analyst's feelings of being humiliated by him; the complementary response followed talion law, a devaluation for a devaluation.

Exploration of his sadistic humiliating fantasies disclosed that he was never fully there with the woman with whom he was having a relationship. His fantasy life while with her was always involved in self-portrayals of being a 'real macho, a stud, a man who has women falling in love head over heels with me'. He described the extraordinary pleasure he felt while masturbating with the perfect imaginary woman in mind. The prolonged analysis of the masturbatory fantasies uncovered that the pleasure originated in the conviction that only the perfect woman could make him feel like a man. That her making love to him would confirm that he was a man.

After persistent but gentle observations on the analyst's part about his fear of being humiliated in analysis he began to ponder if his fear and his need to put down the girlfriends and the analyst could not be a defensive manoeuvre to avoid doubts about himself (signal shame). He began to observe himself in a manner that had not been possible before. He discovered that when he felt something was demanded of him he resorted to sexual fantasies with the perfect woman who made him feel like a man. For the first time he wished the analyst would 'focus' on him because he wanted more objectivity about himself. He asked the analyst to help him look at himself. The request signalled a shift in his dread of being criticized by the analyst and in the underlying fear of being overcome by intense shame. For the first time in his life he did not have to hide what he felt about himself. His request to the analyst that she help him to see himself objectively brought the analysis to the point of developmental fixation when he could not tolerate being the child he was.

Memories of his childhood submissiveness and model child behaviour rewoke childhood memories of violent sadistic fantasies about his parents prompted by 'vitriolic feelings' about being left out. Soon after, Mr B realized that most of his convoluted fantasies, dreams, long stories, and humiliation of the analyst were 'a cover up' for his fear of being 'a dirty boy inside'. *A dream followed in which he had wanted to impress his superiors. However, at the moment of opening his briefcase he found that all he had inside was his dirty underwear.*

New memories followed the dream. He remembered his adolescent fear and wish that his mother would find his underwear stained with semen, as well as several conversations with his father in early puberty and adolescence.

His father had said repeatedly that intercourse was for adults and that children released themselves with masturbation. These memories brought very intense feelings of shame to the analytic moment. He talked bitterly about 'the humiliation of being a child, of having semen in his underwear', the great embarrassment of 'the secret orgasm that always seems so infantile'.

The shame found its source in the childhood disavowal in fantasy, during the phallic-Oedipal phase, that he knew he was in fact a child (Freud 1940: 204). The disavowal had permitted him to convince himself that he could seduce his mother. The shame appeared each time he was confronted with the unavoidable reality that he was 'only a child'.

These revelations were followed by the return of terrifying childhood fantasies and events: panic about a neighbour's dog, dead birds, beheaded kings, dismembered children, ferocious hungry wolves. Analysis of these fantasies uncovered fear of castration, and fear of the destructive phallic woman. He remembered intense unexpressed childhood wishes to be 'number one' and the panic that came upon him on several occasions when the father was away and he felt he could be number one.

The analysis of these feelings and of Mr B's fear of his woman analyst permitted him to experience feelings of closeness with her for the first time. The affectionate feelings brought back the re-experiencing of his tremendous adolescent wishes for the great sexual experience with the perfect woman. He compared himself with the boy in the play *Equus*, feeling that he could not give up his wish. He pleaded with the analyst to give him 'something' not to feel 'like a wimp'. He also experienced great fear and longed for his father's protection. He sobbed for the first time in the analysis: 'I can't permit myself to proclaim my love; I can't tell my mother how much I love her.' He blamed her for it: 'When I want to give her my love she has a hard time receiving it from me.' After several hours of sobbing about his predicament with his mother, new imagery emerged about spiders, bats, crabs and his childhood's 'queasy feelings about vaginas'. Analysis of his fear of the dangerous maternal vagina culminated in a transferential dream. He presented it to the analyst: *You unzipped my fly and put your hand on my penis. . . . We had intercourse. Your being sexually interested in me made me very uncomfortable. It seemed very stimulating but a taboo thing.*

The associations were to the movie *The Graduate*, where the older woman seduces a young man. The dream revealed itself to be the direct and undisguised fulfilment of his core adolescent unconscious fantasy of having his mother wanting to have sex with him. Exploration of the dream made him aware that the obstacle to achieving emotional satisfaction with a woman lay in his internal conflict about what he was, a 'dirty boy' or a 'man'. Mr B acknowledged his dilemma: when a woman gives me the opportunity I am afraid, paralysed with a tremendous wish. I have to run away. I can't perform as a man. I am just a scared kid. I have nothing to offer.

The wish to have the woman wanting him first protected him from the shame of being found wanting without being responded to. The fear of being responded to rested in the disavowed knowledge that he was 'only a boy' who could not handle a woman's complementary response.

Mr B progressively mourned his aggrandizing childhood self-representation until he could acknowledge what he had known all along: that for his parents he was a child and had to accept his fate as second best. He felt the time had come for him to 'face the rough edges of life'.

He was now able to focus on the narcissistic injury prompted by his cowardly feelings towards women. The analysis uncovered the dominating, unconscious fantasy of his early adolescence: that his mother would find him so attractive that she would unzip his pants and masturbate him. He recognized that moping around the house and lying in the living room couch with hurt feelings and seething rage against her was a disguise for his constant invitation to her seduction of him. He had done this for several years while constantly complaining that she did not love him. At the same time he demanded that his father intervene to get her 'off my back'.

The unveiling of these fantasies brought a rush of humiliating self-representations to the analysis: 'a sleazy little creature', 'a rat', 'a disgusting boy', 'a perverse voyeur', 'a slimy little character' who was always secretive and never opened up to older people. To the analyst, Mr B proposed a deal: he would give up the secrets if the analyst gave him 'something'. His rage at the analyst not giving 'it' to him brought out once more intense wishes to humiliate the analyst sexually and in every possible way. The deepest humiliation he felt was having to ask for what he wanted. He believed that he should be given what he wanted without even having to know what it was. He felt he had the right to have a woman be 'crazy about me'.

Recollections of childhood moments of feeling greatly admired alternated with memories of 'the terrible humiliation of being a child' and the intense early childhood wishes of being 'given something'. The unconscious fantasy of his phallic-Oedipal period, now being repeated as a 'deal' in the analysis, conveyed the wish to be given that 'something' a real man, i.e. his father, gets from his wife. The unconscious fantasy was complex and multidetermined. It included (1) the wish to return to great moments of mutual admiration with his mother; (2) the need to preserve a compensatory aggrandized self-representation that denied he was a boy; (3) the wish to have the mother as the father had her; (4) the fear of the phallic castrating woman, and the disgust about female genitals; (5) the awareness of his duplicity behind his good behaviour; (6) the fear of angering the father.

The fantasy intertwined the earliest memories and fantasies with feelings of being entitled to be given everything he wished. The fantasy repeated the search for the narcissistic bliss brought to him by the admiring eyes of his beautiful mother, and the disguised envy of his father who was 'getting it' now. The transformation of the maternal representation in the fantasy became in adolescence the 'perfect woman'. Masturbation with the 'perfect woman' image in mind brought him transient moments of great elation followed by intense shame. The final fixating and fixated organization of the adolescent fantasy depicted the perfect woman seducing him and making him feel like a real man. The constant feelings of humiliation, the endless masturbation with the image of the perfect woman in mind, the need to humiliate and reject women he loved, the inability to be assertive as a businessman, and the need for frequent sadistic revengeful fantasies were all related to that final adolescent fantasy-wish to be seduced by the perfect woman/mother. That fantasy had been the transformation of phallic-Oedipal fantasies of seducing his mother, failing in reality, and repressing the fantasies now transformed into the passive wish to be seduced by the dangerous phallic woman. Near the end of his analysis he put it all together:

> For a long time I was embarrassed communicating with you . . . I did not want to come and be a little boy in your eyes. . . . There is a real problem in being freer. I am so scared of being seen as a little boy that I have to come across as superman, the unapproachable person. . . . My need as a child to create this impenetrable attitude. . . . The defensive superman feeling: I want to have the perfect woman whose perfection reflects on me. It confirms that I am what I want to be. I call that image of myself a defence against the image of the defenceless little boy. . . . In growing up I had intercourse with my fantasy and put a wall around me. The little boy must feel very threatened to need to put on the costume . . . I take myself so seriously; I can't laugh at myself.

Mr B could now give up the key element of the early childhood fantasy, the disavowal that he was a child. The acceptance of having been a child allowed him for the first time to feel like a man with the analyst and with his girlfriend.

Clinical and theoretical conclusions

Mr B's affectionate and stable relationship with parents he loved and felt loved by did not protect him from trauma. His earliest predisposition to shame seems linked to the overstimulation he experienced in being given excessive feedback about his excellence as a handsome, clever, lovely boy. The analysis did not reveal that the parents used him as a narcissistic extension of themselves. It disclosed, instead, that his communicative attempts as a child met an exaggerated response disproportionately intense to his need to recognize himself in them. He perceived that the message sent back to him in such excess meant that he had to be bigger and better than he actually was. He compensated for the difference by identifying with the parental view of him and by creating grandiose expectations and fantasies about himself. The result left him with the conflicting self-representations of being 'just a child' and having to be 'great'. The conflict was aggravated by the parental over-stimulating erotic display of sexual excitement about each other. Mr B felt acutely the reality of his being excluded from their sexual love.

His fear of losing their love and the parents' tendency to talk intellectually in an affectionate manner about his problems inhibited the child's direct expression of his frustration and complaints. He could not put together how he could be so admired and so rejected all at the same time. He drew a correct conclusion: he was only a child. Mr B felt that being a child was unbearably humiliating and, refusing to portray himself as one, he disavowed his know-ledge. He imagined himself a superman capable of doing what his father could do with his mother. Obviously, he failed. The failure became an unbearable secret, and finally a complex, unconscious fantasy of his unsatisfied wish: that his mother – fascinating and frightful as she appeared to him – would want to seduce him, so he could be the man he liked to think he was.

The fantasy did not serve him well. It returned to him from repression in every possible derivative form whenever he feared 'others' would find out he was not a man. With 'them' too, he wanted to be wanted first, so he could be the passive object of their active wanting. Such a wish made it very difficult for him to take the initiative in presenting his work or himself as an active person to his fellow workers and superiors. He perceived himself all the time as a wimp and despised himself for the humiliation of not knowing how to be a man. His tremendously idealized representation of his mother transformed into the 'perfect woman' of his wishes made any relation with real women an incomprehensible mixture of great sexual excitement and love together with a need to reject and humiliate the woman who loved him. Behind it all was the disavowed component of the unconscious fantasy that portrayed him as a frightened boy, longing to be a romantic hero. He needed to have the mother-woman treat him as a man and, thereby, make him into a man. The shame, and the fear of being ashamed, rested on his knowledge in the unconscious fantasy that he was a frightened boy, a cowardly boy afraid of the very thing he wanted. He feared unconsciously that people would see the scared boy. To protect himself he became secretive, evasive, and phobically avoided any exposure that could uncover his secret. He needed the phobic avoidance because the emergence of any derivative of the unconscious fantasy that reminded him that he was such a boy brought to him unbearable humiliation and a compensatory need to humiliate others. The shame resulted from his contradictory self-representations, first that of his ideal-self as a 'stud', a 'superman' and second that of his knowledge in the unconscious fantasy that he was 'only a boy'.

The conceptualization of conflict in the experience of shame in this case suggests that the components of the unconscious fantasies capable of elicit-ing shame come from dynamic sources encompassing several aspects of the psyche. The intensity of Mr B's libidinal wishes conflicted with the superego of the boy who 'made no waves'; his early self-representation of a child everybody is 'crazy' about conflicted with the frustrated child full of 'vitriolic feelings'; his tender and much wanted attachment to affectionate parents conflicted with his wish to have them treat him 'as a man' and with his rage at them for treating him as a boy. His defensive retreat into wish-fulfilling passive fantasies, and revengeful humiliating fantasies towards his parents was an ego defence that did not serve him well. It facilitated his hiding in fantasy while keeping an outward appearance of being a 'model' child. The childhood drama of his unsatisfied narcissistic and libidinal wishes became internalized as part of the repressed fantasies. The overdetermined nature of the fantasies made their constant repression an onerous task. Finally, in early adolescence, their almost direct derivatives weighed heavily on him, making him a prisoner of his fantasized, romantic longings, in shameful masturbatory isolation. Conflicts from all these sources went into the formation of the successive unconscious fantasies and, in my opinion, it was the fantasies themselves that became the source of his disposition to frequent and intense shame. The fantasies included the wishing child whose affect and inviting gestures could not find correspondence either in the affect or in the message of any living woman.

When shame is understood as emergent affect in the context of multi-determined psychic events and factual reality, organized under the guiding form of pre-existing unconscious fantasies, I do not find it possible to understand it from the point of view of a single theoretical model. Drive, narcissistic needs and sense of self, object relations, ego defences and superego demands, pre-Oedipal antecedents and Oedipal configurations are present in the final elaboration of the unconscious fantasy. Pathological shame appears more meaningful if understood as the natural emotion (Basch 1976) of insoluble childhood dramas conflictually embedded in the threads of unconscious fantasies.

Note

1 A longer version of this chapter was first published as Rizzuto, A. M. (1991) 'Shame in psychoanalysis: The function of unconscious fantasies', *The International Journal of Psycho-Analysis*, 72: 297–312.© Institute of Psychoanalysis, London, UK.

References

Arlow, J. A. (1985) 'The concept of psychic reality and related problems', *Journal of the American Psychoanalytic Association* 33: 521–536.

Basch, M. F. (1976) 'The concept of affect: a reexamination', *Journal of the American Psychoanalytic Association* 24: 759–778.

Brinich, P. M. (1981) 'Application of the metapsychological profile to the assessment of deaf children', *Psychoanalytical Study of the Child* 36: 3–32.

—— (1982) 'Rituals and meanings: The emergence of child–mother communication', *Psychoanalytical Study of the Child* 37: 3–14.

Demos, E. V. (1986) 'Discussion of Nathanson's paper: "A timetable for shame" ',
in D. L. Nathanson (ed.) *The Many Faces of Shame*, New York and London:
Guilford Press.

Edgcumbe, R. M. (1981) 'Toward a developmental line for the acquisition of language',
Psychoanalytical Study of the Child 36: 71–104.

—— (1984) 'Modes of communication: the differentiation of somatic and verbal
expression', *Psychoanalytical Study of the Child* 39: 137–154.

Emde, R. N., Gaensbauer, T. and Harmon, R. (1976) *Emotional Expression in Infancy:
A Biobehavioral Study*, New York: International Universities Press.

Fenichel, E. (1945) *The Psychoanalytic Theory of Neurosis*, New York: Norton.

Freud, A. (1946) *The Ego and the Mechanisms of Defence*, New York: International
Universities Press.

—— (1951) 'Observations on child development', in *The Writings of Anna Freud*,
Vol. IV, New York: International Universities Press.

Freud, S. (1910) 'Leonardo da Vinci and a memory of his childhood', S.E. 11.

—— (1914) 'On narcissism: an introduction', S.E. 14.

—— (1916) 'Introductory lectures on psychoanalysis', S.E. 15.

—— (1918) 'From the history of an infantile neurosis', S.E. 17.

—— (1940) 'An outline of psycho-analysis', S.E. 23.

—— (1950) 'Extracts from the Fliess papers', S.E. 1.

Jacobson, E. (1964) *The Self and the Object World*, New York: International Universities Press.

Joffe, W. and Sandler, J. (1967) 'Some conceptual problems involved in the consideration of disorders of narcissism', *Journal of Child Psychotherapy* 2 (1): 56–66.

Kohut, H. (1971) *The Analysis of the Self*, New York: International Universities Press.

Laplanche, J. and Pontalis, J.-B. (1973) *The Language of Psycho-Analysis*, New York:
Norton.

Lewis, H. B. (1971) *Shame and Guilt in Neurosis*, New York: International Universities
Press.

Lichtenberg, J. D. (1983) *Psychoanalysis and Infant Research*, Hillsdale, NJ: Analytic
Press.

Morrison, A. (1983) 'Shame, ideal self, and narcissism', *Contemporary Psychoanalysis*
18: 295–318.

—— (1987) 'The eye turned inward: shame and the self', in D. L. Nathanson (ed.) *The
Many Faces of Shame*, New York and London: Guilford Press.

Nathanson, D. L. (1987) 'A timetable for shame', in D. L. Nathanson (ed.) *The Many
Faces of Shame*, New York and London: Guilford Press.

Piers, G. and Singer, M. (1953) *Shame and Guilt*, Springfield, IL: Charles C. Thomas.

Rizzuto, A. M. (1979) *The Birth of the Living God: A Psychoanalytic Study*, Chicago
and London: University of Chicago Press.

—— (1988) 'Transference, language, and affect in the treatment of bulimarexia',
International Journal of Psychoanalysis 69: 369–387.

Sandler, J. and Sandler, A. M. (1986a) 'The gyroscopic function of unconscious fantasy', in D. B. Feinsilver (ed.) *Towards a Comprehensive Model of Schizophrenia*,
Florence, KT: Analytic Press, pp. 109–123.

—— (1986b) 'On the development of object relations and affects', in P. Buckley
(ed.) *Essential Papers on Object Relations*, New York: New York University Press,
pp. 272–292.

Schafer, R. (1968) *Aspects of Internalization*, New York: International Universities Press.

Sharpe, E. (1940) 'Psycho-physical problems revealed in language: An examination of metaphor', in *Collected Papers on Psycho-Analysis*, New York: Brunner/Mazel.

Stern, D. N. (1985) *The Interpersonal World of the Infant*, New York: Basic Books.

Thrane, G. (1979) 'Shame and the construction of self', *Annual of Psychoanalysis* 7: 321–341.

Tomkins, S. S. (1982) 'Affect theory', in P. Ekman (ed.) *Emotion in the Human Face*, Cambridge: Cambridge University Press.

—— (1987) 'Shame', in D. L. Nathanson (ed.) *The Many Faces of Shame*, New York and London: Guilford Press.

Winnicott, D. W. (1971) 'Mirror-role of mother and family in child development', in D. W. Winnicott *Playing and Reality*, New York: International Universities Press.

Wurmser, L. (1981) *The Mask of Shame*, Baltimore: Johns Hopkins University Press.

Chapter 4

The shame shield in child sexual abuse [1]

Donald Campbell

Introduction

Research has found that between one-third and one-fourth of all sexual offences are committed by young people under the age of 18 (Horne *et al.* 1991; Cawson *et al.* 2000; NSPCC 2002). Home Office statistics for 2005 showed that of the 6400 individuals cautioned for or found guilty of sexual offences approximately 17 per cent were between 10 and 17 years old. Of the approximately 1600 offenders cautioned, the vast majority of whom were male, around 19 per cent were between the ages of 12 and 14 and 13 per cent were 15 and 17 years old (Hutton and Whyte 2006: 115). As a result of their research, Becker and Abel (1984) estimated that the average adolescent sexual offender would during his lifetime commit 380 sexual crimes: 'Criminal statistics refer only to those over the age of criminal responsibility, which varies greatly between jurisdictions, and record only reported offences' (Hutton and Whyte 2006: 115–116). This observation along with the widely held belief that all sex crimes are significantly under-reported support the view that 'research based on crime statistics is likely to reveal only a small proportion of actual incidents of sexual offences' (Hutton and Whyte 2006: 116).

In light of the fact that approximately half the adult sex offenders coming before the courts began their sexual deviancy in adolescence (Davis 1987), one can see the enormous prophylactic potential in work with adolescent abusers. Puberty and the developmental phase of adolescence create internal conflicts that contribute to the adolescent's abusive behaviour. While sexually abusing offenders are caught up in the throes of adolescence these internal conflicts may be more accessible to both the worker and the adolescent.

This chapter will consider only those adolescents who have themselves been abused when they were younger and who are now abusing children outside the family.[2] However, the burden of proof still lies with the professionals who disagree with Freud's (1896) observation that children cannot find their way to acts of sexual aggression unless they have been seduced previously.

An act of child abuse radically affects the victim's psychic organization and requires sensitive understanding and/or psychotherapy if it is not to leave scars or damage future development permanently. I will consider the abuser's experience of being abused in terms of (a) its impact on the sexual body image; (b) the damage done to the shame shield; (c) the defensive use of simulation; (d) its role in behaviour that is abusing.

Shame and the ego-ideal

Shame is an affective response to an awareness of a disparity between expectations of the self and performance that is witnessed by another. Shame occurs from an early age, probably from the time the child becomes self-conscious and aware of being an object of observation for others. It is also likely that the child has achieved a level of cognitive development wherein it can compare its expectations of its own effectiveness with the reality of the effectiveness of its actions. The expectation may arise from the self or a witness. It is an experience of being seen before one is ready, that is, a moment when a weakness (failure to perform a task or compete), a vulnerability (nakedness in public), a mistake (slip of the tongue) or a deficiency (not knowing the answer to a question) is exposed. Sometimes shame is accompanied by shock as with a slip of the tongue or the appearance of a stranger when one expected a familiar face, and at other times shame develops gradually as with a dawning awareness of not keeping up with peers.

Piers and Singer (1953) link shame to the earliest development of the ego ideal. They identify shame as the affective response, which is triggered whenever goals and images represented by the ego ideal are not achieved by the ego. They recognize four characteristics of the ego ideal. First, there is a core of narcissistic omnipotence necessary to establish self-confidence, hope and trust in others and perhaps even 'magic belief in one's invulnerability or immortality to make for visible courage and to help counteract realistic fear of injury or death' (Piers and Singer 1953: 14). Second, the ego ideal is built upon positive identifications with parental images, that is, aspects of the parents that the child does not possess in himself. These identifications gratify the 'child's most intense and most momentous wish' (1953: 237) to be big and be like the parents, especially the parent of the same sex (Freud 1909). While the good-enough parents implicitly and explicitly give their child permission to be like them, the narcissistically oriented parent may impose his or her own unattained ideals upon the child. Third, the ego-ideal contains later identifications, which contribute to the child's sense of his social role and gender role identity. Fourth, the content of the ego-ideal's goals will be based on an awareness of the ego's potentialities, a wish for mastery, maturation and progress – the pleasure derived from the development of one's competence (Piers and Singer 1953). Piers and Singer imply a defensive function for shame when they observe that 'behind the feeling of shame stands not the fear of hatred but the fear of contempt which, on an even deeper level of the unconscious, spells fear of abandonment; the death by emotional starvation' (1953: 16).

Grinker (1955) follows Piers and Singer's view of shame as a response to a disparity between the ideal self as represented by the ego-ideal and the perceived actual self, and emphasizes a response of shame to a particular failure to master a developmental task at a normally expected time. Shame is particularly prominent during latency.

Freud (1908) viewed shame's defensive activity as a reaction formation designed to maintain the repression of forbidden exhibitionistic impulses. He also recognized that exhibitionistic impulses received a powerful libidinal thrust during puberty. Freud (1925, 1926) identified latency as that developmental phase during which the reaction formations of shame and disgust are built up to defend against 'the later tempest of puberty and to lay down the path of the freshly awakened sexual desires' (1926: 210–211). While later writers have built upon and expanded Freud's view of the nature and function of shame, it is his emphasis on the defensive function of shame to maintain repression and instigate reaction formations in relation to genital impulses, particularly during latency, which I want to highlight in this discussion of child sexual abuse. One of the consequences of abuse during latency is the disturbance of the development of such defences as shame.

The shame shield

The word shame is derived from the Indo-European root kam/kem that means 'to cover, to veil, to hide'. Erikson (1977) views reactions of shame, such as putting our hand over our face, as expressions of rage turned against the self. 'He who is ashamed would like to force the world not to look at him, not to notice his exposure. He would like to destroy the eyes of the world. Instead he must wish for his own invisibility' (1977: 227). We feel shame when we are completely exposed, conscious of being looked at and not ready to be visible. It is not uncommon for someone who feels shame to bring their hand up to cover their face reflexively. The accompanying wish to disappear or become invisible may be expressed by wishing the earth would open and swallow them up. Elsewhere I have referred to this aspect of the defensive function of shame as a shame shield (Campbell 1994).

Shame gives an internal signal and an external one. Internally, shame develops as an affect with a signal function, which triggers a withdrawal to protect physical and mental attributes that have been or are in the process of being integrated into a sense of the self. In this way, shame plays a role in development by guarding the child's internal design or biological clock when an object becomes intrusive or makes premature demands, which threaten to disrupt natural development. Hiding prevents further exposure of weakness and/or lack of control, and restores the self to a safe, private, hidden place where it can be reconstituted.[3] In this sense shame functions as a psychic shield.

Fenichel (1937) viewed shame as a specific reaction to scopophilia, that is, projected aspects of the self, which are too conflictual to be allowed into awareness. He draws on mythology to illustrate how castration anxiety is defended against by not looking at Medusa. In the Bible, Lot's wife is turned into a pillar of salt as punishment for looking back on Sodom and God's omnipotent destruction.

However, the shame shield is only partially successful as a defence. A sense of shame confirms our failure to become invisible. We would like to disappear but the best we can do is to hide behind our hands. In this sense, shame not only triggers an internal signal of anxiety, but also manifests an external signal. *The protective function of shame as an external signal depends for its success upon the object perceiving the external manifestations of shame as a shield between self and object which the object recognizes as a signal of failure and respects enough to react sympathetically to the self.*

When the shame shield has been breached and left unrepaired, shame is projected and is not available as a deterrent to enacting conscious or unconscious sadistic fantasies. Ordinarily, a strong sense of shame could deter an individual from acting in a perverse way. Instead, other defences such as repression, denial, disavowal, splitting and projection are used to fill the gap created by the failure of the shame shield.

A child who is subjected to sexual abuse is intruded upon visually and physically before he or she is ready. The shame shield is not respected but is sadistically attacked by the perpetrator who reverses his original passive experience of being abused. As a result, there is no sanctuary for the child to retreat to in order to reconstitute its genital body image. Hence, a common expression for shame, quite appropriate in cases of child abuse, is the popular expression of being 'caught with one's pants down' which reflects the anal regression precipitated by sexual abuse. Erikson views shame as the result of inhibited aggression; a passive ego is overwhelmed and unable actively to fight off an external threat. Aggression is turned from the object to disgust of the self (Erikson 1977: 223).

When the shame shield is breached invisibility is not an option and the ego searches for other means of protecting itself from self-disgust. In tracing the development of the sense of shame, Yorke (1990) compares disgust with shame:

> In the experience of disgust, the subject attempts to place the offending object outside the body, as expressed in his physical or psychological distaste. The object 'stinks', but it does not belong to him: rather, he sees it as if he were thinking: 'I wouldn't like to have that inside me!' The attempt to place the disgusting object outside the body does not do away with the fact that the attempt is an attempt, motivated by the intense dislike of locating the object inside oneself. To this extent the affective but defensive organisation of disgust (reaction formation) is psychically

internal; when the manoeuvre of externalisation fails to work, or cannot be sustained, the disgust of something within oneself is quite overt.

(Yorke 1990: 283–4)

Relief is sought by resorting to actions that project the confusion, passivity and disgust into others. The victim may try to protect himself by splitting off the disgust for himself and projecting that disgust on to the organs exposed by the abuse. Furthermore, the abused child may project his self-disgust via an abusive act on to another's body that is treated with contempt. In this way, the abused child becomes the abuser. The experience of being abused in childhood or adolescence may distort the victim's sexual body image, an aspect of the ego-ideal.

Sexual body image

The child's sexual body image, a component of his ego-ideal, is built up gradually and responds to an 'internal design' or a biological clock which moves the child through age-appropriate phases of development which we refer to as oral, anal, phallic and genital. Stimulation of and pleasure derived from these erotogenic zones in interaction with his parents contribute to the progressive development of the child's image of his sexual body. A child builds up an oral dimension to his body image as he sucks for nourishment, or purely for pleasure, at the breast, teat or beaker, or immediately puts an object into his mouth as a primary means of exploring it. Later, preoccupation with and pleasure derived from defecating as well as conflicts within the child and with others over control of these pleasurable functions and admirable creations enable the child to incorporate his anality into an image of his sexual body.

Increasing awareness of erotic sensations in the genitals, enhanced by childhood masturbation, gives the genital prominence among those three zones of erotic satisfaction, so that it comes to dominate the child's sexual image of his body. This culminates in the child's acceptance of sexual differences, size in relation to the parents, and the reality that Oedipal wishes to kill the parent of the same sex and have intercourse with the parent of the opposite sex cannot be satisfied. A 'bedrock of reality' is created by the acceptance of difference between sexes and generations, that is, 'the inevitable period of time separating a child from his mother (for whom he is an inadequate sexual partner) and from his father (whose potent adult sexual organ he does not possess)' (Chasseguet-Smirgel 1985a: 2). Nevertheless, the oral and anal zones of sexual satisfaction remain with us as adults forming the basis of foreplay and the build-up to genital satisfaction.

An act of child abuse bisects the line of normal development, disrupts the natural timing of the biological clock and turns the Oedipus complex upside down. Incestuous wishes are gratified with parents, siblings or adolescents or adults who are perceived as sibling or parental substitutes. The sexually abusive act overstimulates the mouth, anus or genitals. These traumatized erotogenic zones must be incorporated into the child's sexual body image.

Likewise, the experience of being overwhelmed by a genitally mature person will reinforce passive submissiveness and undermine the development of heterosexual relations in adolescence. As a consequence, the abused child can be expected to think of himself or experience himself in pregenital and pre-Oedipal terms. For instance, a boy who is buggered may feel he has been feminized, used like a woman, and find it difficult as an adolescent to think of using his penis in relation to a woman.

The body, as our representative of the self in the external world, is a stimulus for feedback from others. When the reaction of others is narcissistically satisfying, the ego's cathexis of its sexual body image is reinforced. In this way exhibition of the body plays a role in the ego's perception of itself in light of its ego-ideal. But when the body is the vehicle for public disparagement and rejection by disappointed observers, the ego's narcissistic validation of the sexual body image fails to occur. The failure of exhibition to achieve the anticipated narcissistic satisfaction engenders shame and subsequent regression from a phallic/genital orientation to one's body to the previous anal organization. This regression defends against the narcissistic injury associated with the rejected genitals and reinforces an investment in an anal body image. According to Chasseguet-Smirgel (1985b), a consequence of this exhibitionistic failure and regression to anality is a resexualization of homosexuality. Chasseguet-Smirgel identifies the following sequence: 'the resexualization of homosexuality renders the narcissistic injury equivalent to a castration, and the exhibition to an exposure of the anus' (1985b: 161). Shame, therefore, reflects the proximity of exposure to a sexual fantasy based on the resexualization of homosexual impulses.

The experience of being sexually abused is accompanied by a feeling of shame which brings us a step closer to an essential ingredient in the cover-up of child sexual abuse by victims, perpetrators, relatives, friends and professionals, namely, the fear of seeing and being seen.

Differential diagnosis in adolescence

The physiological changes of puberty, the capacity to impregnate, conceive and bear children, put pressure on the pregenital body image of the abused child. The adolescent who was abused as a child is often anxious about using his genitals in sexual relationships. The individual who enters adolescence with maladaptive solutions to Oedipal conflicts (that is, with a body image that is predominantly oral or anal) will be frightened and despairing in the face of the normal adolescent tasks of taking over his body from his parents and developing heterosexual relationships with non-incestuous objects.

The adolescent who was abused as a child will be confused about his sexual identity, feel guilty about and ashamed of his pregenital fantasies and ill equipped for the tasks of adolescence. He feels a failure and is unable to identify with his peers. When separation from his parents becomes too frightening and the prospect of genital contact with peers is too dangerous, the abused adolescent looks for a sexual partner among children. No two abusers are identical and a differential diagnosis is required if we are to understand the individual abuser. A differential diagnosis should include:

- the study of the abusive act
- a psychosexual developmental history of the adolescent
- a family history of abuse among siblings and parents (for sources of identifications and signs of collusions), gender influences, racial and cultural backgrounds
- the nature of his or her adolescence.

The aim is to develop a picture of the internal world of the adolescent abuser.

Details of the perpetrator's abuse, such as frequency and persistence of the abusive behaviour over time, contain important clues to understanding the nature and function of the abusive act and assessing the adolescent's dangerousness. The setting and the relationship with the victim are also important: was he or she a relative, friend or stranger? How old was the victim? The victim's account and details of the act may also give us clues about the severity of the adolescent's disturbance.

Adolescence is such a turbulent and complex phase of development that it is difficult to categorize adolescent abusers by their behaviour, but it is helpful to try to locate them along a continuum from less to more severe disturbance.

At the less severe end of the continuum are the adolescent abusers whose sexual interest is primarily directed towards girls in their own age group. In their masturbation fantasies and sexual daydreams these adolescents are involved with adult or contemporary female partners. Their sexual abuse of children is infrequent, not persistent, and done in reaction to rejection by or anxiety about approaching female peers. There is no overt violence. Although they relate to the child on the basis of their own needs they recognize that he or she is an independent person and they respond with shame and guilt to their abusive behaviour.

Sixteen-year-old Sidney was babysitting an eight-year-old girl he had known for several years when he fondled her genitals and climbed on top of her. Two weeks earlier his first girlfriend had broken up with him to go out with an older bloke. This was Sidney's first offence. He felt uncomfortable when his parents tried to minimize the incident and sought help so he could have 'a proper girlfriend'.

At the more severe end of the continuum are the adolescents whose sexual fantasies are exclusively about children. Their abusive fantasies and behaviour are frequent, persistent, often accompanied by violence, and function to defend against a psychotic breakdown. They show no concern for their victim.

In contrast to the less severely disturbed abuser, this adolescent sees the child as existing only to gratify his needs. These adolescents are usually lonely, isolated from their peers, and uninterested in adult homosexual or heterosexual relationships.

Harry is 17, unhappy, friendless, unemployed and living in a hostel after his third offence of indecent assault on ten-year-old boys. On the last occasion Harry forced a boy to go on to the roof of a high-rise block of flats. Harry began truanting from school at age 12 and spent his days riding buses around London in order to look at young boys and daydream about buggering them. During my interview with Harry for a court report I discovered that he had nurtured a suicide fantasy and had made a suicide plan. Although I alerted the hostel staff to the risk of suicide, Harry's determination was such that he eluded the staff supervision at the bail hostel and tried to hang himself while awaiting trial.

The boy represented in the case presentation that follows is, on balance, towards the severe end of the continuum. He was an early adolescent who was struggling to separate from his parents, unable to establish himself with peers, and was anxious about violent primal scene fantasies. I will call him George.

The case of George

The referral, history and first impressions

George was referred to the Portman Clinic when he was 14 for a court report after he was accused of buggering four neighbour boys between the ages of seven and ten while he was babysitting. At the time he was apprehended, George confessed for the first time to being sexually abused himself when he was seven years old by a family friend whom I will call Mr Chambers.

When George was a toddler his mother, Mrs Russell, was unable to help her son control himself or protect him from himself. She recounted incidents of his making sandcastles out of flour, sugar and water on the kitchen floor, as well as innumerable accidents including the time when he was two and he fell on the heater and 'burned his private parts. It just missed his little penis and he still has a scar'. It is not surprising that George wet his bed at night until he was nine.

By and large I was given a picture of generational roles turned upside down with George feeling superior to his parents and tyrannizing his mother, who told me, 'I am a miserable woman. As soon as I put a smile on my face George puts me down again.'

After blaming George for the miscarriages she suffered during the previous two years, Mrs Russell haltingly and vaguely shared the secret that her father had sexually abused her. 'No wonder I was hated by my mother. I was my father's favourite but no one understood why. As a child I kept saying to myself, the next time he did it I would cut it off.'

The first thing George told me when we were alone was about the family's card game of fish which they played on the train on the way to the session as well as at other times during the week. The pattern was always the same because, as George said, he was smarter than his parents and usually won.

On the one hand, his parents seemed unable to function as parental authorities, while on the other hand, George clearly saw himself in a rather omnipotent position, that is, as a child who was equal to the parents and, as far as the game of fish was concerned, superior to them. George agreed with my observation that he had to compete for almost everything in the family but there was no one around, no adult, to ensure that he got his share. He always had to do that for himself.

I wondered aloud if he felt he had to compete with and defeat me and doubted that I could help him. It was then that George admitted that he was worried about the violence between his mother and stepfather when he heard them quarrelling at night. He couldn't go to sleep at night because he was wondering about what was going on between them. I commented that adults seemed more like easily overpowered children during the day, but violent and frightening when they went to bed at night.

The first time I met George in the waiting room he impressed me as an appealing lad who looked younger than his 14 years. He had a broad smile, a mop of dark hair, a bouncy step, and was wearing an Arsenal football club jersey. George was eager to come with me but waited for cues from his mother. Mrs Russell was a small, tough, wiry, Cockney lady with a few teeth missing and the gregarious air of a woman experienced in dealing with social workers and other professionals. Mr Russell was a large man with a weak handshake, a pleasant smile and lazy eyelids. He said nothing throughout the family interviews unless actively drawn in by someone, like a child waiting for permission.

Mrs Russell did not differentiate between George and her husband. The boundaries between the generations were easily blurred. For instance, Mother viewed George as being powerful while she herself was helpless in the face of his demands: 'He won't take no for an answer.' Mrs Russell presented George as responsible for everything that went wrong in the family, including the power to generate rows between Mr Russell and herself.

Mrs Russell also relied on projection and introjection to avoid taking responsibility for herself and her son. She gave the impression that she, like her son George, was trapped at home, but blamed this on him. She said she would like to go out to work but didn't dare because she would get it from George when she got in. Then she suddenly said, 'So much hurt. I am frightened to be on my own.' George's stepfather interrupted to say how often he is sent out to look for George. Mother became quite emotional and burst out, 'I don't know what George is doing. That's what buggers me up.' Buggery is an apt metaphor for mother and son's mutual intrusiveness and absence of protective boundaries.

The abuse by George

In our fourth session George was able to talk about his assaults on the younger boys. However, at first he projected his failure to stay in tune with these boys, his failure to protect their bodies, by blaming his own parents for leaving him with those youngsters. Then he blamed the parents of the boys who shouldn't have left them in the first place. The incident occurred when the parents had left George to babysit, or rather to play with the younger children, while the parents went out. He then changed his defence saying that it was the boys' fault because they were playing in their underpants. As he said, 'If you lock up a man and a woman, not a girl, something is going to happen.'

George's association to heterosexual activity provided a clue about what he imagined the violence between mother and stepfather to be about, and the heterosexual fantasy that underlay his homosexual activity with the young boys. It is not uncommon for the homosexual activity between boys in early adolescence, that is, from puberty to 15, to be motivated by heterosexual fantasies. What was worrying in George's case was the absence of peer relationships and his use of boys from a younger generation.

George denied any pleasure when having sexual contact with the boys because they were 'too small'. The pleasure was in misleading the boys into thinking they could beat him up, because he knew that they really couldn't hurt him. The pleasure was also in seeing the shock and confusion in the boys when he turned the tables on them. I took up his sexual play, getting on top of the boys with his penis in their bottoms, as something which made the boys feel small and enabled him to feel big by dominating them with sex. George said triumphantly, 'Yeah, they thought of me as the grown-up.' He reversed what he had set up in the play fights and betrayed the boys just as he felt betrayed and confused at home over who was the grown-up and who was the child. In this way, George clearly identified with the aggressor.

Mrs Russell called just before his next session to say that she had just found out from George that he was due to see me, but she couldn't bring him because she had no money and had not known ahead of time. We arranged to meet again the following week.

The abuse of George

George walked into his fifth session with a bald head, hid his face in his shoulder and looked ashamed. He told me that he had shaved all his hair off because he was impatient with his mum who had delayed giving him a haircut herself. He was also able to acknowledge some anger at her for cancelling his session last week. George went on to tell me about a game he had invented called 'Booby' that he destroyed when his parents wouldn't continue playing. George apparently felt that the most effective way of attacking his parents was to turn his aggression against himself. I took up George's shaving off his hair as aimed at hurting his mother by presenting himself as someone she didn't protect – in this instance from himself. George's defiance gave way to embarrassment about his shaved head. I was reminded of the Nazis shaving the heads of new concentration camp prisoners to shame and depersonalize them. This is what George had done to himself, I said, to show me he felt shame about his own abuse. I added that his abuse of the boys might also have been a way of getting rid of these feelings of shame and being unprotected by making the youngsters feel them.

George then put into words, for the first time, his own experience of being buggered when he was seven (the same age as two of the boys he buggered). 'Everyone had gone out except the kid's dad, Mr Chambers. I was lying on my tummy watching telly. He pulled my pants down. I didn't know what Mr Chambers was doing, but I felt it. Felt his penis . . . cold inside . . . then wet. He left 20p and told me it was just between us. I never turned around. I never said anything because no one would believe me. And there might have been a fight.'

Discussion of the case of George

The abused child must come to terms with a body that has been dominated by someone from an older generation, overstimulated, forced to endure a trauma passively and, perhaps, hurt. The concept of shame as a reaction to the disparity between the perceived actual self and the ego-ideal draws attention to the way in which the experience of being abused influences the perception of the actual self, including the child's sexual body image. Where there is already a weak ego-ideal in terms of gender-role identity the child victim may find that self-contempt for his abused body makes it difficult to maintain an image of himself as active and heterosexual in loving relationships. This appears to be George's experience. George's mother did not have a consistent and clear maternal identity and often appeared to experience George as a more powerful and dominant adult. As a consequence, the incest boundary was porous, which, I believe, made it dangerous for George to develop an ego-ideal that incorporated a strong masculine identity.

Bursten's (1973) views regarding the role that shame plays in understanding three narcissistic types (the paranoid, the manipulative and the phallic-narcissistic) are relevant to understanding George. Bursten notes that in the paranoid type shame results from unrealistic and inappropriate wishes for reunion with maternal and paternal representations, which stimulate anxieties associated with weakness, incest or homosexuality. The manipulative type suffers from poor self-esteem and worthlessness. Both the paranoid and manipulative types resolve internal conflicts by projection. In George's case sexual abuse of the younger boys was the medium for projecting his anxieties about his weak masculine identity, incest and homosexuality. George was also able to project his sense of helplessness and poor self-esteem by, as Bursten writes, 'putting something over' on his victims and controlling them. While shame leads to paranoid and narcissistic deficiencies, Bursten reminds us that shame also destabilizes the grandiose, omnipotent self that is built upon the phallic-narcissistic personality.

George's shame, which emerged in the last assessment interview, was accompanied by the collapse of his omnipotence and manipulativeness, the exposure of his confusion about his masculine identity, and feelings of weakness and worthlessness. George's view of himself reflected the type of grandiose self described by Broucek (1982) in which the 'denial or disavowal of discrepancy between actual self and grandiose self is maintained by a selective inattention to all negatively toned critical reactions of others along with projection of already internalized negative self images' (Broucek 1982: 376). George is someone who initially appeared to be shameless, but on closer examination suffered from the failure of his parents to respond to the defensive function of his shame, which I refer to as the shame shield. George's shame behaviour became more extreme and he shaved his head. This acceleration of his shame alerted me to the presence of shame and the fact that Mr Chambers and his parents had not recognized or responded to earlier signs of shame.

The crisis created by the failure of the parents to protect the child, and the child's failure to work through the trauma of being abused, leads the child to identify with the aggressor in order to defend against the ego-ideal, which is now the source of its shame as well as the representative of earlier identifications with untrustworthy parents. In order to protect the traumatized self from further shame, a split in the ego occurs in which the ego-ideal is disavowed and in its place imitation or simulation is adopted to give the appearance of compliance with authority figures. This represents not only a mocking of the now discredited authority figures (the parents), but changes the self from a denigrated object to a triumphant object that actively deceives its parents.

Furthermore, anal impulses predominate because they minimize the risk of castration and annihilation inherent in genital sexuality, which is most intensely aroused in adolescence, and maximize the assertion of an anal self through defiance, rebellion and triumph over the genital adult. In this way, the anal mode of relating reinforces the development in adolescence of a sexual deviation such as secondary transsexualism, transvestism, fetishism, paedophilia, which, in turn, enables the adolescent to remain oriented to reality, which is essential if he is to read correctly what others need or expect from him.

If one compares a paranoid adolescent with one suffering from a fetish, it is apparent that by containing anxieties within the framework of the sexual deviation, the fetish frees the adolescent to interact safely with the rest of reality. When this is added to the self-preservative function of the sexual deviation it behoves the clinician to consider carefully the consequences of undermining the adolescent's means of protection.

Mr Chambers' abuse of George generated a strong initial feeling of shame. George felt exposed, vulnerable and helpless. He did not turn around because he wanted to hide himself, but he was trapped. Shame gave way to self-disgust as he turned his rage against himself. Otherwise, as he said, 'there might have been a fight'. Shame, the wish to hide, to be invisible, was also part of the reason he could not tell anyone. George also thought his abuse was unshare-able; no one would believe him. I think this was an accurate assessment on George's part of a mother who had to disavow her own abuse, who had not been able to talk about her incestuous relationship with her father.

George has started the painful process of looking at what he could not face before by returning to his own experience of being buggered, and the con-tempt he felt for his body – enacted in graphic self-exposure by shaving his head. The offences cannot be understood in isolation from the feelings aroused by the original abuse, on the one hand, and the crucial developmental issues George faces as an adolescent, on the other. George, the perpetrator, and George, the victim, are inextricably linked. George's abuse by Mr Chambers precipitated an anal regression that undermined George's hetero-sexual fantasies and resexualized his homosexual impulses. Buggering other boys also enabled George to reverse what Mr Chambers and his parents did to him and, thereby, momentarily to get rid of his confusion about sexual difference (was he a boy or a girl?) and generational difference (why did the adults fail to protect his body?), his helplessness and smallness, his shame, rage and self-contempt.

Unconscious incestuous fantasies aroused by puberty and stimulated by his mother relating to him as a dominant peer and noises from his parents' bedroom at night left George feeling that it was not safe to use his penis in a relationship with a girl. While George's penetration of younger boys repre-sented his identification with the aggressor, it also reflected George's attempt to use his penis actively but safely away from girls who, he believed, like his mother wanted to harm him. Regarding his offences George was able to say to me, 'I know what I did, but not why I did it. I tried to stop myself but couldn't because I didn't understand why.'

Implications of psychopathology for technique and management

The abused child will suffer shame, guilt (conscious and unconscious), blame, punishment, imprisonment or fear of retaliation if an abusive act is reported. All this is rekindled and intensified when the child victim enters puberty. If left alone, the child is likely to repress, deny or disavow the traumatic experience. Therefore, most children need the help of a parent, close friend, relative or professional to help them work through the helplessness, betrayal of trust, anger and sexual confusion generated by their abuse.

However, a fundamental reaction to the experience of being abused is a deep sense of having been betrayed by those whom the child sees as responsible for its care and protection. Whatever the relationship between a child and his abuser, the child will directly or indirectly feel that the parents are responsible, if only for failing to protect his body. Behind the feeling that the parents have failed to play the role that is needed and expected of the adult generation is a sense that if the parents had been tuned in to what he felt about his body they would have protected him. The parents who fail to respond appropriately to their child's abuse confirm the child's feeling of abandonment. When the abuse is unshareable, it is unacceptable, and the rage, fear and sexual excitement associated with the abusive act cannot be psychically digested. The feeling of being betrayed by parents, the first authority figures in the child's life, informs the adolescent child abuser's transference to any professional they are involved with. The adolescent child sexual abuser expects their earlier abuse, particularly the experience of betrayal, to be repeated by representatives of society's authority.

Consequently, the adolescent sexual abuser is likely to rely upon compliance, imitation and simulation in order to protect himself from the intrusion and rejection he expects from the authority figures represented by the diagnostician, therapist or any professional, just as he did with his parents. He will be adept at 'reading' the practitioner's valuation of his own work and can readily 'co-operate' with assessment or therapy, and simulate attitudes and behaviour consciously or unconsciously promoted by caretakers.

Those working with adolescents who have sexually abused children will be familiar with this phenomenon. This is not a self-conscious pretence. Just as the adolescent abuser actually believes that he or she is their child victim's best friend, sensitive babysitter or helpful tutor, he or she actually believes they are good clients who are co-operating by acknowledging their abusive behaviour, etc. These simulations are so believable for the professional because the perpetrator is a believer himself. Nevertheless, the true self beneath the compliance will wage a guerrilla campaign against the therapeutic process that, he believes, aims to take him over completely, just as his abuser had. The subtle or gross signs of resistance offer the professional a more reliable clue to the whereabouts of the true self which may be so deeply buried that even the adolescent has lost contact with it. It is unlikely that the seriously disturbed sexually deviant adolescent will ever find his way back to his actual self without the help of a professional.

However, any individual or group treatment or management programme that adopts a macho or authoritarian role or focuses exclusively on behavioural change without understanding the individual's internal conflicts and anxieties is in danger of being sabotaged by the abuser's capacity to adopt language, concepts and whatever is suggested as normative behaviour, in the same way as the chameleon takes on the colour of its environment as a protection against attack. Since the change is based on simulated attitudes and behaviour, it only appears to be change. Momentarily, one will see changes in the abuser's behaviour as the result of this kind of identification with the therapist, probation officer or child care protection worker, but, since underlying anxieties are not affected, the abuser is at risk of returning to abusive behaviour once the external supports have been taken away and old anxieties re-emerge. Put into the language of child abuse, any treatment or management programme that does not take the abuser's internal world into account is very likely to be victimized by the abuser in the same way as the child victims are, that is by being deceived by the outwardly positive but inwardly fraudulent behaviour of these clients. When professionals discover they have been deceived they should guard against reacting in an abusive way by abandoning their adolescent clients or adopting a punitive attitude. Those in positions of authority are also likely to be deceived by late adolescent or adult child sexual abusers who regularly seek out employment which brings them into 'legitimate' contact with children as police officers, teachers, child care workers or social workers ostensibly 'caring' for the children who become their victims. Newspapers regularly report that a child psychiatrist, a director of social services, head of a children's home or another professional has been found guilty of child abuse while working in a position of care and protection of children. Ironically, many adolescent abusers were first abused themselves while living in children's homes or residential treatment settings.

The abuser also plays a role in his subsequent abuse. The adolescent abuser not only expects the therapist or social worker or 'the system' to relate to him in an abusive way, based on his experience of the way his mother and father related to him, but will attempt to provoke the professional into a response of punishment or collusion (such as feeling sorry for the abuser in such a way as to avoid his maliciousness), in order to confirm the abuser's expectation that he won't be taken seriously.

Summary

Research indicates that a high proportion of child molestations are committed by adolescents. This chapter draws attention to the need for a differential diagnosis to be made when assessing adolescent child sexual abusers. Puberty and developmental conflicts, which occur during adolescence, create internal conflicts that may contribute to the adolescent's abusive behaviour. In particular, the role of the ego-ideal, sexual body image and shame are considered as they are affected by the experience of being abused and the victim's subsequent abusive behaviour, and are illustrated in the report of an assessment of a 14-year-old male adolescent child abuser. Finally, broader transference and countertransference dynamics are considered as they affect other professionals and institutions that are involved with adolescent child sexual abusers.

Notes

1 This chapter builds on a previous paper on this subject (Campbell 1994) and represents my current thinking.
2 The clinical experience, upon which this chapter is based, is derived from the author's assessment and treatment of adolescents over 30 years who had been referred to the Portman Clinic. The Portman Clinic is a National Health Service outpatient clinic that specializes in the assessment and psychoanalytically oriented psychotherapy of adults, adolescents and children who have experienced psychological and/or physical pain associated with perverse actions or have engaged in acts of delinquency.
3 See Freud's (1911) views of the Schreber case and Victor Tausk's (1953) discussion of the 'influencing machine'.

References

Becker, J. V. and Abel, L. G. G. (1984) *Neurological and Ethical Issues in Evaluating and Treating Adolescent Sexual Offenders*, NIMH monograph, Bethesda, MD: National Institute of Mental Health.
Broucek, F. J. (1982) 'Shame and its relationship to early narcissistic developments', *International Journal of Psycho-Analysis* 63: 369–378.
Bursten R. (1973) 'Some narcissisteic personality types', *International Journal of Psycho-Analysis* 54: 287–300.
Campbell, D. (1994) 'Breaching the shame shield: Thoughts on the assessment of adolescent child sexual abusers', *Journal of the Association of Child Psychotherapists* 20 (3): 309–326.
Cawson, P., Wattam, C., Brooker, S. and Kelly, G. (2000) *Child Maltreatment in the United Kingdom: A Study of the Prevalence of Child Abuse and Neglect*, London: National Society for the Prevention of Cruelty to Children.
Chasseguet-Smirgel, J. (1985a) *Creativity and Perversion*, London: Free Association Books.
—— (1985b) *The Ego Ideal*, London: Free Association Books.
Davis, G.E. (1987) 'Adolescent sex offenders', *Psychological Bulletin* 101: 417–427.
Erikson, E. (1977) *Childhood and Society*, 2nd edn, St Albans: Triad/Paladin.
Fenichel, O. (1937) 'The scopophilia instinct and identification', *International Journal of Psycho-Analysis* 18: 1–34.
Freud, S. (1896) 'Heredity and the aetiology of neurosis', S.E. 3: 141–156.
—— (1908) 'Character and anal erotism', S.E. 9: 167–176.
—— (1909) 'Family romance', S.E. 9: 235 ff.
—— (1911) 'Psychoanalytic notes on an autobiographical account of a case of paranoia', S.E. 12: 3–82.
—— (1925) 'An autobiographical study', S.E. 20: 20–90.
——(1926) 'The question of lay analysis', S.E. 20: 179 ff.
Grinker, R. (1955) 'Growth inertia and shame: Therapeutic implications and dangers', *International Journal of Psycho-Analysis* 36: 242–253.
Home Office (1988) *Criminal Statistics: England and Wales* (CM 847), London: Home Office.
Horne, I., Glasgow, D., Cox, A. and Calam, R. (1991) 'Sexual abuse of children by children', *Journal of Child Law* 3: 147–151.

Hutton, L. and Whyte, B. (2006) 'Children and young people with harmful sexual behaviours: First analysis of data from a Scottish sample', *Journal of Sexual Aggression* 12 (2): 115–125.

NSPCC (2002) *Child Protection Research Findings*, London: NSPCC.

Piers, G. and Singer, M. (1953) *Shame and Guilt*, Springfield, IL: Charles C. Thomas.

Tausk, V. (1953) 'On the origin of the "influencing machine" in schizophrenia', *Psychoanalytic Quarterly* 2: 519–556.

Yorke, C. (1990) 'The development and functioning of the sense of shame', *Psychoanalytical Study of the Child* 45: 377–409. A shortened version of this paper appears in this volume, Chapter 2.

Chapter 5

Shame

What psychoanalysis does and does not say[1]

Malcolm Pines

Shame, the 'Cinderella of the unpleasant emotions' (Rycroft 1972), has not been well served by psychoanalysis: only in recent years has more attention been paid to this neglected affect. Before considering the nature of shame and what we know of its psychodynamics, I shall consider the reasons for this neglect.

There are two factors to be considered. First, there is the weakness of the psychoanalytic theory of affects. As long as psychoanalysis was a 'one-body psychology' (Rickman 1957), based upon Freud's neurological model, it was restricted to considering affects as discharge phenomena, as the responses of an organism attempting to reduce tensions and to bring them to a manageable level. As psychoanalysis became a multibody psychology, the theory of affects shifted significantly and the great complexity of affect psychology was more fully grasped. Affects cannot be reduced simply to discharge phenomena: while psychoanalysis persisted in this, the distinctions between shame and guilt, for example, went largely unrecognized. Shame and guilt seemed to be more alike than distinct. Both were guardians of morality – dams to the discharge of primitive libidinal and aggressive drives (Freud 1909).

The second factor to be considered is an aspect of Freud's own personality. For so long psychoanalysis was his own personal creation, and as Freud paid more attention to guilt than to shame, psychoanalysis followed in his footsteps. Why should Freud have paid far more attention to guilt than to shame? In his earliest writings shame was given a prominent place: 'Shame, disgust and morality are like watchmen who maintain repressions, dams that direct the flow of a sexual excitation into normal channels instead of reactivating earlier forms of expression' (Freud 1909: 45). Thus Freud proposed morality as the motive behind shame, and later the superego as the agency through which this is regulated. As Freud developed the structural model of guilt, the internal guardian of morality, mediated through the severity of the superego, it was given prominence over shame. Guilt fits much more neatly into the tripartite structural model; it is less intimately and closely connected with self-referential properties than is shame. In shame the target of the reproach is the self, a self flooded with painful feelings that surge beyond the boundaries of any structural model. Since shame is so largely connected with the whole feeling about oneself, it brings immediately into focus questions such as those of *self* and *identity* with which psychoanalysis has found it hard to grapple. Shame is not experienced by the ego but by the self. With the rise of self-psychology, the self-referential qualities of shame have begun to find a place within the house of psychoanalysis.

This does not answer further probings into the question of why Freud did not direct his own powerful 'beams of darkness' (Bion) into the murky areas of shame. I speculate (but I think there are grounds for this speculation) that Freud himself was a shame-sensitive person who avoided dealing with this issue and who consequently turned his attention to guilt, which has less painful, self-referential qualities. Shame is very much caught up with vision, whereas guilt can, in a broad generalization, be conceptualized as being more auditory. In shame we avoid the eyes of other persons: they are spectators of our state of distress, of our incompetence, ugliness, loss of self-control. The few references that Freud makes to his own visual appearance as seen in mirrors show how much he disliked what he saw. He saw an elderly, ugly man and at times failed to recognize and to own the image as himself. In considering guilt we can take our eyes off our own self-image: guilt can be shared and, in the sharing, we can be equal in the eyes of others. Guilt can be revealed and shared with less affect than in the examination and elation of shame. For instance, Freud was very shame sensitive over his Jewish identity. In his adolescence he raged at his father for failing to uphold what Freud felt were the proper standards of courage and manliness in the face of anti-Semitism and his ego-ideals; his heroes were all powerful men who fought against kings and giants and who released the Jewish race from some of the discriminatory burdens that had been placed against them. His heroes included the Semitic warrior Hannibal; Napoleon, who emancipated the Jews from many medieval restrictions; Oliver Cromwell, who overthrew the king and allowed the Jews to return to England; and Napoleon's marshal, Massena, whom Freud mistakenly thought to be a Jew, because of his name (Klein 1985; McGrath 1985). We know that Freud feared that psycho-analysis would be lost if it remained identified with Jewishness and that he fought desperately to bring Jung and his fellow Christian Swiss into the psychoanalytic brotherhood. Thus there are reasons to suppose that Freud himself was shame prone and shame sensitive and that he retreated from the active struggle with this affect into the more neutral area of the study of guilt.

Emotions

In order to deal properly with shame as an affect, we must seek adequate models for the emotions. I consider the two following definitions to be useful tools for our study.

1   An emotion exists whenever a person is moved, whenever his relationship to the world is transformed (De Rivera 1977).
2   Emotions are self-concerning, partly physical responses that are at the same time aspects of a moral or ideological attitude; emotions are both feeling and cognitive structures, linking person, action and sociological milieu (Levy and Rozaldo 1983).

What do these definitions highlight? First, that emotions represent movements. We are moved by our emotions: we are *in* motion and through our emotions our relationship to the world is transformed. We change our form and the form of our relationship to the world is changed. Second, that emotions are self-concerning, that they always have a reference to the self, that they are physical responses and that they are patterned by our cultural milieu. Cultural experience affects both the field and the structure of the actor; hence culture significantly organizes emotions.

I shall shortly consider the important and finer differentiations between shame and guilt, but at this point I consider them together:

> In both shame and guilt there is a tension between the private and public aspects of self. In different cultures there are to be found differences in the nature of what is private and what is public in the self concept, emotions and relationship and therefore there will be different experiences of shame and guilt.
>
> (Levy and Rozaldo 1983: 131)

Our anthropological colleagues, from whom these ideas are taken, are quite clear about the major differentiations between shame and guilt, and state:

> Shame and embarrassment have positive aspects of shyness, social sensitivity and modesty. These are virtues. Guilt has the principally negative connotation of banning someone or something. Guilt invites retribution or protective atonement. In shame others are visualised as audience or spectators; in guilt others are visualised as victims and sufferers.
>
> (Levy and Rozaldo 1983: 131)

Levy and Rozaldo bring their anthropological perspective to bear upon our particular and peculiar western experiences:

> The Western model of emotions portrays varied feelings of shame and guilt which are needed to protect the individuated self from dangerous and asocial acts of impulse, lust and violence. These represent the experience of a closed social self in the individuated Western society and can be contrasted with the open self of different cultures.
>
> (Levy and Rozaldo 1983: 136)

In group analysis we start from the proposition that we are social creatures and that we are all bound up affectively with each other in a social nexus. Thus, our emotions are always linking us with other persons and their emotions link us to them. We are intrinsically in the realm of what is partly, but not exclusively or comprehensively, covered by object relations theory. De Rivera states that emotions move us in our relationships with other persons and that they represent transitions between person and environment, organizing the relation between the person and the other so that the response itself gives meaning to the stimulus situation. Thus an emotion is not simply a discharge phenomenon, it is always a meaningful response to a situation. This is an important contribution to psychoanalysis and group analysis. De Rivera proposes three principal modes of our relating to others:

- belonging (a horizontal mode of relating)
- recognizing (a vertical mode of relating)
- being (an opening or closing of oneself to the other).

These three modes of relating naturally all have positive or negative qualities. In wishing to belong to another person, or wishing the other person to belong to us, we move towards them in psychological space or desire to move them closer to us. The affects of love and desire represent these movements in horizontal space. However, if we have anger or fear towards or for the other person we will want to move away from them or to have them move away from us in psychological space.

In giving recognition to other persons or wishing them to give recognition to us we will look *up* to them with esteem and admiration or will look *down* upon them with contempt or horror. In wishing to *offer* the depth of our being to other persons or to be *open* to the depth of their being, we will experience or wish for acceptance, experience wonder or the painful negative affects of rejection and dread.

De Rivera links these three principal modes of relating (belonging, recognizing and being) to the three aspects of self that were outlined by William James (1957): the *material self* (that which I am and that which belongs to me), the *social* self (that which I am for society and which society grants to me) and the *spiritual* aspect of being that relates me to the wider, encompassing and mysterious world that surrounds and is greater than myself.

Thus all affects links us to the other, an implicit or explicit other. The emotions are always structured in terms of our moves towards or away from the other represented in ourselves, or represent the moves of the other-representation towards or away from our own self-representation. Regarding the specific topic of shame, if the other moves towards us and offers us admiration then we move towards that person with pride. If, however, the other withdraws from us with contempt, we attempt to hide away and withdraw into ourselves with the affect of shame. In shame we withdraw from the gaze of the other who is experienced as more worthy. This other may be the unconscious implicit other or may be an actual real other with whom we are engaged at that moment, but who also reactivates earlier representations of shaming persons.

De Rivera suggests that guilt is linked with a relationship in which the other regards us with horror and would not have us exist in his or her own affective and experiential world. I find this a questionable concept, for alternative approaches to the differentiation of shame and guilt emphasize that in guilt we are pursued by the other or that we wish to move towards that person with confession. The other is angry with us and wishes us to pay our debt to society in order that we may atone and become at one again with society.

Self-esteem and shame

One way in which different authors agree is that the shame experience can be significantly linked to loss of self-esteem, to feelings of inferiority and failure, hence to the psychoanalytic field of narcissism. They see the pain of shame as linked with the failure of that which we are and that we would wish to be, either for ourselves or for others. This is expressed by different authors in terms of the ego-ideal contrasted to the ego, the ideal self contrasted to the actual self, or the grandiose self as related to the central self. All these are concerned with some notion of ratio, a measurement of one against the other. The closer the two approximate to each other, the greater is the sense of satisfaction and loss of tension within the organism. Theoretically, these ratios can be measured, as in some Rogerian experiments on self-esteem, where a person is asked to show by putting two pointers at an angle how much the person feels that in any particular and specific respect their achievements match up to their ideals. Thus individuals may feel that they may match up to their ideals in a particular aspect almost 100 per cent yet may only score 10 or 15 per cent, or indeed nothing at all or have a negative score, in relationship to some other aspects of self. In that way, using the model of the hands of a dial, shame is viewed analogically. There are shades and differentiations of shame along very many subtle dimensions, as are shown by the many words in language to represent these different qualities. We talk of bashfulness, shyness, embarrassment, coyness, self-consciousness, awkwardness, humiliation, mortification and so on. Is this the case when we turn to consider the nature of guilt? Guilt is more directly related to a juridical model in which the alternatives are a verdict of guilty or a verdict of not guilty, a declaration of innocence. Language is not nearly so rich in the description of shades of guilt feeling as with shame feeling. We have to differentiate between feelings of guilt and a sense of conviction of guilt, a differentiation which Freud used in German although the Strachey translation loses these distinctions (Lewis 1983). Thus guilt can be seen as being digital rather than analogical in that it represents an either/or and on/off situation that does not offer the same possibilities of shade and measurement as does the self-experience of shame. In the eyes of the law a person is either guilty or not guilty. It does not really make sense to ask 'how guilty' a person is unless we take a very sophisticated view about the distribution of guilt between all the parties involved.

Using these models of analogical and digital modes of experience and noting the nature of the differences in our language, we may speculatively link shame and guilt experiences with predominantly left and right cerebral hemisphere functioning. The dominant hemisphere, usually the left hemisphere, is the centre for our decision making, our logical thinking, our precise evaluations and our judgements. The non-dominant hemisphere, more usually the right hemisphere, is much more closely linked with the sources that govern affect and present us with a different mode of experience that is more diffuse, global and encompassing. Thus speculations that shame may be a more basic affect than guilt and concerned with a total organismic sense of distress make good sense when linked up with these two models. Indeed, we have had the suggestion of Broucek (1982) that shame differentiates from early stages of organismic distress, that later become organized into discrete affects of which shame is among the most prominent.

Developmental aspects of shame

It has been argued by Broucek (1982) that shame arises from and later becomes differentiated from the 'acute distress state' of infants which is linked with stranger anxiety and can also be linked to the child's beginning to experience mother herself as a stranger. This occurs when the infant expects responses to its own communications that fail to arrive, leading to disappointment and to shock. This acute distress state occurs prior to the emergence of the self as self-representation, which we can begin to see happening in the second year of life. However, it has been argued, particularly by Emde (1983), that the precursors of the self are in existence prior to the emergence of this recognizable self-representation, so that what later can be labelled as a distinct affect can be traced to its earlier stages.

Shame, a highly affective state, brings about a great awareness of bodily experiences and of autonomic reactions and involves some cognitive recognition of a sense of deficiency of the self. As this happens the sense of self moves suddenly from background to foreground awareness and the person is caught up in a sense of subjective self-awareness and self-consciousness, experienced as a painful intrusion into a previously quiet, smoothly operating sense of self as background, as a context or framework for experience. Spiegel (1959) has called this the 'fly-wheel' background sense of self that always operates smoothly until it is disrupted and we then become suddenly and painfully self-conscious.

Developmentally we can see how between the ages of 18 and 24 months self-consciousness begins to appear as a painful state when the child is either exposed to its own image in the mirror or feels itself not to be the object of approval in the eyes of the mirroring parent or caretaker. At that point the sense of 'objective self-consciousness' obtrudes over a more pleasurable state of 'subjective self-consciousness'. In other words, the child begins to recognize that he or she is now an object in a world of other objects, visible in a world of other visible persons, and that he or she can therefore be the object of the scrutiny of others in a disappointing or critical manner.

At this stage the child becomes acutely aware of its smallness, weakness and relative incompetence in the larger scheme of things. This sense of smallness destroys the inevitable fantasies of grandiosity that the child is living out and the sense of collapse and deflation of the self is extremely painful. Against this, defences develop which can take many forms. Much has been written on the relationship of shame to narcissism; narcissism as representing an aspect of the feeling tone of the self. Bursten (1973) has written:

> Shame experiences disrupt the silent automatic functioning of the sense of self and shame is considered to be the basic form of unpleasure in disturbances of narcissism. The grandiose self is viewed as evolving compensatory formations instigated in large parts by primitive shame experiences.
>
> (Bursten 1973: 287–300)

It is necessary to recall here that Freud linked the sense of narcissistic vulnerability and a sense of narcissistic inferiority to femininity and to the experience of genital deficiency. In his view this rendered women more narcissistic, more liable to narcissistic object choices, which had cultural consequences in that their contributions to civilization were limited by attempts to conceal the inadequacy. Freud also considered that this led women to be more envious than men in all aspects of mental life and generally less fair in their judgement, to have a more inadequately formed superego. The consequence of this was that female morality was in some ways deficient in guilt and overcompensated by shame. Thus the primary shame of genital deficiency led to a secondary shame with the character traits of vanity, jealousy, revengefulness, secretiveness, passivity and submissiveness. Freud was aware that this concept would arouse hostility and would not always sound friendly.

Anthony (1981) has reviewed Freud's contribution to the study of shame and femininity and has pointed out that when feminine shame, which is often of very great importance in the early stages of analysis, is overcome, women show many strengths as analysands and are then able to form stronger transference than many men can. Following Susan Miller's useful review (1985), I now pose certain questions, to see what answers psychoanalysis has to offer.

Is shame a reaction formation?

For some writers, principally Freud, shame functions directly as a reaction formation against exhibitionistic impulses, obliterating the awareness of forbidden wishes.

> Shame, disgust and morality are like watchmen who maintain repressions, dams that direct the flow of sexual excitation into normal channels instead of reactivating earlier forms of expression. The first diminishing, self-hiding quality of shame represents its function as a dam against immoral, exhibitionistic excitement.
>
> (Freud 1909: 45)

Freud proposed morality as the motive behind shame, the superego in the role of its agency. Nunberg (1985) designated castration anxiety as the motive and the ego as the relevant agency. In both cases, indulgence in exhibitionism brings about attacks from within in the form of guilt or the threat of attacks from without in the form of castration. These approaches, as Susan Miller (1983) points out, have studied a particular function of shame, as a guardian of morality, but have neglected to study the shame experience itself. They present shame as an experience of personal inferiority that does nothing except represent the negative conviction behind the self, shame signifying attempts to deflect attention away from the impulse to exhibit an erotically viewed self or body. Exhibitionism itself is simply explained as the strength of a particular component instinct.

Does shame function in a homeostatic manner?

Other writers who see shame as a sort of brake applied against various forms of exhibitionistic excitement do not posit morality as the exclusive motive. They point to the ego-destructive impact of overstimulation and to the need for a mechanism to reverse highly stimulated states. Thus shame here has a function to counter sexuality and is a protection against the loss of self-boundaries implicit in some forms of sexual fantasy, such as those of observing the sexual behaviour of others; or it serves as a feeling state which functions to ground a person who is so overstimulated by feelings of omnipotence that these feelings threaten the capacity for safe existence.

Is the concept of self and of identity a useful one in conceptualizing the nature of the shame experience?

Some writers define shame as an acute experience of inferiority feelings that may refer to any aspect of self or to the self experienced as unity. Thus shame experience refers to the self as a whole. Kohut (1971) views shame as a collapse of self-esteem which is developmentally linked to parental failures to respond attentively and appreciatively to the child as a whole human being rather than as a collection of bodily parts and functions: one stands revealed to oneself as a person with an excess of crude, unutilized, exhibitionistic libido. Here exhibitionistic shame relates not to the genital but to the whole self.

Alexander (1938) views shame as resulting from the failure to develop mentally to the point where one no longer gives in to regressive wishes, such as to be small protected or sexually undifferentiated.

Shame and intra-psychic conflict: superego, ego-ideal and ideal-ego

Shame does not fit comfortably into the model of a conflict between superego and ego. This is more the province of guilt and was extensively developed as the structural theory evolved with a dynamic of the aggressively invested superego turning against the ego. However, with the concept of the ego-ideal and with the related concept of idealization of the superego, the beloved and loving superego of Roy Schafer (1960), shame once again finds a place in the structural model.

For Piers and Singer (1953) the stage of disparity between the perceived actual self and one's ideal self, one's ideals and one's actual behaviour, gives rise to shame. This does not belong exclusively to sexuality but can occur in any area of life whether it be that of sexual performance or of moral integrity. Shame is the failure to reach one's ego-ideal, falling short of an aim, whereas guilt is an active violation of the principle that one values. Both shame and guilt respond to internal standards: the relevant standards differ.

Morrison (1983) has argued cogently that ideal-self is a more useful concept than ego-ideal in assisting our understanding of shame. The *ego-ideal* represents the classification of goals, ideals and valued object-representations which we internalize as a checklist against which to compare ourselves. The *ideal-self* is the more subjective, less specific and cognitive, sense of self to which we aspire with regard to ideals and standards. Failure to reach the ideal-self representation reflects, therefore, a subjective sense of self-defeat and short-coming, experiences central to the shame experience. Kohut's contributions to the psychodynamics of narcissism are central to this construction of the shame experience.

Chasseguet-Smirgel (1985) extensively develops the argument about shame and the ego-ideal in a way that merits attention from group analysts. For her, self-esteem is based upon the way in which the ego lives up to the standards of the ego-ideal and our performance; our success or failure in reaching to those standards is measured through the image that is reflected back upon us by our peers. We see what we actually do and whether or not we fall short of our aims and goals through what is mirrored back to us in our interpersonal experience.

In what way do peers act as mirrors, as reflectors of the psyche? The answer lies in the difference between the body ego and the psychic ego. Our bodies, being physical, we can see, touch and feel: we do not need mirrors to confirm through external reality that such a thing as a body exists, with the exception of our faces and our backs, which we are not able to perceive for ourselves. But there is no external object corresponding to the internal representation of the ego; we are invisible to ourselves in the sense that there is no external representation of the self in the way that there is of the body; thus it is through the responses and evaluations of others that we actually see ourselves. Persons are invisible, they gradually become visible through the experience of relatedness. Thus we actively seek psychic mirrors for reflections of the psychic ego: through being seen by others we know that we exist. But, for these very reasons, it is through the reactions of others that we can feel shame at falling short of our ideals or of the ideals which are held up for us by membership of a group.

Chasseguet-Smirgel argues that exhibitionism is more narcissistic than any of the other component instincts and is therefore more linked to the regulation of self-esteem. This creates a potential situation of psychic danger, of narcissistic trauma. But added to this danger is that which arises through the fact that the psychic ego, having no external representation, can make use of the body ego with which it identifies to represent it. Thus the body ego carries the exhibitionism of the psychic ego and leads to the confusion of moral and aesthetic values: 'A beautiful body implies neither a beautiful soul nor extraordinary abilities' (Chasseguet-Smirgel 1985: 154).

Here we must digress back to the issue of genitality and of the phallus which Freud invoked in describing female shame. For Chasseguet-Smirgel the link between shame and genital exhibitionism is not simply and directly related to the Oedipal fantasies associated with exhibitionistic wishes. Chasseguet-Smirgel links up the concept of the psychic ego with homosexuality, for Freud said that social feelings have roots in narcissism and in homosexual libido. Narcissism has a direct route to homosexuality in that the person seeks for the object that has similar genitals in order to ward off castration anxieties and to reinforce the sense of safety of the self. Thus at the unconscious level peers approximate to narcissistic homosexual doubles and it is in relationship to them that we gauge the performance of our ego. Chasseguet-Smirgel argues that the penis can represent a miniature 'double' of the ego and therefore can be used to evaluate the status and performance of the ego, as in phallic narcissism. This genitalization of narcissism leads to significant differences between males and females, in that the absence of the penis in women leaves them more at the mercy of 'opinion' and reinforces dependency and the need for narcissistic confirmation from others.

Chasseguet-Smirgel developed the argument that later stages of development, those of secondary identifications, following the primary identification with mother, allow for better and more realistic evaluations of the psychic ego. These relationships with the others who are the objects of secondary identification have actually been relationships with separate external objects and have been subjected to reality testing. However, the latent homosexuality underlying libidinal investment of peers will always play a part in the relationship to them and, therefore, in the regulation of self-esteem which, as already argued, is related to psychic mirroring by our peers. Peers are homosexual doubles who act as mirrors and if the needed narcissistic satisfaction is not achieved then states of shame ensue. Shame is related both to narcissistic failure and to the vicissitudes of unconscious homosexuality. The experience of shame through narcissistic failure leads to regression, to resexualization; in mirroring, fantasies of castration, of helplessness reappear; the person therefore becomes subject to fears of passive penetration, which adds to the whole shame cycle. Thus embarrassment, the loss of face in shame, the reddening of the face, is seen by Chasseguet-Smirgel as displacement to the face of conflicts belonging to anal phases of development; the anus becomes the face and the face becomes the shameful rear.

Shame, dependency and passivity

The argument that shame is intrinsically linked to passive receptive phases of development has been put forward most strongly by Gilligan (1976). Shame arises as the motive of defence against the passive libidinal needs of oral, anal and phallic-urethral stages, whereas guilt arises as the motive of defence against the active aggressive drives associated with these phases of development. Oral suckling, passive anal-erotic and passive urethral wishes are defended against by shame; oral biting cannibalistic drives, anal sadistic drives and phallic competitive drives give rise to guilt as the motive of defence.

Using a broad canvas to delineate the differences between shame and guilt cultures, a distinction which is not nowadays upheld by anthropologists, Gilligan nevertheless makes some important points about the differences between ethics which are based upon shame and those which are based upon guilt. In the shame ethic the worst possible experience is that of humiliation and shame, and the most positively valued personal quality will be that of pride. Thus in these cultures love of self, egoism, pride, competitiveness and the urge to mastery will predominate. This is the master–slave morality of Nietzsche. Others will be experienced as contemptible and hate-worthy. Hatred and aggression will be directed towards others and this will be reinforced by the values of the culture which will also minimize the return of hatred towards the self. It is others who are to be despised, not the sacred vessel of the self. Hence the qualities of altruism, of otherness, of sympathy and compassion, pity and fellow-feeling will receive scant consideration and will always be based upon narcissistic identity. Cannibalistic tribes that seek out others as prey are cited as examples.

Table 5.1 Distinguishing between shame and guilt

	Shame	Guilt
Feeling (a)	Always implied: for example, to be (feel) ashamed.	Feeling not intrinsic: for example, to be guilty is not necessarily to feel guilty. To feel guilty is not to be guilty.
Feeling (b)	Self-referential. I am ashamed of something I have done (or someone with whom I identify).	Feeling guilty does not necessarily involve a wholesome feeling or concept.
As a verb	I can 'shame' another – make the other feel ashamed.	I cannot 'guilt' another.
To be without	Shameless reveals the inner self: not a virtue.	Guiltless is a virtue: does not relate to inner self.
Sense of identity	Bound to.	Not bound to.
Relation to society	Not rule bound: linked more to inner self.	Transgression of moral rules.
Relation to peers (a)	Peer pressure very high.	Peer pressure not as salient.
Relation to peers (b)	Peers as mirrors	–
Relation to body	The principal object	–
Physiology	Highly reactive. Almost impossible to control or conceal.	Less reactive. Can be controlled or concealed to a considerable extent.
Facial involvement	Very high.	May not be revealed facially.
Relation of response to size of offence	Very variable. A very small offence may produce a very marked shame response, for example, embarrassment, humiliation.	Response may well be proportionate to the offence.
Discharge from affect	Through repair to self-image.	Through payment of debt: 'at-one-ment', penance, punishment, confession.
Openness	Flight from into silence and concealment.	Sought in confession.
Response to humour	Protective, reparative.	Not susceptible.

Source: Adapted from Thrane (1979)

By contrast, in a guilt system the worst evil is pride and the highest goal is humility, which can be self-humiliation. Each value system will contain its unconscious opposite: behind the conscious humility of the guilt ethic is unconscious pride; behind the conscious pride and arrogance of the shame ethic is unconscious shame.

Conclusion

Psychoanalytic understanding of the meaning and motivations of shame has travelled a long way from Freud's starting point: shame as a guardian of morality. The greater sophistication of the psychoanalytic model of the personality has enabled us to comprehend the complexity and importance of the shame experience. The framework of self-psychology and the study of narcissism has contributed greatly to this progress. Group analysis has to take further account of the ubiquity of the shame experience and contribute to this important area. Shame is fundamentally a social phenomenon: our field of observation is social; we should have much to contribute. (See Table 5.1.)

Note

1 This chapter was first published (1987) in the journal *Group Analysis* 20: 16–31. © The Group-Analytic Society (London), 1987, by permission of Sage Publications Ltd.

References

Alexander, F. (1938) 'Remarks about the relationship of inferiority feelings to guilt feelings', *International Journal of Psychoanalysis* 19: 41–49.

Anthony, J. (1981) 'Shame, guilt and the feminine self in psychoanalysis', in S. Tuttman (ed.) *Object and Self*, New York: International Universities Press, pp. 191–234.

Broucek, F. J. (1982) 'Shame and its relationship to early narcissistic development', *International Journal of Psychoanalysis* 63: 369.

Bursten, B. (1973) 'Some narcissistic personality types', *International Journal of Psychoanalysis* 54: 287–300.

Chasseguet-Smirgel, J. (1985) *The Ego-Ideal*, London: Free Association Press.

De Rivera, J. (1977) 'A structural theory of the emotions', *Psychological Issues* 40.

Emde, R. N. (1983) 'The prerepresentational self and its affective core', *Psychoanalytic Study of the Child* 38: 165–92.

Freud, S. (1909) *Five Lectures on Psychoanalysis*, S.E. 11.

Gilligan. J. (1976) 'Beyond morality: Psychoanalytic reflections on shame, guilt and love', in T. Lickonc (ed.) *Moral Development and Behaviour*, New York: Holt, Rinehart, Winston, pp. 144–158.

James, W. (1957) *The Principles of Psychology*, London: Dover.

Klein, D. B. (1985) *Jewish Origins of the Psycho-Analytic Movement*, London: University of Chicago Press.

Kohut, H. (1971) *The Analysis of the Self*, New York: International Universities Press.

Levy, R. and Rozaldo, M. Z. (eds) (1983) Issue on 'self and emotion', *Ethos* 11 (3).

Lewis, H. B. (1983) *Freud and Modem Psychology*, New York: Plenum Press.

McGrath, W. J. (1985) *Freud's Discovery of Psychoanalysis: The Politics of Hysteria*, London: Cornell University Press.

Miller, S. (1983) *The Shame Experience*, Hillsdale, NJ: Analytic Press.

Morrison, A. P. (1983) 'Shame, ideal, self and narcissism', *Contemporary Psychoanalysis* 19 (2): 295–318.

Nunberg, H. (1985) *Principles of Psychoanalysis*, New York: International Universities Press.

Piers, G. and Singer, M. B. (1953) *Shame and Guilt*, Springfield: Charles C. Thomas.

Pines, M. (1984) 'Reflections on mirroring', *International Review of Psychoanalysis* 11: 27–42.

Rickman, J. (1957) 'Number and the human sciences', in *Selected Contributions to Psychoanalysis*, London: Hogarth Press.

Rycroft, C. (1972) *A Critical Dictionary of Psychoanalysis*, Harmondsworth: Penguin.

Schafer, R. (1960) 'The loving and beloved superego in Freud's structural theory', *Psychoanalytic Study of the Child* 15: 163–188.

Spiegel, L. (1959) 'The self, the sense of self and perception', *Psychoanalytic Study of the Child* 14: 81–112.

Thrane, G. (1979) 'Shame and the construction of the self', *Annual of Psychoanalysis* 7: 321–341.

Part II

Visual culture

Chapter 6

The visual poetics of shame

A feminist reading of Freud's *Three Essays on the Theory of Sexuality* (1905)

Griselda Pollock

I was in Hong Kong for the first time in February 2005. I listened to the news on CNN in my hotel room. Being in Hong Kong, I got the Asian news broadcasts I normally do not hear in Northern European and American time zones. They reported the unexpected, hence tragic, death of a young woman. Her name was Lee Eun-joo. She was one of the young superstars of contemporary Korean cinema. She had committed suicide. Her brother found her hanging in her walk-in closet. Later it was reported that there was a three-page suicide note. It was said that she had killed herself for shame. Shame is deadly. Clearly, we sometimes mean it when we say 'I almost died of shame.'

I am a person full of shame.

Shameful. This makes shame sound like a substance that can fill me. Shame floods, colouring the outer surface of the body with its visible sign: blushing. We *burn* with shame. It is like a fire within. These bodily signs write my body with my shame. But it can also be the hidden shame that no one knows. It is other. The Other that can heat and colour my body and silence my tongue. Shame is such that often we cannot speak of that which shames us. Shame plants itself in the body and yet it is a silencing. It numbs the subject, it dumbs the subject who cannot speak of what is shameful. Is shame an emotion, an affect, or a condition? Shame makes it dangerous to explore aspects of ourselves, bodies, imaginations and desires. Shame is the mark of an inner conflict. But it is also the instrument of the cultural police, internalized conscience, a persecuting superego that seems to enter us from without, a foreign force, an occupier and regulator.

The superego is the internalization of social or cultural mores, the prohibiting voices of the socializing agencies through which the archaic animal-infans becomes a socialized adult, a sexual, speaking subject. It can be a strong or a weak force, depending on the contingencies of each of our historical pathways through the normative processes of child-rearing and parenting that pattern the relations between the amoral intensities of the pleasure principle and the ego, negotiating the inner and the outer worlds in the name of the reality principle. The socialized subject is the potential site of a perpetual struggle. Remnants of the revolting infans – shameless as Freud will teach us – battle the voicing of prohibition which monitors the borders of our bodies and its fleshly dimensions, contributing to the transformation in the name of culture of its biological processes – such as ingestion, defecation and the flow of various bodily fluids and incitement of organs – into those psychic theatres of animating pleasure and *emotional* conflict. Shame is both an instrument of socialization and an emotion produced in that contest between infantile pleasures and human accommodation to societal adulthood. Shame silences the subject in the name, or voice, of an Other now situated within, creating, I suspect, one of the most violent and painful of all experiences of the subject at war with itself, divided between its boundless drives and monitoring colonizer: culture. The emotion of shame is the register of that interface of subjectivity and sociality. Shame as emotion plays an active role in depression, related to and even generating the self-hatred that can lead one part of the self to target itself for destruction in suicide – an act that is both an attempt to escape shame and one that is seen, socially, as deeply shameful. Shame is always there waiting to engulf the mistake, the failure, the lack, the unacceptable, registering itself in us as aphonic anxiety. There is shame and there is shamefulness. How useful is it? How deadly?

This area of social shame is explored by Martha Nussbaum in her book *Hiding from Humanity* (2004). Nussbaum suggests close links between disgust and shame in that the former is a defence against internal shame which is directed outwards to an other who inherits through social engineering the shameful traits – leading to both anti-Semitism and misogyny: the Jew and the woman as leaky, open, animalized figures. Disgust is thus the dominant group's fear and loathing of its own shaming animality and mortality. This will make shame a feminist issue as well as one deeply linked with the effects of racism. Homophobia stalks in the same forest as these other mythic figures of projected shame.

Shame, however, has deeper roots in human infancy according to Nussbaum. She relates it in a similar fashion to a protective rejection by the infant of feelings of vulnerability and neediness – rendering shame a 'way of hiding from humanity' and an awareness of our needs and powerlessness. This view of shame as an indication of human problems with mortality and physicality is widespread and renders our sexuality also susceptible to shame. Freud's arguments, however, lead in a radically different direction that I aim to plot out against this vision of shame in social and political discourse. There is also the realm of historically induced post-traumatic shame, discussed so painfully and courageously by Primo Levi in his writings as a survivor of the dehumanizing concentrationary universe. Although liberated physically from camp life and its daily form of dying, the survivor is, according to Levi, irredeemably altered by an experience of having his or her humanity violated from which there is no escape. The experience of dehumanization through torture in the concentration camp leaves the survivor chronically shamed: 'Coming out of the darkness, one suffered because of the reacquired consciousness of having been diminished' (Levi 1989: 56).

I am a person full of shame.

As a result I cannot speak of it at all. It is the hardest thing of all to admit to another. I am fascinated by the power of the internal barrier – the shame itself – that makes me silent, that strangles the words in my throat, that renders me inarticulate when sharing this hidden anxiety, a communication that might lead to release from the power of the superego that has damned me in both senses of the word.

So I become interested in shame intellectually. I agree to attend an academic conference on shame and sexuality in honour of the centenary of the publication of Freud's most scandalous and radical book *Drei Abhandlungen zur Sexualtheorie*, known in English as *Three Essays on the Theory of Sexuality*, first published in 1905. In preparation for the conference I propose a Research Salon at AHRC Centre for Cultural Analysis, Theory and History. A Research Salon assembles an informal group of staff and graduate students to undertake a close week-by-week, word-by-word reading of the selected text. Reading out loud, this process takes place over many months.

The Research Salon on *Three Essays on the Theory of Sexuality* is, quite simply, riotous. As the leader of this reading group who must both read the text aloud and provide commentaries for those new to psychoanalysis and Freud, I am made utterly shameless, obliged to follow Freud into conversations about the eroticism of bowel movements, coprophilia, and a range of sexual excitations that are not normally the topic of academic discussion at 5 pm on a Thursday afternoon. Freud's text lured us into transgression of the monitor that usually silences us. His book bypassed our shame by means of a carefully constructed and argued *writing* of the conditions under which it will emerge as one of the three *disgraces* that accompany the formations of sexuality. Freud's text creates a picture of the sexuality of human subjectivity that suspends the inner voices of culture's moral police so as to be able to acknowledge the very condition of *human sexual* formation (the two terms being profoundly interconnected for Freud). Shame is irrelevant here since there is no normal, no proper, no acceptable sexuality but only a complex and variable trajectory from the need for animal sustenance to the ability to love and experience pleasure with ourselves and later with another by means of the formations of the drives, their varied aims and unpredictable objects:

> Popular opinion has quite definite ideas about the nature and characteristics of this sexual instinct. It is generally understood to be absent in childhood, to set in at the time of puberty in connection with the processes

of coming to maturity and to be revealed in the manifestations of an irresistible attraction exercised by one sex upon the other; while its aim is presumed to be sexual union, or at all events actions leading in that direction. We have every reason to believe, however, that these views give a very false picture of the true situation. If we look into them more closely we shall find that they contain a number of errors, inaccuracies and hasty conclusions.

(Freud 1905: 1)

Freud takes aim at 'popular opinion' and its 'views', the locus of the accepted social ideologies of reproductive, heteronormative sexuality that posits an innocent childhood, pubescent development into adult sexuality with its exclusive Malthusian aim of the genital sex between a man and a woman. In this paragraph we can find elements of what Michel Foucault would later plot out in identifying the 'four strategic unities' of the nineteenth-century European bourgeois discourse of sexuality in which the idealized Malthusian couple stands surrounded by the failing and the aberrant: the frigid wife or hysterical daughter, the masturbating child and the perverse adult. Foucault identified thereby the classificatory mechanisms of social regulation of the productive-reproductive couple (the family) and those deviations and hence medically and psychiatrically defined abnormalities to which social power would self-legitimatingly apply their varied expertises in a riotous explosion of discourse (Foucault 1978: 104–105).

Within the next, only the third paragraph of the book, Freud undoes the 'strategic unities' and their personifications by introducing the sexual drive, not as the unitary instrument of social ideology, but a complex force characterized by its own economy of object and aim, the former 'being the person from whom the sexual attraction proceeds', the latter being 'the act towards which the drive tends':

Scientifically sifted observation, then, shows that numerous deviations occur in respect of both of these – the sexual aim and the sexual object. The relation between these deviations and what is assumed to be normal requires thorough investigation.

(Freud 1905: 2)

Donning the cloak of 'scientifically sifted observation', Freud prepares to do battle with 'popular opinion', in order to speak of human sexuality in a radically new way: not as the source of shame to be managed by social experts such as doctors and psychologists. In Freud's writing, sexuality becomes an animating, creative and intensely human aspect of subjectivity. Not at all the residue of an animal past, it is the produced condition of a creative humanity. Yet clearly 'popular opinion' has it locked in a cage whose sentries Freud will repeatedly list as the trio of 'shame, disgust and morality'

(Freud 1905: 30). Here, I would disagree profoundly with those who see in shame the human expression of anxiety in sexuality as a reminder of our animality. Quite the opposite is true. Our perplexity before our own desire lies in its specifically *human* and *humanising* generation, without which we would have an action without the condition of consciousness, self-consciousness and repression (the unconscious) that makes us the *subjects* of sexuality rather than subjected to what so many mistake as an alien, pre-human, shamefully non-human/animal force.

Prefaces

In our Salon, we start at the beginning. Thanks to the editors of the Standard Edition, Freud's *Three Essays* are prefaced by a title page that provides us with the history of the publication of the text. It informs us that between 1905 and 1925 there were six German editions, and a final posthumous publication in 1942. English translations begin only in 1910 and undergo four editions by 1930 followed by a reprint in 1938 and the appearance of the Standard Edition in 1953 with a version in 1949 published by the Imago Publishing Company. We track the appearance of the book in French, Spanish and Italian as a cultural history of uneven dissemination and of censorship.

My edition also prints three prefaces. Reading the three prefaces to the editions of 1909, 1914 and 1920 is instructive. Dated Vienna, 1909, the first preface to the second edition is but a short, and we might say, confident paragraph. The author concludes: 'It is his earnest wish that the book may age rapidly – that what was once new in it may become generally accepted, and that what is imperfect in it may be replaced by something better' (Freud 1905: xiv). From Ernest Jones's biography of Freud (1967), we glean that psychoanalysis and Freud himself were under attack from opponents in the medical, psychological and scientific communities of Germany and even the United States. Since *The Three Essays* had appeared at the same time as the 'Dora' case study, 'Jokes and their relation to the Unconscious' and but five years after *The Interpretation of Dreams*, a substantive body of argument about the central role of sexuality in the unconscious and in the aetiology of neurosis as well as everyday life was already in the public domain. What clung to Freud, however, was the *stain* of sexuality, so different from the sexuality that for Freud, in attempting to analyse it in his patients and himself, ceased to be a stain, or a source of shame. It might appear that the internalized shame of a culture towards sexuality not only blinded its scientists but led them to attempt to silence the one of their community who dared to break ranks and speak of it, shamelessly. Thus the brevity and apparent confidence of the 1909 Preface to a second edition seems disingenuous, calm amidst a storm of vile accusations – 'it rains abuse from Germany', wrote Freud in 1910 (Jones 1967: 389). His critics (see Kiell 1988) projected Freud as a 'Viennese libertine' (Jones 1967: 392) to which he added:

There one hears just the argument I tried to avoid by making Zurich the centre. Viennese sensuality is not to be found anywhere else. Between the lines you can read further that we Viennese are not only swine but also Jews. But that does not appear in print.

(Jones 1967: 387)

Freud's hope for quick acceptance, however disingenuous, faded by 1914. In the tenth anniversary edition, Freud made some remarks 'intended to prevent misunderstandings and expectations that cannot be fulfilled'. The unrelenting years of abuse and misrepresentation must now be faced. Freud's new preface is on the defensive about psychoanalytical theories of sexuality which have been challenged on the grounds of their differing from the findings – the givens of popular opinion which is in fact the mindset of the scientific establishment – of biology. If theology appeals to a transcendent creator for its truth, science invented nature and in this realm set up its own fictions of the biological as the final defence against the self-analysis that is at the heart of an atheist and modernist project: psychoanalysis. One way to delegitimate psychoanalysis, seeding a doubt suffered by Freud himself, is to question his scientific knowledge of biology. Freud, therefore, had to insist that he knows of what he does not write about, that he has made choices in his structure and topics that are being dealt with *psychoanalytically*. In this gap between the hegemonic mode of knowledge rooted in a biologistic determinism and the tentative, experiential hermeneutics of psychoanalysis lies a much deeper struggle not only for some delusion of final understanding of ourselves, but for a political emancipation of human sexualities not dictated by the elevation of a sovereign construction of the biological. This is neither libertarianism, nor the misguided abuses of sexuality typical of the 1960s sexual liberationists. It marks the attempt to refashion that deeper intimacy within our experience of a self, to escape its deformations by the double force of shame as the socially monitoring outsider and an internally self-hating emotion.

In affirming his fidelity to a distinctively psychoanalytical approach, Freud is deeply defensive – the years leading up to 1914 were a period of difficulty in the public reception of psychoanalytical interpretations of sexuality (Tichy 1999). We might include here the violent response in another academic community, that of art history, to his reading of the work of Leonardo da Vinci, published in 1910, where Freud was shockingly attacked for besmirching this glorious artist by daring to speak of his homosexuality as if the latter was a kind of dirt that itself sprung from the sexual filth of Freud's own 'Jewish' mind. In all of this the politics of both homophobia and anti-Semitism constantly chime as undercurrents of the assault on psychoanalysis. Shame is used to silence that which hegemonic culture dares not face.

The preface to the fourth edition, dated 1920, much longer than either of the preceding two, reveals what amounts to a significant pattern in which the pious hope of easy acceptance and advance of the theory put forward expressed in the second preface has clearly failed to materialize. Instead Freud notes:

> Now that the flood waters of war have subsided, it is satisfactory to record the fact that interest in psycho-analytical research remains unimpaired in the world at large.
>
> But different parts of the theory have not at all had the same history. The purely psychological theses and findings of psycho-analysis on the unconscious, repression, conflict as a cause of illness, the advantage accruing from illness, the mechanism of the formation of symptoms, etc., have come to enjoy increasing recognition and have won notice even from those who are in general opposed to our views. That part of the theory, however, which lies on the frontiers of biology and the foundations of which are contained in this little work is still faced with undiminished contradiction.
>
> (Freud 1905: xvii)

Freud's theory of sexuality – registering a certain instability of the boundaries between the psychic and the biological – continues to generate resistance, despite the increasing acceptance of many of psychoanalysis' central propositions. One of the reasons Freud advances to explain this difference concerns the central thesis of the *Three Essays* on the proposition of the origins of sexuality in infancy. As we shall see, the complex layering of advent, repression and return of sexuality constitute a structure both leaning on and inscribed on to the body in a phantasmatic mapping of its zones, movements and surfaces. It develops across a barrier of amnesiac registration and anamnesic return on the other side of the cataclysmic submission to the Oedipus complex – the mechanism of cultural structuration of subjectivity and sociality. This picture of an historical configuration of sexuality through different sites and discontinuous moments will form the primary scandal of the book itself as well as the condition for psychoanalytical work as an archaeology of subjectivity.

A secondary scandal is indicated in Freud's final paragraph which also marks the enormous cleft his work created between biology (as a mastering scientific discourse and as a field of life processes) and psychoanalysis as a decentring of mastery in pursuit of reflexive but observably testable self-knowledge. Freud writes:

> It must also be remembered, however, that some of what this book contains – its insistence on the importance of sexuality in all human achievements and the attempt it makes at enlarging the concept of sexuality – has from the first provided the strongest motives for the resistance against psychoanalysis.
>
> (Freud 1905: xviii)

Liberating sexuality from biology also liberates humanity from a division in which that which is most intensely associated in 'popular opinion' with a predestined biological function, in fact, becomes that which most distinctively defines us as achieving humans. By theorizing sexuality psychoanalytically, sexualities become the hallmark of the human in which that itself means the capacity to transform the drives necessary for keeping the organism alive into psychic, intersubjective and other/object oriented work and creation. It is the motor of dynamics – change, work, thought and creativity as well as love and pleasure.

Freud inverted existing models: sexuality is not the recalcitrant remnant of our animality, heteronormatively confining human sexuality to the service of reproduction of genes or species. Precisely because it is a psychological effect, it relates to the creation of the psyche that marks the gap between the infans-animal we are born as and the human subject we become. Sexuality is one of the modes of that humanization, and it is the energy and force that drives our most human activities: creation, ambition, thought as well as that other distinctive human condition: neurosis and psychic pain. Thus we can see how wrong are the traditional accusations of 'pan-sexualism' and the 'senseless charge against it of explaining "everything" by sex'. Against these charges Freud defended himself by referencing Schopenhauer and Plato – but in passing he reminds us of those topics which make his book astonishing and so much misread and resisted: the sexuality of children and of 'what are called perverts'.

In his contributions to the theory of sexuality – lying on the borders of biology and psychology – Freud has been attacked for overemphasising the importance of sexuality. His arguments, misread and misrepresented, produce the caricatured and still popular idea that Freud based everything on sex, i.e. reduced human dignity to its most base instincts. This preface marks a historical development in the reception of Freud's theory which accuses Freud of the very inverse of what his *Three Essays* in fact argue. Since sexuality is not a biological but a psychological effect at the interface of fantasy and the drives, it is a human achievement, not a pre-psychological given. There can be no reduction of everything to sex: Freud's aim is precisely to discover its dynamic foundations in intersubjective psychic life and to trace its varied manifestations. It is with the vicissitudes of this archaic intersubjective formation of the infant's psychic life and the social management of sexual desire that impinges upon us firstly with the Oedipus complex and secondarily with the transformations of puberty that Freud devotes his carefully plotted arguments.

These prefaces are historically interesting as they chart the increase rather than the fading of resistance to Freud's 1905 theorization of sexuality. It is the element against which culture in its public form resists Freud's revelations as if what Freud dared to say shamed the culture that turned back its disgust on to Freud and psychoanalysis to make his claims themselves appear shameful.

The architecture of the argument

In our Research Salon, we next considered the question of the architecture of Freud's writing. Why *three* essays? What were the three topics and why were they laid out in that order? Through what movement of thought would the reader be led by the tripartite structure? What does the structure of the book in these three parts reveal about the very process Freud is exposing to analytical discourse: not visually showing it but speaking its complex articulation as at once both structure and history, both drive and social moderation?

The first essay is titled 'Sexual Aberrations'. I have already quoted the opening paragraphs. Its first footnote references an impressive array of established experts in the field of sexology: Kraft-Ebbing, Moll, Moebius, Havelock-Ellis, Schrenk-Notzing, Löwenfeld, Eulenberg, Bloch, Hirschfield, editor of the *Jahrbuch für sexualle Zwischenstufen*. Are these the intended interlocutors, the supporting 'fathers' or those who will be invoked in order to be transcended in the production of a new, psychoanalytical discourse on sexuality which must first deal with that of sexology: the classification of sexual types and disorders?

The writing of this essay is primarily a wonder of deconstruction – disassembling the everyday and common-sense ideas about fixed sexuality. 'Popular opinion' is introduced as a key protagonist whose misguided assumptions will be systematically demolished in a fine display of inconclusive evidence that serves to destabilize any certainty. The moral convention that establishes a normal against an abnormal sexuality, legislating against that abnormality as that which must be policed and excluded from the normal, is utterly undone by allowing into view an accumulation of documented possibilities in both aim and object. The mechanism is based on providing a theory of sexuality as a drive – generated by a lack (need) structured by an aim – the achieving of satisfaction (defined as the meeting of a need and removal of a lack) by means of an object, none of which is given by any prior order or inherent rule. Observation of human sexual activity reveals that the sexual instinct and the sexual object are not soldered together with a pre-given telos – such as popular opinion will assume to be adult heterosexual reproductive genital activity. Equally the instability of the sexual aim undoes what popular opinion deems to be the single and proper aim, genital sex and its reproductive potential. This expanded concept of sexuality eroticizes both touching – the skin – and seeing, rendering the eye itself an erotic organ: scopophilia. Here Freud is also able to demonstrate that these 'perversions' in the sexual aim often exhibit two different forms, active and passive, and it is in the midst of this elaboration that he concludes: 'The force which opposes scopophilia, but which may be overridden by it (in a manner parallel to what we have previously seen in the case of disgust), is *shame*' (p. 23). Disgust is raised in terms of the eroticized mucous membrane of the mouth and oral cavity. Disgust 'protects' the subject from accepting sexual aims of the kind in which the lips of one person come into contact with the genitals of another. These limits are purely conventional, remarks Freud of a man who may kiss a girl but feel disgust at using her toothbrush. 'Disgust seems to be one of the forces which have led to a restriction of the sexual aim . . . [but] the sexual drive in its strength enjoys overriding this disgust' (p. 18). Disgust and hence shame in this early essay appears as a 'force' countering and often overridden by the 'strength' of the sexual drive. Conventional and hence cultural, it is also co-present with the emergence of the sexual drive as a mirror of its own eclectic investment of every surface, cavity, organ with the potential for gratification. Is it, therefore, an instance of pure conflict? In providing an interim conclusion to this essay, Freud has this to say:

> Our study of perversions has shown us that the sexual instinct has to struggle against certain mental forces which act as resistances, and of which shame and disgust are the most prominent. It is permissible to suppose that these forces play a part in restraining that drive within the limits regarded as normal; and if they develop in the individual before the sexual drive has reached its full strength, it is no doubt that they will determine the course of its development.
>
> (Freud 1905: 28)

The positing of 'forces' that function as resistances introduces a kind of mechanics into the preliminary plotting of the aims and objects of the sexual drive which might seem at first sight non-psychoanalytical. I wonder if the use of this vocabulary of forces and resistances is required in order to create a discourse that does not yet personify sexuality, identifying it always and already with the anthropomorphic image of the heterosexual couple and the bourgeois family framing of sexual productivity. The terms give sexuality an impersonal quality of an energy incited by and eroticising the body that is being mapped erotogeneously by the patterning of the drive across its surfaces, interiors, sphincters, cavities, fluids, none of which are at all related to anything conventional wisdom knows as sexuality. The second conclusion uses what we might call another kind of constructive metaphor.

> In the second place we have found that some of the perversions which we have examined are only made intelligible if we assume the convergence of several motive forces. If such perversions admit of analysis, that is, *if they can be taken to pieces*, then they must be of a composite nature. This gives us a hint that perhaps the sexual drive itself may be no simple thing, but put together from components which have come apart again in the perversions. If this is so, the clinical observation of these abnormalities will have drawn our attention to amalgamations which have been lost to view in the uniform behaviour of normal people.
>
> (Freud 1905: 28)

By this means Freud demolishes the tenacious belief in a unitary sexual drive with its single valorized aim. It also undoes a fixed distinction between normal and abnormal. Sexuality is *constructed* out of component elements; it is neither given nor merely derived but produced in a process subject to considerable accident (the history of each individual) in the process of construction. The difference between the normal and the perverse is a mere degree of visibility of the shared building of the drive out of its pre-sexual or even non-sexual components that fasten on to every and any potential.

Thus the neurotics become the resource for a clinical study of sexuality because in them *their sexual life takes the form of their symptoms*. Symptoms are a form of visibility of both what human sexuality is (where normality is mere assimilation to the point of rendering its own formations invisible) and evidence not of its diversity (the happily perverse are not neurotic as the sexologists would claim) but of the cost of adversity. The symptom is formed as a mental substitute or 'transcription' for 'mentally cathected processes, wishes and desires, which by operation of a special psychical procedure (repression) have been prevented from obtaining discharge in psychical activity that is admissible to consciousness' (Freud 1905: 30). One group of neurotics, the hysterics, are significant here. They exhibit or suffer from a combination of excessive repression and 'an intensification of resistance against the sexual drive (which we have already met with in the form of shame, disgust and morality)' (p. 30). We shall have to wait until the final chapter to explain this enigma which touches upon what is scrupulously excluded from this first essay, for good reasons: sexual difference with regard not to the origins of the components of sexuality but the social sphere in which the subject's experience of its own forces and resistances encounters the powerful pressures of its engendering, normalizing culture.

At the end of Freud's calculatedly destabilizing demonstration, logic forces us to admit that so widespread are what popular opinion might have generally called *perversion* that perversity in fact 'forms part of what passes as the normal constitution' (p. 30). Psychoanalysis, far from reducing everything to a fixed origin, functions as a countertheory. All is accident, i.e. each of us is shaped by what has happened to us – a historical figuration that can, however, only be deciphered against a ground of the structural functioning of the mental processes. Thus what Freud has done in this first essay is to elaborate so complex a picture of the aims and objects of the sexual drive that any notion of a single, innate sexuality is impossible. Yet he will play games with his opponents, who propose innate sources and admit that there must be something '*innate in everyone*' if every one of us is more or less subject to what is now in place as a generative perversity. Some use elements of this to develop specific sexual activities; others – neurotics – transpose the sexual energy into their symptoms. 'Normal sexual life' lies somewhere between the two framed 'by effective restriction and other kinds of modification' (p. 37).

By means, therefore, of the existence of those in whom we may study the persistent or fixated perversions – the neurotics – (perversion in the popular sense of referring to non-heterosexual reproductive sexualities having now been completely displaced) the next move can be made to suggest that the sexuality of neurotics only reveals to us regression towards or persistence from the constitutive space of our non-determined sexualities: namely the infantile state of polymorphous perversity.

Troubling infancy

> One feature of the popular view of the sexual drive is that it is absent in childhood and only awakens in the period of life described as puberty.
>
> (Freud 1905: 38)

Freud has brilliantly led the 'popular' thinker to the core of his scandalous assertion that, beyond even the displaced idea of normal/abnormal, he is prepared to undo the child/adult division and with it the idea of childhood innocence and the Christianocentric idea of a corrupting fall into adult sexual knowledge which surrounds the advent of adult sexuality with its moralizing shame. In a sense Freud's new theory simply abolishes the myth embedded in both the Hebrew and Christian Bibles that something significant has to happen to introduce otherwise innocent children to the knowledge of their own sexuality – the oral incorporation of the fruit that is instigated by the woman and is offered by her to her man, *ish*, to share. Fascinating as it is to work over the texts of the book of *Bereshit/Genesis* in order to reinterpret in less misogynistic terms the coming of moral adulthood and moral choice by the act of disobedient desire, Freudian theory simply debunks the entire problematic and with it the basis of shame-inducing misogynistic morality contained in a notion of adulthood, or maturity, as a matter of control over the contaminating sexual drive.

If sexuality is constituted *in infancy*, it is constituted both auto-erotically and relationally across the generations, in trans- and hence non-gendered ways, or rather in what Teresa de Lauretis might name, *sexual indifference*. It is, therefore, constituted precisely as the transitional space created between the biological body in its struggle to maintain itself in life and the social, intersubjective, already cultural conditions under which the human infant experiences that struggle. Freud's definition of the drive as a psychical representative of an endosomatic 'continuously flowing source of stimulation . . . lying on the frontier of the mental and physical' tries to create a concept through which to think both a passage and a constitutive condition of psychological embodiment. The child thinks the only way it can: with a body, or with body parts, zones, pleasures, movements, spaces, limits, borders, ingestions, expulsions, contents, edges, stimulations, pulses, repeats, release, emptiness, fullness, and of course, bits and pieces and surfaces of its flesh that seem particularly intense in generating supplements of pleasure. Thus Freud would arrive at his proposal about the oral, anal and genital phases and the idea of erotogenic zones: a mapping of the body around pleasure/unpleasure indifferent to anatomical coherence or function, grooved like well-worn stones by the flowing currents of its animating energies.

Freud has, however, to contend with a major problem. His hypothesis, reasonable as it may be, is supported by no report from within it because of what he names infantile amnesia 'which turns everyone's childhood into something like a prehistoric epoch and conceals from him the beginning of his own sexual life' (p. 42). Thus to the fractured character of the component drives, Freud is now adding the irregular patterns of activity and latency in the formative period of sexuality: 'this oscillating course of development' (p. 42). We can begin, however, to observe the sexual life of children around three and four years old.

This period becomes significant in our study of shame and sexuality for it is during this period that 'are built up the mental forces which are later to impede the course of the sexual drive and, like dams, restrict its flow – disgust, shame and the claims of aesthetic and moral ideals' (p. 43). Freud dismisses the suggestion that these dams are the product of education; they are 'organically determined and fixed by heredity'. This seems deeply puzzling. How can a psychoanalytical theory of the construction of sexuality – given all these mechanical and architectural metaphors – nonetheless be subject to organically determined and hereditarily fixed resistances? How can they not? If there is an energy, there must be a resistance without which energy would itself be self-identical. But what is the function then of the particular forms of damming: disgust, shame and now this new sense of an 'aesthetic ideal'? The passage in which these phrasings occur concerns a speculation on the diversion of sexual energy towards other ends: sublimation, another borrowed term, this time from chemistry. Sublimation results from two sources, according to Freud here. One is that there is a sexual drive but the means of its realization in what will later be full adult sex is necessarily deferred. The other is that the polymorphous perversity of the sexual drive in that condition may arouse unpleasurable feelings against which the subject erects its mental dams: disgust, shame and morality. Thus shame and its partners are both party to sublimation but distinct, as fundamentally reaction-formations, again suggesting an intimate coexistence inside the subject with sexuality, with shame registering as the symptom of a conflict within.

The nature of this conflict comes into view several sections later when Freud is discussing the effect of 'seduction' which can make children polymorphously perverse. For the most part, his concept of infantile sexuality renders it auto-erotic, a matter of stimulations of surfaces, interiors and organs of the child itself that bring satisfaction. Seduction, even if it introduces prematurely an other object, only confirms children's aptitude to further excitements which, however, at this stage, meet little resistance because 'the mental dams against sexual excesses – shame, disgust and morality – have not yet been constructed or are only in process of construction according to the age of the child' (p. 57). But Freud then continues:

> Moreover, the effects of seduction do not help to reveal the early history of the sexual drive; they rather confuse our view of it by presenting children prematurely with a sexual object for which the sexual drive at first shows no need. It must, however, be admitted that infantile sexual life, in spite of a preponderating dominance of erotogenic zones, exhibits components which from the very first involve other people as sexual objects. Such are the drives of scopophilia, exhibitionism and cruelty, which appear in a sense independently of erotogenic zones; these drives do not enter into intimate relations with genital life until later, but are already to be observed in childhood as independent impulses, distinct in the first instance from erotogenic sexual activity. *Small children are essentially without shame*, and at some periods of their earliest years show an unmistakable satisfaction in exposing their bodies, with especial emphasis on their sexual parts. The counterpart of this supposedly perverse inclination, curiosity to see other people's genitals, probably does not become manifest until somewhat later in childhood, when the obstacle set up by a sense of shame has already reached a certain degree of development.
>
> (Freud 1905: 57–58, my italics)

Shame is emerging only slowly in these curious passages as a kind of pre-ego. Mirror of and for the sexual drive, it is also a regulator of excess. To be shameless is associated with a confidence about exhibiting oneself and significantly that which is most intensely pleasurable and narcissistically significant. The child offers its body, its sex, itself to an other for the pleasure of showing and being seen. Adult shame will focus acutely on exposure, being seen naked outside of the covenantal space of sexual play. Thus what appears from the plotting of these terms in Freud's text is a history, a set of relations between elements sharing their originating disposition but emerging at different times in opposing forms so that drive-energy and resistance-dam are different facets of a common genesis.

In a brilliant conclusion to this section on infantile sexuality, Freud reclaims a means of analysing this mysterious zone subject to amnesia, latency and irregularity, by arguing that the pathways of the formation of sexuality 'are traversable in the opposite direction' (p. 71). Thus far from reducing everything to sex in some essentialist reduction, Freud suggests that he can track backwards down the formative grooves and trenches from adult neurotics in whom their symptoms, often somatic, are 'the counterpart of the influences which bring about the production of sexual excitation' (p. 72).

It all goes off in puberty

It was the same year, 1905, in which Freud's *Three Essays* appeared that a British scientist identified the chemicals Freud was already hypothesizing as causing the onset of adult sexuality during puberty – hormones. Ernest Henry Starling introduced the term hormone in his Croonian lectures to the Royal College of Physicians in June 1905. Previously Claude Bernard (1813–78) and Charles Edouard Brown-Sequard (1817–94) had introduced the idea of internal secretions, but neither had thought of them as specific chemical messengers (Eaton 2005).

Chemically switched back on, at the moment of a physiological development that acts directly upon the genitalia and sexual morphology of children's relatively non-different bodies to produce adult, sexed men and women, sexuality runs smash up against culture during puberty in ways which actively differentiate between boys and girls and what boys and girls are allowed to do with whom:

> Since the new sexual aim assigns very different functions of the two sexes, their sexual development now diverges greatly. That of males is more straightforward and the more understandable, while that of females actually enters upon a kind of involution.
>
> (Freud 1905: 73)

Freud's study of 'The Transformations of Puberty' simply shows that as girls emerge into womanhood their access to sexuality is censored so that what they experience as sexuality is its shaming, its silencing, its unspeakability. Hystericized, however, their bodies speak of nothing else – but only indirectly, and backwards as it were, reversing down the channels of damned becoming.

What remains during latency of 'infantile florescence of sexuality' is the affectionate current. Children ceased to desire but come to love their parental figures. Affection now must be joined to the newly restimulated sensual current that has, however, as its aim in men the discharge of sexual products – quite distinct from the infantile sexual pleasures focused entirely on the attainment of pleasure. Freud will go on to argue that puberty marks the differentiation between men and women, allowing 'sexuality' to become detached from its genesis. Nonetheless, there are signs of what will become masculine and feminine dispositions during childhood: what are these?

> The development of the inhibitions of sexuality (shame, disgust, pity, etc.,) takes place earlier in little girls and in the face of less resistance than in boys; the tendency to sexual repression seems in general to be greater; and where the component drives of sexuality appear, they prefer the passive form.
>
> (Freud 1905: 85)

This is set against the fact that 'auto-erotic activity of the erotogenic zones, is, however, the same in both sexes, and owing to this uniformity there is no possibility of distinction between the two sexes such as arises after puberty' (p. 85). Precocious predisposition to sexual inhibition or shame and preference for the passive could be red rags to feminist cows. The latter is important to redress since Freud's discussion of the sexual component drives carefully reveals that there is only ever one originating form: active. Passive is not its opposite but its involution or even complement. Thus active refers to a muscularity associated with mastery in defecation, for instance, while passive refers to the pleasures associated with surfaces: Freud's supreme example – he is discussing the sadistic-anal phase – is the mucous membrane of the anus. Unattached to conventional, cultural and figurative notions of heterosexual genital couples, active and passive are alternating mechanisms of pleasure resting upon different components of the non-gendered body. What entrains these pleasures of contracting muscles and stimulated surfaces to gendered sexual identities is the imposition of the imagery of gender during puberty. The proclivity of the girl-child towards inhibition and shame seems to me to smack of a retrospective projection down the reversible tunnel from the social world to the susceptible, other-oriented child, who if female is constantly under the added pressure of the women tending her who are themselves already formed by convention and acting as society's agents of gendering and policing.

It is in this context that Freud argues that libido – the Latin name he has given the sexual drive – is 'invariably and necessarily of a masculine nature, whether it occurs in men or in women, irrespectively of whether its object is a man or a woman' (p. 85). To this passage Freud added a long footnote in 1915. He distinguishes between three uses: in the sense of activity and passivity, biologically, and sociologically. The first is the usage preferred by psychoanalysis because the drive is always active, even when it has a passive aim. The biological terminology concerns sperm and ova and although there are many cases in which the functions resulting from their presence generate masculine activity, this is not at all the invariable case across all species. At the sociological level, when actual people are observed there is no pure masculinity or femininity but countless unpredictable mixtures of traits which do not tally with biological one (i.e. having sperm or ova in the body).

Nonetheless, the conclusion we can draw from this study is that what differentiates the sexes so markedly at puberty is not their biologies which clearly only offer the potential for certain kinds of outcomes. It is more than the vicissitudes of their passage through infancy and latency in which, independent of the sexing of their bodies at birth, is uniform in its eroticization of oral, anal and genital as well as skin, vision and movement. It would seem to be that girls/women are formed/deformed at the point at which the internal conflict between the sexual drive and the spontaneously formed resistances that act like mental dams encounter the shaming of active sexuality at the point of its biochemical reincitement at puberty. As hormonally reawakened sexuality floods the body with its own intensities of desire for pleasure and for an Other, Freud remarked factually on the wall built by misogynistic patriarchal culture against which female sexuality smashes. The wall is not just the incrementally installed mental dam but actual social surveillance and even surgical or psychological suppression that has built an entire phantasmagoria of images, words, and modes of actual bodily punishment to terrorize women into a shameful fear of betraying their desire. Even with the women's movement and all the acts of aesthetic, theoretical and cultural transgression that involved challenging the deepest taboos by flashing their bodies like shameless little children, this deep structure has not been seriously undermined. Shame is, therefore, a central feminist issue: and, as the site of the physical formations of her sexuality, the body of the adult woman becomes infected with shame.

This chapter gestures towards the larger project for which it has plotted out the theoretical ground by a reading of Freud's *Three Essays*: a feminist analysis of the visual poetics of shame in contemporary art and visual culture. My opening epigraph points in one direction: an event in visual culture which prompted my reflections on shame, namely the death of a Korean movie star, apparently shamed by a recent part she played as both a lesbian and a pregnant, heterosexual adulteress in a film titled *The Scarlet Letter* (Daniel Buyn 2004). The title, knowingly, invokes the nineteenth-century American novel by Nathaniel Hawthorne in which Hester Prynne is forced to wear the badge of her 'sexual shame' in the form of an embroidered red letter 'A' for 'Adulteress' on her clothing. Her shame is, in fact, published by the child, Pearl, she bears out of wedlock, fathered by a man she would not name to maintain his honour in the community which thus pillories her. In the film's final scene the woman and her lover are locked into the boot of car where she miscarries her 'Pearl' and is shot in the head, covering both herself and her lover with her life blood. The film almost biblically images the trauma of masculine encounter with the 'shame' of female sexuality that is played out in grandiose melodrama and visual excess that leaves the viewer perplexed as to how to read its project that associates the sexuality of women with temptation and final catastrophe.

For the most part, the other works of visual art that I aim to explore further intervene against this imaginary, teasing out both a different perspective and a different aesthetic process. Perspective and process converge in aesthetic attempts to engage the viewer with the subjectivity, the position as subjects, of women negotiating the imposition of shame occasioned largely by the traumas of ethnic, racist political violence and its aftermath. The work of Penny Siopis on shame in post-apartheid South Africa forms part of this volume. Lubaina Himid's installation *Naming the Money* (2004) seeks to situate the wandering viewer in a brilliant crowd of African creative people whose entrapment and transportation into slavery in Europe and its colonies imposed the shame of slavery involving the loss of name, of past, but not of memory which Himid poetically reconstitutes as counterforce to the reduction of person to the status of a chattel. Bracha Ettinger's paintings cover with a veil of longing the traumatic shaming of women appearing in a grim photograph of the Holocaust where they were forced to strip naked in midwinter amidst unknown men who are to be their murderers. Images of victims of the Holocaust are often exhibited in order to document a horror whose impact on the individuals thus exposed once again to a deadly gaze is left unconsidered in the need for historical proof. How can we look upon any persons so violated precisely by afflicting them with shame amidst the terror of imminent death without participating in the sadism of that genocidal gaze? How can we negotiate the relations between trauma and shame in the field of history when we look back?

While these final indications of other pathways seem to lead away from the theses on sexuality proposed by Freud, almost returning to the territory of social shame discussed by Primo Levi and Martha Nussbaum which I bypassed at the beginning of this chapter, I would like to argue that they do not. Freud's analysis of the formations of subjectivity force us into knowledge of ourselves, our capacities, our responsibilities. Freud's work on subjectivity and notably on sexuality are about acknowledging as necessary an adulthood that takes upon itself an ethical responsibility for its actions, thoughts and feelings even while acquiescing to knowledge or rather lack of knowledge of the unconscious at work. Freud's attempt to renegotiate an understanding of sexuality as the life force, the energy that patterns us with later psychological possibilities for both love and pleasure and creativity and thought, tends in a direction that refuses us the comfort of thinking that beneath the veneer of civilization lurks a force we cannot control, a power that is the ultimate 'truth'. It is that tenaciously held belief (of a sex beyond us [men] that must then be socially controlled in some [women]) that negates the ethical demand Freud's production of self-knowledge makes upon us. To know ourselves through these curious and often disturbed formations as historically made subjects, to know the vicissitudes and variations that fall within those possibilities, is to encourage us to avoid the egregious prejudices and wilful, racist, homophobic and sexist cruelties of 'popular opinion' and, at the same time, to recognize that for all their creative perversity, human sexualities always take place in social, cultural and historical worlds.

The architecture of Freud's book is a political architecture, moving from critical deconstruction to challenging self-knowledge and onto cultural situation. To the ethics of self-understanding and granting life to all others resulting from our acknowledgement of the meaning of infantile sexuality, we must then add the politics of taking responsibility for making changes to those aspects of cultural and social practice that are deadly when sexuality returns in puberty and encounters the force of culture. Shame lies precisely in the fold of the ethics and politics of sexuality that Freud's little book is all about.

References

Eaton, L. (2005) 'College looks back to discovery of hormones', *British Medical Journal*, 330: 1466.

Foucault, M. (1978) *A History of Sexuality, Volume I: Introduction*, trans. R. Hurley, Harmondsworth: Penguin.

Freud, S. (1905) *Three Essays on the Theory of Sexuality*, S.E. 7, New York: Basic Books, 1962.

Jones, E. (1967) *The Life and Work of Sigmund Freud*, ed. and abridged L. Trilling and S. Marcus, Harmondsworth: Pelican.

Kiell, N. (1988) *Freud without Hindsight: Reviews of his Work 1893–1939*, New York: International Universities Press.

Levi, P. (1989) 'Shame', in P. Levi *The Drowned and the Saved*, trans. R. Rosenthal, London: Abacus.

Nussbaum, M. (2004) *Hiding from Humanity: Disgust, Shame and the Law*, Princeton: Princeton University Press.

Tichy, M. and Zwettler-Otte, S. (1999) *Rezeption des Psychoanalyse in Osterreich 1895–1938*, Vienna: Sonderzahl.

Chapter 7

The Garden of Eden

Sex, shame and knowledge

Claire Pajaczkowska

The structure of Paradise

It was Proust who, in his concluding thoughts to *À la recherche du temps perdu*, while exploring the enigma of time, noted that 'The true paradises are the paradises that we have lost' (Proust 1923) and it is this paradox of the imaginary presence of paradise as an experience of a space and time that is also, and simultaneously, a symbol of a world once possessed and now lost, that I want to explore here. In fact it seems that the condition for the existence of paradise is that it has been lost. It is also likely that the loss of a paradise is a prerequisite for the beginning of narrative, and of self-consciousness, an ego or subject-self that exists only in a world of language, divisions, rules, time and frustration. Loss is what opens up a space that allows narrative to move forward. The experience of loss as a precondition for the internalization of a structure that articulates reality through the symbolic representation of space and time is something that can be found not only in Proust and modern reflections on the subjectivity of memory but, more fundamentally, in all origin myths.

Collecting origin myths from different cultures and religions one finds repeated and recondite motifs: the insufficiency of solitary existence, the base facts of embodiment and the fantasies this generates, the enigma of sexuality, the antithetical emotions of pride and shame in creation. And beyond the repeated elements and themes one finds a bewildered intelligence that tries to grasp and make sense of the unknowability of humans' relations to the world, to each other and to themselves. Not all are as mournful or as prolific as Proust. One cheerful origin myth from Ancient Egypt describes a lonely god who masturbated until he reached orgasm, whereupon he sneezed out the universe through his nose. There are very many charming stories from Ancient Egypt, none more so than the story of the manifestation of Ra as a dung beetle who rolls his home across the desert as the sun rolls across the sky, the ball of dung that is both food and home and the nest for the eggs, and from which hundreds of tiny scarab beetles emerge as they hatch. But it is the Judaic tradition that I want us to consider here.

The book of Genesis in the Old Testament of the Bible has much in common with Sophocles' *Oedipus Rex* – both are narratives about the origins of the human subject as a self-conscious subject. Both involve hermaphrodites, talking animals with monstrous destructive appetites, protagonists with curiosity that leads to strange sexual practices, a transgression of a divine law and a terrible retribution or punishment implicating sight and its negation. Adam and Eve hide their eyes in shame, and Oedipus puts out his eyes, blinds himself, and is led by his daughter Antigone through the wilderness.

The elements of the narratives are interesting in themselves and we shall have time to consider some of these in depth, but it is in the patterns that combine these elements that we find what is the most compelling and satisfying meaning. This is the way that stories can create a space through narrative structure. Narrative is itself a structure which has been created through a space that was opened up by loss. As one space of possession is lost, a new narrative space is created that models the architecture of the cultural space which someone like Emil Durkheim might have called 'society'; a set of rules and a pattern of emotional relationships that circumscribe our relationships to one another and define our relation to ourselves. The new space is 'grasped', metaphorically, as 'meaning'.

The idea of a bounded space – and our term 'paradise' is the Persian word meaning walled garden – is one example of the significance of this synaesthesia produced by stories that creates a double register of sensory experience. The idea of wall as boundary also exists, for the representational world of the listener, as a metaphor for other meanings of limits and liminal experiences. We shall explore some of the meanings of the bounded, as spatial, temporal calibration and as ethical or rule-bound reality. The spatial boundedness of paradise, which Genesis describes as provided by walls, rivers and geography, is metonymically and simultaneously the boundary set by the prohibition that regulates the humans' relationship to nature. All those who tell and listen to stories know well that a prohibition is always followed by a transgression, just as a loss is always followed by a journey to make good that loss. It was Roland Barthes in his essay 'The Structural Analysis of Narrative' (1977) who concluded that it is interesting that at the age of three the small human simultaneously stumbles upon three structures: the sentence, narrative and the Oedipus complex.

We find that this is true of both the Genesis and the Oedipus myths. More than this similarity of narrative patterns, what interests me about these myths is the simultaneity of spatial, symbolic and temporal experiences of limits and thresholds. This boundary of wall, and of interdiction spoken by the voice of the father, is also experienced as the boundedness of time, which includes within it the awareness of mortality.[1] Knowledge of death is central to the enigma that holds together the elements of space, law and time. When Oedipus enacts the patricide foretold by Tiresias the blind seer and hermaphrodite oracle, it is at a crossroads. The omphalos as a navel, or narrative punctum, is like the tree at the centre of a walled garden that is itself placed at the imaginary centre of the world. There is reference to death at the centre of meanings that radiate outwards through metonymic and metaphoric displacements and condensations.

The Garden of Eden is thus a concept that exists as an articulation of space and time, within a textual structure of story that specifies a past anterior tense, a space that once was and no longer is, except as a painful memory of a lost happiness (see Figure 7.1, colour plate section).

Infantile amnesia

In 2005 the Freud Museum in London celebrated and commemorated the centenary of Freud's writing of *Three Essays on the Theory of Sexuality*, in which he formulated the theory of infantile sexuality. Freud realized that he would gain little gratitude or acclaim for this work, and that it might not be the work that scientists would be most proud of. But what could account for the complete silence that greeted this centenary event? The general public is not historically ignorant; Einstein's theories of relativity also date from 1905, and were much discussed and commemorated. But even in the year that saw the occupying army in Iraq taking photographs of ritual humiliations of prisoners, saw the trial of numerous music celebrities for child sexual abuse, saw the Catholic church in the USA devastated by claims for the compensation for sexual abuse of children by priests, to mention just three examples of the irruption of unconscious libidinal economy into public life, the world of public honours paid no heed to the book that gave us the most valuable and least understood concept of the twentieth century. The Queen hosted a party for the hundreds of Olympic medallists who had brought pride and honours to Britain and 2005 was also the centenary of the British Olympic Association. The centenary of the *Three Essays on the Theory of Sexuality* passed in relative silence. We might well ask why.

The concept of infantile amnesia, or primal repression, is one that has found expression in all cultural forms, and it is to Freud that we owe its first, clearest and finest formulation. The book of Genesis and *Oedipus Rex* give us narratives in which protagonists struggle with this paradoxical relationship that we have to the knowledge of our own origins and to self-consciousness, and they are evidence, if such were needed, that religion is a precursor of science. It is the law of infantile amnesia, as irrevocable as the law of gravity, that is one of the prohibitions we have to face if we want to complete our journey into the discovery of the meaning of this origin myth.

What the defence of repression and infantile amnesia conceals is still very much open to debate: for some it is the elaborate structures of developmental libidinal economies and their corresponding fantasies; for others it is the oscillation between paranoid-schizoid and depressive anxieties; for others it is a tripartite unconscious divided into its symbolic, imaginary and real vectors.

Each theory has its own proofs through years of carefully documented clinical practice which is considered the laboratory and the crucible of psychoanalysis, where theory and practice find their testing ground and their efficacy. As I am not a practising psychoanalyst I can offer these thoughts that emerge from the crucible of everyday life and the 'garden shed' of the teacher's study. That there is something actively repressed by the blankness of infantile amnesia is indisputable, as to what it may be I suggest that it is evident everywhere around us (and within us), and a fertile source of analysis is in what might be called infantile textuality, the traces of Oedipal and pre-Oedipal fantasy, anxiety and libidinal economies as these are manifest in the stories and images of the culture that surrounds us. In the *Three Essays* Freud notes:

> I believe then that infantile amnesia, which turns everybody's childhood into something like a prehistoric epoch and conceals from him the beginnings of his own sexual life, is responsible for the fact that in general no importance is attached to childhood in the development of sexual life. The gaps in our knowledge which have arisen in this way cannot be bridged by a single observer. . . . As long ago as 1896 I insisted on the significance of the years of childhood in the origin of certain important phenomena concerned with sexual life, and since then I have never ceased to emphasize the part played in sexuality by the infantile factor.
>
> (Freud 1905: 176)

Oedipus and Genesis

Now another confession – I did not know, despite a sound Christian education, that there were two trees in the Garden of Eden and I am grateful to anthropologist Audrey Cantlie for pointing this out to me. Even when I returned to reread Genesis, and found a story quite different from that which I remembered, and which circulates in popular consciousness, the status of the first tree, the tree of life, seemed much more prone to oblivion than the memorable and dangerous tree of the knowledge of good and evil, the tree that is iconic of the Garden of Eden. Only the negro spiritual keeps it firmly in mind, embodied in the rhythms and bodily vibrations of song rather than in the optical visions of picture:

> The hardest tree in paradise is the tree of life.
> All my trials Lord, soon be over.
> Too late, my brothers . . . too late, but never mind.
> All my trials Lord, soon be over.

The tree of life was not an object of interdiction for Adam and Eve until the moment of expulsion, at which point God protected it from the reach of the couple by means of a cherubim armed with a flashing sword. What is the meaning of the cherubim with the flashing sword protecting the tree of life? Is it something to do with the infantile energies that are made to die the death of castration and are resurrected in adulthood in the form of unruly sexuality?

In the Genesis story, as in the Oedipus myth, there is morning and there is evening. The events of the narrative are framed within the course of the rising and the setting of the sun. There is east and west, and the knowledge of this orientation is taken from the direction of the sun. The mythical couple Adam and Eve, once expelled from paradise, become fertile and leave to start the family of man through work and through sadness in the land of the rising sun, in the dawn of time, east of Eden. This makes us wonder why it was necessary to roll back time, as it were, in order to place the birth of humanity sometime before its *lapsus*.

Oedipus has to solve the riddle of the Sphinx: 'What is the creature that walks on four legs in the morning, two legs at noon, and three legs in the evening?' The answer requires an understanding of the metaphor of the course of the sun in the sky through the day as a symbol for the lifespan of man, the enigma of time, temporality, human ageing and its relationship to symbolism. Father Time wields a scythe, castrating and prefiguring mortality.

For the Greek myth morning and evening have the significance of infancy and old age, and mark an awareness of the irreversibility of time and death in the midst of self-conscious existence. Besides this almost inconceivable reality the idea of talking animals, blind seers, incest, divine creation and monstrous beasts seems simple and transparent. The coexistence of 'being and nothingness' requires abstract thought that leads us beyond imagination and into a consideration of the paradox of the sublime. We grow 'up' as time goes 'by', and there is no way to understand this paradox except through thinking about time as an external and, to some extent, abstract reality. It is this inadequacy of subjective experience to grasp, in thought, the reality of its own conditions of existence which leads the subject across the abyss that differentiates embodied knowledge from abstract thought. This is the gap which generates the space of narrative and the sublime sublimations that span human endeavour from the Egyptian origin myths to Proust and beyond.

Before nineteenth-century science, discourses of philosophy and theology bore the weight of defining or explaining states of mind. In many parts of the world religion is still the primary means through which states of mind are defined and evaluated, and Genesis, like the Oedipus myth, accounts for a moment of the dawn of self-consciousness or self-knowledge. For Adam the realization of nakedness and shame results in the need to hide, first behind trees and then behind the leaves of trees sewn together to make garments; in Masaccio's early Renaissance painting he is hiding his eyes, while Eve hides her breasts and pubic hair. The man is portrayed as suffering the shame which is directed at his gaze, the woman is suffering the desire to hide her exhibited body. The pattern of activity and passivity is already given a gendered inscription.

For Oedipus the connection between self-knowledge and sight as a trauma is subject to a temporal displacement. The monster whom he defeats with his intelligence is the monster of unsightliness and spectacle (Warner 1998), the castrated mother who reappears in stories and fantasies as the phallic mother. Oedipus, having conquered the Sphinx, wins the prize of Queen Jocasta in a moment of triumph that is simultaneously his moment of catastrophe, and when he realizes his implication in the monstrosity of his own desire he blinds himself by piercing his eyes. The pain of self-consciousness and of shame, the first emotion of self-consciousness, which precedes guilt and the superego, is figured, for both Oedipus and Adam, as physical pain that castrates them from the potency of symbolic fatherhood. Oedipus is led by Antigone, his daughter, who has to mediate the world for him. Adam must work for a living tilling the soil and having children only through the bodily pains and sorrows of Eve.

Shame

It has been pointed out that shame is a more painful emotion than guilt as it derives from an earlier pre-Oedipal dynamic where experience is less differentiated and less amenable to rational thought – therefore more visceral and overwhelming. Freud notes, in the *Three Essays* that, at this stage, shame is a reaction formation along with disgust, and with aesthetic and moral ideals:

> It must be insisted that the most striking feature of this sexual activity is that the instinct is not directed towards other people, but obtains satisfaction from the subject's own body. It is to use Havelock Ellis's term 'auto erotic'.
>
> (Freud 1905: 181)

This feature of being directed at part-objects rather than at another person means that the reaction formation of shame is less focused on a particular event or specific relationship, but is more indistinct and more total, overwhelming the whole subject in a global dawning of consciousness of a self that had not previously existed as an object of self-consciousness. Perhaps this is why shame is more difficult to locate, to specify and contain than is, for example, guilt.

Shame appears to be visited upon the subject from the outside, just as awareness of the self requires the existence of an other through whose eyes the subject acknowledges himself as 'being seen'.

For Lacan (1979) shame is etymologically and conceptually derived from sham, the deception and facticity that is a symptom of fetishism. The sham is the illusion, which subtends the fetishistic illusion, requiring the suspension of disbelief or the disavowal: 'I know but nevertheless.'

The erect phalli that adorn the lintels of Roman homes preserved in Pompeii are fixed to the home to 'ward off the evil eye' of *invidia* or envy. Here the connection between envy and sight is made manifest.

In the *Three Essays* Freud states that shame is the organically given reaction that opposes scopophilia or visual pleasure. The scopic drive is not centred on organ pleasure, as are the other partial drives, but is object related from the outset, like exhibitionism and sadism, suggests Freud. Is it this proximity of visual pleasure to sadism that makes it allied to shame?

In shame the connection between humiliation and oneself seen in the sight of others is made metaphor, through being transmuted from the corporeal world of external gaze into the 'inner' or representational world of meaning. *Honte*, in French, is a sixteenth-century term from the same root as honour, an antithetical concept in which the twin terms of pride and abjection are combined. The dishonour of shame is intricately connected to family honour, and the sense that the propriety of self-identity is shared with the confusion of identities in which self is merged with family, is vividly evoked by eighteenth-century French dramatist Corneille, when he writes: '*Viens mon fils, viens mon sang, viens reparer ma honte*' ['My son, my blood, absolve my shame!'] (Corneille, cited in Robert 1973).

Is it the tree of life, the family tree that depends for its development on the reparative feelings unleashed by the catastrophic fall from grace that precedes it? Is it the green eye of envy that creates the conditions for the greening of the arid wastelands east of Eden? Here we follow Longinus writing on the sublime, who was the first, long before Milton, to claim that Genesis is a sublime work of literature, and to note that sublimity is the greatness that arises from the flaws and weaknesses of our subjectivity. Greatness is not, according to Longinus, the opposite of the abject, as the Romans asserted, but is an outcome of abjection. If there is no sublimity without abjection this is because, as Freud noted a hundred years ago, there is no sublimation without the polymorphous perverse and its base admixture of sadistic and libidinal appetites directed at narcissistic part objects, half differentiated in the primeval dusk of unbounded energies.

The Greek term 'hypsous' gives us our word 'up' and from this we infer that sublimity is, metaphorically, an upward movement. The Latin word sublime means 'up to the lintel' and we note the significance of the threshold as a liminal space from which one can be e-liminated, marking a spatial axis of horizontality. The axis of above and below is also present in the concept of the lintel or doorway through which we pass. Remember the Roman phalli that adorned the lintels of the threshold, to ward off the evil eye of invidious outsiders? Remember the pre-lapsarian paradise from which Adam and Eve are eliminated at the point at which they become self-consciousness through the emotion of shame. We will return to explore this liminality and its relationship to the sublime.

The enigma of sex

The Genesis story makes no mention of sex; there is no copulation or sexual desire before the moment of expulsion. There is man, and 'Adam' means bloke; an Adam with a definite article is a generic term for man, Adam without the definite article becomes a proper name. God shows him the animals for him to name, and naming acquires the power of dominion over. Eve is created but not named until after the expulsion from Eden. The female companion without a name, produced from the torso of the unconscious man, is, before the fall, not a differentiated person or sexually distinct other. In fact before the fall there is no sex. There is appetite, which is created through the cathexis of hand and eye fixed on a fruit. It is an appetite as indistinct as the infant reaching out to grasp the good object. A part-object of oral and tactile gratification. To grasp as the babies in the Paddington clinic grasped the shiny spatula in D.W. Winnnicott's child consultations. To grab with the hand is the infantile prototype of the adult's ability to grasp a concept intellectually. This is the reaching for knowledge, the infantile appetites that underlie adult desires, either sexual or sublimated, that propel us through the condensations and displacements of language, as we cultivate our gardens east of Eden.

There is, in Genesis, no mention of sex. We somehow understand the plucking of the fruit to have sexual meaning. But where is the sex? Is the sex in the hand reaching to touch? Or in the fruit put to the lips of the man? Or is it in the woman listening to the words of the seductive serpent? Or in the awareness of nakedness? Is the sex in being seen? Is the sex in the sewing together of the fig leaves to make clothes? Sexuality is not implied until it is denied and negated, outside the Garden of Eden, by the fig leaves, sewn together by Adam and his newly named Eve, to hide both nakedness and shame. Sewing together leaves is an act of manufacture through which nature is transformed into culture. This is the work that humans have, henceforth, to do. This is the significance of the radical break from the prelapsarian harmony between man and nature. Sewing is an act that, paradoxically, uses penetration to unite two edges, to suture the gap between different edges in a contradictory process of making holes and erasing difference.

The fig is a luscious and evocative plant, combining masculine and feminine associations of genital and pregenital configurations. Not only are metaphorical relations between fruit and fertility embodied in this image but there are richly allusive synechdocal meanings that connect the outline of the leaf edge with the contour of the penis, the tendrils of the climber with the curl of pubic hair. The complex androgyny or hermaphroditism of the plant is an echo of the hermaphroditism of the serpent, a beast that is not easily sexed, and whose limblessness reduces it to a body without organs, defying castration, differentiation, schism and separation. This serpent, sometimes understood as a dragon, a feminine being with wings and teeth, is a hybrid monster, like the Sphinx, that is both animal and human. It can speak like a human but retains the amoral beastliness of the dumb animal. It is superhuman in its evil cunning and seductive shamelessness and it is the most abject of all creatures, unable to walk and sliding along on its belly, the most successful of all predators, inscrutable in its invulnerability.

The serpent incites the woman to pick the fruit from the tree, and woman takes it to Adam and puts some fruit into his mouth before she too eats of the fruit. It is not in the eating that self-consciousness emerges, as the two are happily walking through the garden until the evening wind sounds through the leaves. As God was heard walking around the garden in the evening, Adam and his naked companion became aware of their nakedness and of their shame. It is only with the proximity of the gaze of the other, the God, that there is the panic-stricken, painful realization of self-consciousness, and the need to hide.

What is sexuality before the man knows that he is different from the woman? What is a man when he is still indistinctly undifferentiated from the mother that feeds him before he knows he is hungry? What is a subject before it assumes responsibility for its own appetites, needs and desires? It is that shameless, pre-Oedipal monster of exhibitionism, voyeurism, activity, passivity, hybridity and unbounded drives that are organized into the schism of positive and destructive fantasies aimed at the same object, the primal fused parent of the phallic mother or maternal father. With the ambition to become as one with the loved and hated object, to deny difference even more totally, comes the realization of the failure of the perverse power; and with the gradual capacity to tolerate frustration comes the differentiated ego abilities of mastery over the body, its organs and impulses and then the attempt to master and to designate the outside world. The interdiction of eating the fruit of the tree of knowledge of good and evil was a rule that stood for maintaining the difference between God and man, the difference between the parent and the child. When the man transgresses the rule he expresses his infantile ambition to become the parent, to take his place, to take his power in the confused appetite of the child who wishes for omnipotence and the abolition of all frustration. This is not a sexual ambition, and sex can exist only after the loss of the omnipotence fantasy, once difference is accepted, the woman named and recognized, one's place taken alongside the other. That ambition is not a completely negative thing as it is what motivates the journey outwards into the world of work and into the need to cultivate the barren soil in order to grow the tree of his own life story. As Longinus points out, Genesis is sublime, and nothing is more sublime than the fall from grace, the expulsion from Eden in a moment that is both terribly shameful and generatively fertile. Infantile omnipotence is no more, like the hermaphroditic serpent which represents it, and in its place there is sex, there is an other, there is Eve, there are babies – but these are not magical God-given creatures, they exist only because there is work and pain and what Freud once called 'the vicissitudes of life'.

Freud called this odyssey that follows the moment of loss, the Oedipus complex, after Sophocles' narrative, and he knew why he idealized the culture of classical antiquity over the Judaic tradition.

As Lévi-Strauss concluded from his analysis of the Oedipal myth, the question to which the myth provides an answer is the question of the autochthonous origins of human beings: are we born of one or born of two? (Lévi-Strauss 1953). How is it that our birth as humans requires bio-logical conception, gestation, delivery but that it also requires psychic con-ception and self-representation which takes place through the emotion of self-consciousness, shame, and which is formulated through the uniquely human evolutionary adaptation that is articulate language, that represen-tational world of imaginary autonomy that did, in fact, evolve from our capacity to sustain infantile dependence through patterns of nurturing and parental, maternal nurturing.

In the same way Genesis provides us with an answer as to how the world of oneness is not a fertile world, and that to protect the tree of life the cherubim must show us the flashing sword of separation, the sword that cleaves, that separates and divides in order that sex may exist and that the two sexes may reproduce and bear their own fruit.

French anthropologist René Girard would have much to say about the pointing finger of the cherubim in Masaccio's fresco. According to Girard, the pointing finger is the gestural, iconic, precursor to the word (Girard 1979). It is the gesture of ostracization that forms the social unit as united in its selection of a common object nominated as 'outside', the newly formed boundary of social cohesion. For Girard the first object is a sacrificial object. The first word is also an accusation, a projection of unwanted sadism from the ritually cleansed representational world.

Lévi-Strauss may have been the first to put this into words but the frescoes of the chapel and the stories of Genesis demonstrate that he was not the first to begin to ask the question and to risk transgressing the divine prohibition of self-knowledge. The stories and their pictures are the other that we need in order to know ourselves and through this to know others. This ambition to know implies an encounter with shame, death, sex and fear, and this is why the journey towards knowledge is sublime.

Shame and guilt

To conclude, some thoughts on the relationship between shame and guilt. If shame is an emotion that results from a pre-Oedipal libidinal economy in which the ideal ego is inaugurated, visually, as a precursor of the superego, the dynamics of shame revolve around the world of sight and of being seen. Hence the pain of shame is in the subject imagining himself as seen by the gaze of the other. The humiliation of shame is visible in the blushing, or is experienced in the surfaces of the self as a sense of being publicly available to the critical gaze of others. The sense of being flayed alive, of being unprotected, is made corporeal in Massachio's image of Eve hiding beneath her hair, of Adam shielding his gaze. It is rendered in the biblical narrative of the couple manufacturing clothes by sewing together the leaves of the fig to hide their nakedness. Shame is meaningful in a universe of vision, and as an ethics of the pre-Oedipal scopophilic fantasies.

Guilt, which is an element of an Oedipal libidinal economy, has a relationship to language; to the diction and interdiction that issues from the voice and the word of a paternal universe. The transgression of a law results in guilt because the law has been experienced as an internal resonance of the voice, and in the interior universe of invisible privacy. The guilty are not seen to be guilty, but have evidence furnished of their guilt, whereas the shameful are seen to be shameful, like the scarlet letter of the adulteress.

Guilt may be a reformulation of shame, distilled into another vessel, the container of the Oedipal ego that orients itself as much through an interior compass of moral cardinal points as through the vision of external spectators and their imaginary ethics. Or guilt may be a different emotion entirely that can coexist with shame in different proportions according to the admixture of impulses and fantasies that comprise the cocktail of libidinal appetites, to which it is a response. There are anthropologists who are interested in the difference between shame cultures and cultures of guilt. And art historians who are interested in the difference between religions that use imagery to explicate their teachings, and religions that are iconoclastic or have strict prohibitions on the use of graven images. It is interesting that the iconoclastic religion of Islamic fundamentalism requires public and highly visible rituals of humiliation: beheadings, floggings and stonings as punishments for those that transgress its moral codes. Historians such as Michel Foucault have traced the development in Europe, from a mediaeval culture of public humiliation through to the eighteenth-century panopticon that heralds the internalization of the moral eye as a psychic agency, which he connects to the fantasy of Enlightenment culture within the western episteme (Foucault 1977). The interplay between an ethics of visibility and an ethics of the word are as complex as the boundary between them is highly permeable, with constant interaction and through-flow.

Psychoanalysts have long been interested in the way in which shame and guilt can exist in the psyche independently of any external correlative moral flaw; unconscious shame and unconscious guilt that can make criminals of us all. In this way they challenge the ethics of religion that would maintain the structural position of 'original sin' in us as the mainspring of our search for atonement through religious ritual. For those who disagree with religion there is no reasoning a believer out of his faith, the ideas must become decathected from the inside rather than reorganized rationally.

Liminality and the sublime

The positioning of the fresco of the expulsion from paradise is significant as it is placed at the threshold of the entrance to the church. On either side of the threshold that is both entrance and exit from the building it gives embodied form to the experience of community and culture; the fresco makes the biblical narrative a frame for the believer who enters and leaves the chapel. As an expulsion the biblical story is an *insignia* that marks the threshold of the church for the congregation. The church and its embodiment in the architecture of the chapel is a reconfiguration of the walled Garden of Eden, the bounded space that is lost and can be recovered only through picture, story, song, prayer and other illusions, fetishes and shams which embody our relation to God.

As we stand at the threshold, the liminal space allows us to contemplate our relation to the maternal body, and the prohibitions, fears and physical insufficiency which separate us from it. We rediscover a connection in the form of sublimations that we make through art, work, science and love. In sublimation another object is found in the world 'out there', which we cathect or invest with the meanings that were once attributed to our original objects of desire, our Oedipal objects. Sublimation makes links between the prehistory of our infantile passions and the real world of the 'here and now', resurrecting a lost origin in the form of a new meaning. As Adrian Stokes suggests, architecture is the mother of the arts, and the doorways of the churches and chapels of Renaissance Italy, dark against the sunlit environment of an agricultural economy, are mouths that swallow and disgorge those that enter and leave them (Stokes 1945). The frescoes are visual displays, like the flying phalli of Pompeii that ward off the evil eye of envy, like the visibility of the monsters that demonstrate to us, as they seduce and fascinate the protagonists of their narratives, the origins of subjectivity. The pictures that accompany religious ritual are the prototype of our civilization and for most of the earth's six billion inhabitants are still the main source of their culture.

Note

1   The wall as symbol of father is noted by Glasser (1989).

References

Barthes, R. (1977) 'The structural analysis of narrative', in R. Barthes *Image, Music Text*, trans. S. Heath, New York: Hill and Wang.

Foucault, M. (1977) *Discipline and Punish: The Birth of the Prison*, trans. A. Sheridan, New York: Vintage.

Freud, S. (1905) *Three Essays on the Theory of Sexuality*, S.E. 7.

Girard, R. (1979) *Violence and the Sacred*, trans. P. Gregory, Baltimore: Johns Hopkins University Press.

Lacan, J. (1979) *Four Fundamental Concepts of Psychoanalysis*, trans. A. Sheridan, New York: Norton.

Lévi-Strauss, C. (1953) *Structural Anthropology*, Vol. 2, New York: Basic Books.

Longinus (c. 213–273 AD) *On the Sublime*, trans. G. M. A. Grube, Indianapolis: Hackett, 1991.

Proust, M. (1923) *Á la recherche du temps perdu*, Paris: Bibliotheque de la Pleiade, Gallimard, 1954.

Robert, P. (1973) *Dictionnaire Alphabetique et Analogique de la langue Francaise*, Paris: Société du Nouveau Lettre.

Stokes, A. (1945) 'Venice', in *The Critical Writings of Adrian Stokes, Volume II, 1937–1958*, London: Thames and Hudson, 1978.

Warner, M. (1998) *No Go the Bogeyman: Scaring, Lulling and Making Mock*, London: Chatto and Windus.

Chapter 8

Shame in three parts at the Freud Museum

Penny Siopis

My engagement with shame began in 2000 as an ongoing series of small 'shame' paintings and installations of found objects, all of which I expanded in my multimedia exhibition *Three Essays on Shame* (2005). Curated by Jennifer Law, the exhibition took the form of an intervention in the Freud Museum in London. The site itself presented a special challenge in materializing shame. This was not only because of the symbolic weight and myriad associations of Sigmund Freud's house, its contents and location, but because shame is relatively invisible in his writings.

I want to ponder here on how shame came to 'breathe' in my intervention in the Freud house. I say 'breathe' not only because I want to convey something of the creative inspiration for *Three Essays on Shame*, but also to capture the aliveness of the relation between intensely subjective feeling and an exterior social world. Shame lives with one foot squarely in each. Art mediates these worlds, and is particularly apt in embodying the contradictions and ambivalences of this dual register of experience.

I also want to speak emphatically as an artist here; partly to avoid the post-mortem feel that so often pervades retrospective reviews of exhibitions and to resist a certain kind of extended self-analysis. The grounds for such an extended analysis are most likely present in what I say and do, but this is not my primary focus here. I want rather to give a strong sense of what stimulated and energized this intervention in its complexity, and to stress the power and potential of unruly, animated 'association' over stabilizing narrative or analysis. The intervention was a place- and time-specific creative response to and reflection on site and space, on material things, and on temporality. Part of the temporality was the obvious coincidence of the exhibition and the centenary of Freud's 1905 publications *Three Essays on the Theory of Sexuality* and 'Jokes and their Relation to the Unconscious'.

I should also say I have always been taken as much by Freud's stories and his sheer literary power as by his psychoanalytic philosophy of human consciousness. His writings are so rich in allusion and so ripe for elaboration. He imagines the dynamic processes and structures of psychic life in terms of deeply affecting, ancient mythologies and with a narrative vitality that for me remains unparalleled in psychoanalytic writing.

Baubo

To prepare the exhibition I asked Michael Molnar, director of the Freud Museum, for a tour of the house. As we went through the hallowed spaces and Freud's extraordinary collection of antiquities, I searched for a sign that would trigger my imaginative energies and also connect with one or both of the centenary publications. As we worked our way through the house, a sign duly emerged from the shadowy recesses of Freud's study. Squatting on a shelf was a dark terracotta female figurine. She sported a broken leg and a cheeky grin. One hand lifted her skirt to expose her genitals, the other gesturing to the site of exposure. She appeared the perfect embodiment of a joking sexuality (see Figure 8.1, colour plate section).

This is reputedly a Baubo figurine and belongs to a class of fertility objects (c. fifth century BCE) excavated in ancient Egypt and Greece and Asia Minor. How this Baubo found herself in Freud's collection remains a puzzle. As far as I was able to establish there is no reference to her in his inventory of purchases. She may well have been a gift from a reader of Freud's (1916) paper 'A Mythological Parallel to a Visual Obsession' in which Freud actually refers to and illustrates 'a Baubo'. The paper focused on a young man suffering from an obsessive disorder. Freud writes:

> Whenever he saw his father coming into the room, there came into his mind in close connection with each other an obsessive word and an obsessive picture. The word was 'father-arse'; the accompanying picture represented the lower part of a trunk, nude and provided with arms and legs, but without the head or chest, and this was the father. The genitals were not shown, the facial features were represented on the abdomen.
>
> (Freud 1916: 345)

Freud continues in his inimitable way; 'father-arse' was soon explained as a jocular Teutonizing of the honorable title 'patriarch'. In a footnote he elaborates: 'German for "father" is *Vater*, for "arse", *arsch*; hence *Vaterarsch*, *Patriarch*' (Freud 1916: 345–346). The caricature struck Freud as extraordinary, but as he says: 'Chance then brought to my notice an antique instance of it which shows complete correspondence with my patient's obsessive image' (Freud 1916: 346). Not quite so complete a correspondence; the illustration in the paper *does* suggest female genitals, even if manifesting at once as a V shape, a smile or an absent penis. It corresponds to the 'Baubo' to which contemporary writer Aileen Ajootian refers: 'her body itself . . . compressed visually into its essential components; her sex itself, not the lifting of the dress, central to her meaning' (Ajootian 1997: 224). This reminds me of Freud's essay 'Femininity' in which he writes that shame 'is considered to be a feminine characteristic *par excellence*'. '[B]ut', he continues '[this] is far more a matter of convention than might be supposed' and 'has as its purpose . . . concealment of genital deficiency' (Freud 1933: 430). Deficiency is Freud's problem, but his casting of shame as a female characteristic – and by extension that of feminized people – seems to have become a commonplace.

'Baubo' 's origins are ancient Greek, and, like so many overdetermined classical myths, different aspects of her story shape her in different tellings. But basically she is an ordinary older woman with a bawdy bent who exposes herself to fertility goddess Demeter in order to cheer her up. Demeter had been distraught as she searched for her daughter Persephone, abducted and raped by Hades and incarcerated in his underworld. As Ellen Handler Spitz says:

> Demeter's response to Persephone's disappearance has elements of both narcissistic and object loss: she becomes by turns sorrowful, depressed, and bitterly indignant. Wandering over land and sea in an effort to discover the whereabouts of her beloved child, she enacts a sequence that uncannily prefigures the stages of mourning and melancholia Freud outlined in 1917. Turning her aggression inward, she tears the covering on her hair, refuses both food and drink, and ceases to bathe.
>
> (Spitz 1991: 162)

Demeter's link with Persephone frequently stands for the mother/daughter relationship in psychoanalytic writing, and for some offers an alternative matriarchal shape to Freud's patriarchal Oedipus complex.

In lifting her skirt Baubo lifts Demeter's spirit. Demeter laughs. Why Baubo's vagina is funny is anyone's guess. But whatever the case, laughter did not cover shame in this instance. As contemporary writer Catherine Blackledge notes, vaginas were reputedly less associated with taboo in ancient times than with heroic, dangerous genital might: '[d]riving out devils, averting vicious spirits, frightening carnivores and scaring opposing warriors and threatening deities' ways' (Blackledge 2003: 8). Herodotus is said to have given the act of lifting of skirts associated with this kind of genital exposure he witnessed in Egypt a special name: the Greek, *ana-suromai*, which literally means 'to raise one's clothes' (Blackledge 2003: 12). The *ana-suromai* of Baubo was a key feature in the fertility initiation rites of Eleusis, and involved pigs, sacrifice and blood (Blackledge 2003: 22). The advent of Christianity transformed this genital might into shame. Witnessing such an initiation ritual, the early Christian writer Arnobius observes: '[S]he pulled up her gown revealing her thighs and pudenda. . . . Thus they gave her a name, which covered her with shame. In this disgraceful manner the initiation ceremonies came to an end' (Blackledge 2003: 23).

Whatever Baubo is, or is taken to be, like so many myths she provides an emblem and a structure through which to mediate the contradictory and contending impulses we experience in art and in life. My interest in Baubo lies specifically in her personification of 'shame' as an emotionally and semiotically complex feeling. Baubo's act discloses a keen knife edge between affirmation and negation, between assertive agency and vulnerable victimhood. Shame may be ambivalent at its core, a form of double bind. Jacqueline Rose captures this quality well when she writes that '[s]hame relies on the art of exposure, even if exposure is what it hates most, and most militantly struggles against' (Rose 2003: 1).

Few would see anything positive about shame, shame being extreme humiliation, psychological nakedness, traumatic loss of face, of voice. It is the opposite of dignity (Gilbert and Andrews 1998; Nussbaum 2004), a visceral emotion that signifies the risk or reality of a collapsed subject-object relation. Self is turned inside out, exposed for all to see. For clinician Phil Mollon shame stems from an infantile loss of connection with the other (the mother): 'Instead of the responsive "gleam in the mother's eye," Heinz Kohut speaks of, the shamed infant encounters only a void' (Mollon 2002: 32). Charles Rycroft labelled shame 'the Cinderella of the unpleasant emotions' because it has 'received much less attention than anxiety, guilt and depression', but he also notes in his definition of shame that '[i]f faced up to, shaming experiences increase insight and self-awareness' (Rycroft 1995: 169).

Shame has, indeed, recently attracted interest, which credits it with more positive potential (Probyn 2005). One could argue that Freud himself saw shame in this way: as a 'force' inhibiting the sexual instinct, but crucially necessary for the psychic development of the subject. It would be a 'civilizing' force. Writing on infantile development in *Three Essays*, Freud speaks of shame as one of three 'mental forces' (the others being 'disgust' and 'the claims of aesthetic and moral ideals') which function 'like dams' restricting our sexual instinct and enabling the psychic and social growth necessary for survival (Freud 1905: 177).

Referring to infantile sexuality, Freud suggests that 'small children are essentially without shame, and at some periods of their earliest years show an unmistakable satisfaction in exposing their bodies, with especial emphasis on the sexual parts' (Freud 1905: 192). Small children have little capacity to identify, to empathize, to sympathize with the other. This is linked to their sense of omnipotence and cruelty. For Freud such cruelty 'comes easily to the childish nature, since the obstacle that brings the instinct for mastery to a halt at another person's pain – namely a capacity for pity – is developed relatively late' (Freud 1905: 192–193).

Let us return now to our walk through Freud's spaces. With Baubo having now colonized my creative thoughts and thoroughly coloured the context, all manner of images spun before me. Baubo's story triggered multiple exposures: connecting, detaching, overlaying and turning into one another. Her grin seemed to echo Helene Cixious's *Laugh of the Medusa* (1975). Her intimate morphology smacked of Luce Irigaray's famous 'two lips' in *This Sex which is Not One* (1977). Her irreverence found a home in Sarah Lucas's *Chicken Knickers* (1997). Charcot's famous hysterics also came to mind, lifting their skirts, baring their breasts, freezing and seizing gestures in acts understood by feminists as defiance of and resistance to patriarchal power. Closer to home, a video titled *To Walk Naked/Uku Hamba 'Ze* in which numbers of black women stripped and lifted their skirts to protest the destruction of their houses and forced removals in Soweto also tracked across my mind's eye.

At this point in my experience of walking through the space sexuality trumped jokes (whatever their underhand ties), and so Freud's *Three Essays on Sexuality* best set the tone. It is worth noting that Freud worked on both manuscripts simultaneously. Ernest Jones tells us that 'Freud kept the two manuscripts on adjoining tables and added to one or the other according to his mood' (Jones 1955: 13). My show became *Three Essays on Shame*, and in it I echoed the three-part structure of the essays. The three spaces which suggested themselves were Freud's study, his dining room, and his bedroom. That is: the place he worked, the place he dined, the place he slept. In a strangely appropriate way the last, the bedroom, is the current exhibition room at the museum.

Three essays on shame

Essay 1: Study (Voice)

Entering the study is like entering a deep, red cave. Freud's famous couch dominates the space, symbolically if not physically. The study is a reconstruction of Freud's consulting room in Vienna; how he transposed it to his new home in London. Still it stands for the invention of psychoanalysis and the talking cure. But more interesting to me is the memorial quality of the room, an atmosphere in which the presence of absence is palpable. The room also feels haunted by the ageing, ill Freud suffering stoically in the face of the virulent cancer in his mouth. His mouth was a malignant wound, a source of shame expressed in his deep upset at his beloved dog turning away from him to avoid the stench.

Freud decamped to London to escape the Nazis. As we might imagine – notwithstanding his Anglophone affections – it was hard to uproot and move. Sick, old and exiled, Freud, writing to the psychoanalyst Raymond de Saussure soon after arriving in London, spoke of one loss in emigrant experience being especially painful, the loss of language:

> The loss of the language in which one lived and thought and which one will never be able to replace with another, for all one's efforts at empathy. With painful comprehension I observe how otherwise familiar terms of expression fail me in English.

> (Molnar 1992: xvi)

Not wanting to overtly disrupt Freud's space, but rather to mark the inter-action of the psychological and social, I decided to use sound. Sound is an invisible medium and the disembodied human voice offered a perfect way to fill the room. Also, the voice not only invokes the talking cure but, when recorded, is a profound statement of belatedness, of loss. Each recorded utterance is a memorial to that loss. The recording shares something of the 'after the factness' of loss wrought by the chemistry of light we know to be photography.

The ritualistic, affect-laden element of the human voice reiterated over and over was an important consideration in my choice of medium. What com-pelled me was the processual nature of medium and mediation, the subtly inflected articulation of pitch, tone and timbre, the glosses and hesitations in searching for the right words, and then getting them out. We struggle to voice feelings and to speak of shame.

My choice of voice – or voices – came from my experience of political turmoil in South Africa articulated through oral testimonies during the Truth and Reconciliation Commission (TRC). The TRC was set up in 1996 to uncover the facts of apartheid crimes, to give a voice to victims, to provide perpetrators a chance to tell all for amnesty, and more besides. The TRC was itself the child of political compromise during the negotiated settlement that ended apartheid. It turned away from the punitive precedent set by Nurem-berg after World War II, and also from just giving blanket amnesty to all who committed political crimes in the three decades of apartheid (Posel and Simpson 2002).

The specific voices I chose represented a complex mix of personal and political commitments and emotions. The people I approached were willing to be 'exposed' because they saw the potential for agency, for action in such a process. Some even saw exposure as the kind of visible ventilation – cath-artic – necessary for social transformation. For this part of the project, I approached seven well-known South Africans who had publicly voiced views and feelings on or about shame. I asked all to consider if and how shame connected with sexuality in their speaking. Some made a direct connection with genital sexuality and others spoke in more libidinal terms. I edited my voice out, but the audio traces from the context of communication remain present. Initially I was the only audience for these words, but, through record-ing, siting and playing them in Freud's study in London, other audiences, other publics were created.

Each voice could be heard through individual sets of earphones attached to portable CD players. These players were perched on plinths that were part of the cordon around 'no-go' areas of the study. At the opening, though, the voices played out as ambient sound – loud, public and intense. The spectator/audience could not look at Freud's desk, his couch, other things without the accompaniment of voices audibly pondering attitudes to personal shame and the shame of others. In an important sense each listener/viewer was poised

Figure 7.1 Adam and Eve banished from Paradise, c.1427 (fresco) (post restoration) by
Tommaso Masaccio (1401–1428). © Brancacci Chapel, Santa Maria del Carmine,
Florence, Italy/The Bridgeman Art Library.

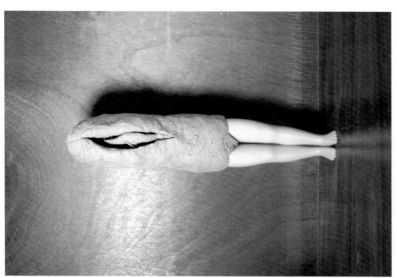

Figure 8.2 Clay moulded vagina on 'found' doll's legs in one of the cupboards in the *Dining Room* part of Penny Siopis's installation *Three Essays on Shame* in the Freud Museum.

Figure 8.1 'Baubo', a terracotta figurine in Freud's collection of antiquities, exhibited in a glass vitrine in the *Dining Room* part of Penny Siopis's installation *Three Essays on Shame* in the Freud Museum.

Figure 8.5 Jenny Haniver, a flattened skate fish artfully manipulated by sailors to look like a grotesque female body in one of the cupboards in the *Dining Room* part of Penny Siopis's installation *Three Essays on Shame* in the Freud Museum.

Figure 8.6 One of the cupboards in the *Dining Room* part of Penny Siopis's installation *Three Essays on Shame* in the Freud Museum.

Figure 8.7 Selection of shame paintings from the *Exhibition Room* part of Penny Siopis's installation *Three Essays on Shame* in the Freud Museum.

Figure 8.8 Selection of shame paintings from the *Exhibition Room* part of Penny Siopis's installation *Three Essays on Shame* in the Freud Museum.

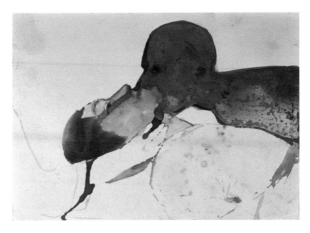

Figure 8.9 Selection of shame paintings from the *Exhibition Room* part of Penny Siopis's installation *Three Essays on Shame* in the Freud Museum.

Figure 9.4 Mona Hatoum, *Measures of Distance*, 1988. Colour video still, sound, 15 minutes. A western Front Video Production, Vancouver. Courtesy Jay Jopling/White Cube, London.

Figure 9.2 Shirin Neshat, *I Am Its Secret*, 1993. RC print & ink (photo taken by Plauto) Edition of 10 Copyright Shirin Neshat 1993. Courtesy Gladstone Gallery, New York.

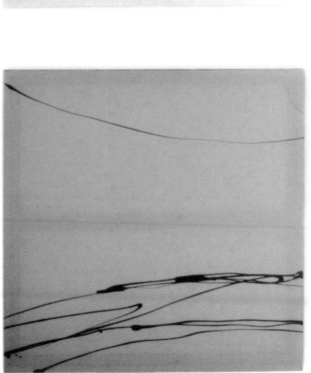

Figure 11.1 Maria Chevska *Perpetua [Books (i)]*, 1994. Paint, cotton, polyester, bandage, tea. Two panels each 92 × 92 cm. Photography: Eileen Tweedy.

Figure 11.4 Anne Wilson *Edges, no. 5,* 2001 (detail). Cloth, hair, thread. 10.25 × 75.75 inches. Copyright 2001 Anne Wilson. Collection David and Bobbye Goldburg. Photo by George Bouret. Anne Wilson's artwork is represented by Rhona Hoffman Gallery, Chicago and Paul Kotula Projects, Detroit.

uncomfortably between being voyeur, witness and participant in a public space. Onlookers could feel caught listening. Listeners could feel caught looking. After the opening, the sound manifested as a cerebral, emotional, individual headspace through the isolating headphones. This isolation and individuation meant privacy of a sort, and encouraged a more intimate and visceral connection with shame for each listening body.

This complex scenario shared something with what actually happened in the TRC hearings themselves. Shame was staged in very public, emotive, almost theatrical ways during oral testimony. The setting allowed exposure of the most private and intimate 'self' in a public drama of confronting sometimes inconceivable hurt, and of acknowledging complicity in the hurt of others. This drama was expressed in the sometimes dreadfully limited language of human suffering, including apologetics, confessions, protestations of good faith, denials of bad faith. Some of the testimony got deep under the skin. It was physical. Vocality was decisive in the actual hearings and in the radio and television reports of the hearings. Much of this oral testimony was also doubled or replicated in simultaneous translation into different languages, all of which is also available now, long after the completion of the TRC's work. The following individuals were recorded.

Edwin Cameron, widely respected Justice of the Supreme Court of Appeal, self-declared as HIV positive, and a courageous AIDS and gay activist. Edwin speaks of the stigma of AIDS and how this stigma is invariably sexual as it stems from the fact that the disease is sexually transmitted; of how terrible shame falls upon those afflicted with HIV/Aids, and of how this shame can stop treatment even starting (Cameron 2005). In a sense, the AIDS-afflicted can die of shame.

Fatima Meer, an outspoken sociologist and icon of the struggle who was imprisoned during her activist years. Fatima speaks of the terrible exposure she felt in prison; the physical invasiveness as warders probed vaginas of inmates to see, in her words, 'if they were hiding anything there'. She also speaks of her shame as a young girl when she started menstruating, an experience of shame still much more common than it should be.

Antjie Krog, respected poet and author of *Country of My Skull* (1998) which was one of the very first sustained, individual responses to the TRC. Antjie's voice became familiar (as Antjie Samuels) on radio as she reported daily on the TRC hearings for as long as they lasted. She speaks of her personal shame connected to being a white Afrikaner, the group which bore the major responsibility for apartheid, and from whose ranks many of the perpetrators came. Antjie also speaks of the shame she now feels in ageing.

Pumla Gobodo-Madikizela, a clinical psychologist and academic at the University of Cape Town, also served on the TRC's Human Rights Violations Committee. She is the author of *A Human Being Died That Night* (2003), a probing account of her 46 hours interviewing arch perpetrator of apartheid terror Eugene de Kok – otherwise known as 'Prime Evil'. De Kok is serving

212 years in prison for crimes against humanity. In this book and in the recordings she recounts an incident under apartheid in which an older black woman is subjected to violent sexual abuse at the hands of young white soldiers. The shame this woman felt was less the humiliation of having a man 'insert his hand into her vagina' and more the indignity presented by the man's youth. He could have been her son!

Irene Stephanou, actress, comedienne and playwright, talks of a degenerative illness which afflicts her body, and the sometimes shameful effects of this affliction. Irene also reflects on being Greek and the manifest gendering of shame – *dropi* in Greek – that happens within this community.

Kgomotso Motsunyane, a sharp, outspoken young woman who edits the South African *Oprah* magazine. Kgomotso represents a new generation, a generation that must deal with the legacy of apartheid in this moment. She speaks of the sexual abuse of young women and children that has come to be such a visible part of this society, spoken of as 'the shame of our times'. The increasing visibility and incidence of rape, of violence against women and children has led to profound questions of value being asked of post-apartheid South Africa.

My final selection is the Reverend Paul Verryn, long-serving activist minister of the Methodist Church. I want to explore his story in greater detail here, because it shows the complex entanglement of shame, sexuality, aesthetics and politics that these recordings embody. And because of how the particular emotional register of his testimony became a kind of prototype for these recordings.

Paul Verryn lived in a Methodist manse in Soweto, not far from Winnie Madikizela-Mandela's home. Madikizela-Mandela's home was also the home of her infamous Mandela United Football Club, a group of youths whose behaviour was 'frequently described by community residents as a "reign of terror" ' (Truth and Reconciliation Commission 1998: 555).

In 1988 13-year-old Stompie Seipei, who lived at the manse with other homeless children under the protection of the church, disappeared. After an intensive search he was eventually found dead. Winnie Madikizela-Mandela and her football team were suspected of abducting and murdering the boy, ostensibly because he was an informer. Just before the TRC hearing on Stompie Seipei, a defiant Winnie Madikizela-Mandela announced publicly that she had removed the child from the manse to protect him from Paul Verryn who she accused of sodomizing the black children who lived there. This accusation proved false, and was presumably intended to deflect criticism of her and her possible culpability in the case. But Paul Verryn's name became linked with Stompie Seipei in this way, notwithstanding his innocence. By the time Verryn testified at the TRC he had become a bishop. He spoke of his hurt, offered Madikizela-Mandela his forgiveness. More importantly, he expressed his sense of shame not in relation to the false accusations Madikizela-Mandela had made, but in not doing enough to protect Stompie

Seipei. In my later recordings Paul reflects this time as 'the darkest period' of his life, but also the most extraordinary in how he was able to publicly lift the burden of his feelings through the exposure offered by the TRC.

The TRC opened the floodgates of long-repressed feelings, and some hard truths had to be faced. The exposure the hearings entailed – however painful – made it possible for us to imagine new forms of agency, of social power, and the prospect at least of moving on. Even if uneven and hesitant, the forward movement of mourning can slowly replace the paralysis of melancholia. The TRC posed fundamental questions of the collective psyche of the nation. The suffocation of the dignity of millions is a shame, a disgrace. The self-reflection and introspection provoked by the TRC certainly caused many white South Africans to finally see themselves as shameful, although not always and everywhere. The unrehabilitated still stick defensively to their guns, and admit neither shame nor guilt for the atrocities carried out in their name. They are trapped in racist melancholia but are fast decaying into mere historical residue of a past that is finally past.

I want to end now by shifting to a very personal register again. An incident I experienced in 2000 provoked my connection with shame in art. I was living for a short period in Amsterdam at the time. One day I went to a screening of the documentary *A Long Night's Journey Into Day* (2000). Directed by Francis Read and Deborah Hoffman, the film focused on four cases of the TRC, all asking impossibly painful questions about culpability, shame, confession and the violent breach between private and public the TRC itself embodied (Dawson 2005: 473–486). As I watched the documentary I felt drenched in shame. Why? I don't know. I was familiar enough with these stories. I had watched news inserts and full programmes documenting the TRC's relentlessly traumatic stagings of our inhuman conduct during apartheid. None of this prepared me for this feeling. The shame I felt perhaps had something to do with a strong sense of identification and empathy paralysed by an unexpected sense of complicity and association with the negative. Being away from home and isolated most likely made me more thin-skinned.

Going back to my apartment I came upon a shop where rubber stamps were made and sold. I handwrote the word 'shame' for the assistant, and asked if it could be made into a stamp. I bought some glow-in-the-dark ink, thinking I would stamp the word over my body and then photograph myself in the dark. This was the image the documentary wrought for me. In the end I never carried out my plan, but did eventually use the shame stamp in the first of my shame paintings in 2000 that I started in my room in Amsterdam. These paintings placed shame outside my body but still psychologically close, allowing me to engage it in shared social space, and so deal with it in a creative but also critical way. Reflecting on this process suggested a conscious link to Freud's work on mourning and melancholia. I felt that the unrelenting, frozen, circular, self-consuming grief that unresolved traumatic fixation follows in the wake of unbearable loss could be shifted, and my collapsed sense of self regain some composure, however provisional.

In this experience shame seems linked with guilt. Speaking psychoanalytic-ally, these two 'moral emotions' have been cast in different ways. This differ-ence is important insofar as it relates to my *Three Essays* exhibition. The analytic distinction between shame and guilt is contentious, but shame is arguably distinctive in being very visceral, a quality intensified by the fact that the feelings are often associated with bodily exposure and sexuality. Shame feels primary, primitive. For psychologist Erik Erikson shame comes before guilt. As Kalu Singh notes:

> Erikson pairs [shame] with 'doubt', and contrasts them both with 'autonomy', the attainment of a sense of integrity, skill and self-sufficient power with regard to bodily functions of eating and excretion. Shame is the sensation consequent upon the *exposure of failed autonomy* or hubris.
>
> (Singh 2002: 157, my italics)

For Erikson, 'visual shame predates auditory guilt, which is a sense of bad-ness to be had all by oneself when nobody watches and when everything is quiet except the voice of the superego' (Singh 2000: 157). My experience in Amsterdam and the voices on the exhibition indicate that shame feels rawer than guilt.

Essay 2: Dining Room (Gesture)

Freud's dining room becomes Baubo's room – I removed her from Freud's study and displayed her in a glass case as befits her status. Out of the shadows now, her presence begs the question: why did she have no place on Freud's desk or in his cabinet of treasured things? Was she too common as object? A mere bauble? At odds with Freud's phallocentric focus, the vagina not being an object of envy? These questions, with Baubo's assertive physicality, with her edgy power and vulnerability in exposing her 'shame', speak volumes. The cupboards and closets in this room add a volume or two of their own.

Around her vitrine, Freud's nineteenth-century, hand-painted cupboards are flung open to expose a series of 'transcultural' objects. These include news-paper cuttings, film, documents, photographs, other people's artworks, objets trouvés and my own crafted and found things. Listing some of these will give a strong sense of the tone I sought in the installation. Many of the news-papers, documents and photographs relate to current racial and sexual vio-lence in South Africa. One clipping, for example, shows a young naked man painted completely silver. This was punishment exacted by the owner of a shop for an alleged theft, and was meant to shame him publicly. Other clip-pings show the ongoing saga of Sarah Baartman, the so-called 'Hottentot Venus', with information on the repatriation of her bodily remains sans her genitalia to South Africa where she is now buried with due dignity. Baartman's genitals were referred to as her 'veil of shame' in much of the literature associated with her and were a source of intense 'curiosity' to western eyes. These 'curiosities' disappeared somewhere in Europe. Shameful sexual and racial violation converge in Baartman's body, her story and their aftermath. South African writer Zoë Wicomb sees Baartman's brown body as exemplifying 'the body as site of shame'. In being a visible sign of miscegenation, 'coloured' identity (in South Africa) emblematizes 'the shame invested in those (females) who have mated with the colonizer' (Wicomb 1998: 92). Shame in this unrelenting scopic scenario is 'identified as the recognition of being the object of another's shame' (Wicomb 1998: 97).

Another source was the intense debate about the 'black vagina' artwork by Kaolin Thomson that went all the way to parliament. Controversy erupted after this small ceramic sculpture – a vagina – sporting a Gaulois Blonde cigarette was exhibited in a gallery at the University of the Witwatersrand, Johannesburg in 1996. A critic for the *Mail and Guardian* newspaper, Hazel Friedman, framed the work as a 'black' vagina, and this caused offence. The subsequent debate was caricatured by prominent political cartoonist Zapiro in the same newspaper. In my installation I place this caricature as well as photographs of the offending artwork near two framed photos of a nineteenth-century hermaphrodite and a copy of Jeffery Eugenides's book *Middlesex* (2002). Above is a photograph of a painting of Charcot showing off an hysteric exposing herself to his group of male scientists.

Included in various cupboards are early editions of Alan Paton's *Too Late the Phalarope* (1953) and Wulf Sachs's *Black Anger* (1947). A South African feminist journal *Agenda* published in 1994 is opened with an article titled 'And what do Zulu girls have?' by Makhososana Xaba (Figure 8.3). The article deals with the sometimes anxious shame-laden naming of female genitals in Zulu culture, but also has a humorous side. Included in these object-installations are alien or sexually suggestive found objects: a Jenny Haviner (see Figure 8.5, colour plate section) a strange flattened skate fish from the depths of the ocean that has been artfully manipulated by sailors to look like a grotesque female body, and the more familiar if exotic coco de mer. There are also partly made, partly found 'things' – a vagina on doll's legs (see Figure 8.2, colour plate section) not unlike the image invoked by Freud's obsessive patient I mentioned earlier, a human bone with two false blue eyes inserted into its cavities. These connect sexuality with monstrosity and manipulate the boundary between reality and fantasy, and involve phantasmagoric projection. Not far away, below a shelf with two books, a Princess Diana-like doll lifts her skirt on a replica of Buckingham Palace. One of the books is open at a reproduction of Gustave Courbet's *Origin of the World* and the other shows Sarah Lucas's *Chicken Knickers*. Elsewhere sexualized monsters in miniature lie around. Two small plastic shapes which 'grow' in water refer to the South African urban legend of Pinky Pinky; a transsexual, 'poly-racial' creature

in brief

And what do Zulu girls have?

*If English speakers are in a state of denial about girls' genitalia (see previous in brief), it would seem that indigenous cultures in South Africa have similar inhibitions. **Makhososana Xaba** asked around, and produced laughter and embarrassment - but few technical terms*

Figure 8.3 Detail of the South African journal *Agenda* in one of the cupboards in the *Dining Room* part in Penny Siopis's installation *Three Essays on Shame* in the Freud Museum.

that terrorizes prepubescent girls on their visits to school toilets. These 'things' overlay a child's handwritten account of Pinky Pinky. Other things include over a hundred fake eyes, a pair of cut-off 'black' cast feet, a 'black' cast face, a Zulu pregnancy apron of animal skin and an array of Baubo replicas.

Finally, a monitor in one cupboard screens the short documentary I mentioned earlier titled *To Walk Naked/Uku Hamba 'Ze* (1995). Directed by Sheila Meintjies, Jai Maingard and Heather Thompson, this work documents a group of black women from Soweto who, in an incident in 1990, stripped in front of policemen set on destroying their homes under apartheid legislation. This highly unusual communal gesture attempted to shame the authorities into restraint or even retreat. The film juxtaposes archival footage of the event with interviews with the women, all of whom reflect on both the power and the pain of their acts of self-exposure (Figure 8.4).

The objects in the closets create a network of associations which turn on the psychosocial state of shame. Whether historical traces or invented 'things', they intensify the unstable process of 'free association' that lies at the heart of psychoanalysis. These objects are neither labelled nor categorized, but 'float' symbolically, much like many of the more arcane objects in Freud's collection

But through my
nakedness I got my reward

Figure 8.4 Still from *To Walk Naked/Uku Hamba 'Ze*, a short documentary by Sheila Meintjies, Jai Maingard and Heather Thompson (1995), shown on a monitor in one of the cupboards in the *Dining Room* part of Penny Siopis's *Three Essays on Shame* in the Freud Museum.

of artifacts; they are fundamentally open and eternally 'unfinished' (see Figure 8.6, colour plate section).

Essay 3: Exhibition Room (Memory)

The exhibition room was once Freud's bedroom. We moved his deathbed – which looked uncannily like his couch – from the attic storeroom into the centre of the space, and I hung a series of 'shame' paintings in a low, continuous frieze around the walls. The paintings are small and intimate, imaginings of childhood sexuality and dread. Imagining in paint can be troubling. Painting, for me, can materialize otherwise invisible or even unthinkable trauma. In a way there is a parallel here in the fate of Freud's seduction theory, where what was symbolic (imagined) and what actually, physically happened was a matter of profound contention.

It is in how we see our childhood hurts, real or symbolic, that shame comes over us again and again in adulthood. There is often an actual or implied viewer (adult or child) in the shame paintings, and sometimes this position extends out to the actual viewer. This is unnerving. If the anxiety of being looked at is distinctive in shame, then the viewer is not a passive onlooker, but a sometimes uneasy witness, an uneasiness which may arise from a sense of being complicit in the shaming: 'I should not be seeing this.' In this disavowal lies an intensity that can be associated with the child's disturbing witness of the primal scene; a disturbing sexuality with shame potential. In this context but with a slightly different emphasis, Phil Mollon notes: '[T]he child is cast into the place of the stranger, the outsider, the one who is excluded from the paradise of union with the mother' (Mollon 2002: 21).

The verbal texts imaged in all the paintings are made from rubber stamps bought from craft shops. The phrases are sentimental, clichéd love talk. Set in a pictorial context of sexual violence, these sweet phrases turn sour, becoming at once more ironical and more true to life. These are words incarnate, frequently repeatedly overstamped, a process which harks back to the hysteric's incessant reiteration of the language of trauma. The often mannered gestures also conjure up the clichéd body language we might read as 'shame form'. Hanging our heads in shame is the form Silvan Tomkins points out. This somatization seems especially intense – even required – when language fails.

But the iconography of body language is not the only thing worth commenting on here. My process of creating and clarifying imagery is equally important. Many of the paintings begin as 'blots': formless, splashes, drips and drags of coloured liquid that runs, pools and ultimately congeals. This raw, clotted, liquid matter is profoundly suggestive, and allows the thoughts and feelings pressing against my consciousness a medium and a space – a stage – for unfolding and playing out my imagery. Paint has – for me at least – always operated as a physical emanation of entangled thoughts and feelings. In this way, the work of paint becomes a carnal document. It is not for nothing that these are paintings, not photographs or some other kind of image process which I may use elsewhere. Painting offers me the prospect of touching on something primary, on elemental states, processes, visions. The initially amorphous liquid process I encourage sets conditions for figuring unspeakable things, taboos, like the still shameful 'curse' of menstrual bleeding, for example, and for manifesting sensations of dissolving or congealing into visceral 'stuff', being flooded or drenched in shame (see Figures 8.7, 8.8 and 8.9, colour plate section).

Turning now to Freud's deathbed exposed so starkly in the centre of the exhibition room, my strongest feeling was of something 'pathetic'. This feeling seemed embodied most in the ornamental reddish brocade of the mattress, an elaborate decorative attempt to dress up the bed. But the bed – however overlaid – marks the stark primitive terror of the iron truth that all bodies will die and decay in time. The body is a leftover of death, a shameful leftover in that we have little if any control over our post-mortem display or disposition. We will be exposed to others raw. Indignity threatens the body we leave when we die, and we worry about this. We cannot witness this final self-shame, but we can imagine it, and must rely on the kindness of others to ensure that our imagining does not become real.

Coda

Loss is central to shame. Shame is a necessary part of mourning but loss of shame, according to Freud, is a mark of melancholia. Freud observes:

> The shame before others that characterizes [mourning] is missing [in melancholics], or at least not conspicuously present. In the melancholic one might almost stress the opposite trait of an insistent talkativeness, taking satisfaction from self-exposure.
>
> (Freud 1917: 207)

Freud's comment about self-exposure is important, for all that its alleged satisfactions are not always clear. What is more to the point for me though is that the melancholic's self-exposure seems not to offer the transformative potential that the self-exposure of shame – for all its contradictory qualities – might deliver. Perhaps shame was only partially explored by Freud because of his gender bias, and like his work on hysteria shame can be understood more productively than he may have thought possible. Perhaps this is why Freud never really developed a theory of shame per se, or why he never gave shame an ennobling Greek name.

In South Africa the word shame is colloquially an expression of sympathy for, and identification with, someone else's pain, usually public. If you should fall in the street, people might exclaim 'shame' or cry out 'sorry', even though they are clearly blameless. There is also an Afrikaans word *siestog* which does something similar. While it can be intoned as an ironical expression of sentimental kindness, my interest is in its ambivalence. The combination of disgust ('sies') and pity ('tog', although this is difficult to translate) seems to me to articulate this ambivalence very trenchantly.

That a person might feel shame on behalf of another is empathetic and suggests strong identification. Speaking speculatively, shame seems both profoundly individual and social. In her recording Antjie Krog echoes something Jacqueline Rose says, and something which bears repeating here: 'shame requires an audience' (Rose 2003: 1). Baubo did, after all, engage with Demeter, and the story of that engagement requires readers. Shame is a form of human relation.

References

Ajootian, A. (1997) 'The only happy couple: Hermaphrodites and gender', in A. O. Koloski-Ostrow and C. L. Lyons (eds) *Naked Truths: Women, Sexuality and Gender in Classical Art and Archeology*, London and New York: Routledge.

Blackledge, C. (2003) *The Story of V: Opening Pandora's Box*, London: Weidenfeld and Nicolson.

Cameron, E. (2005) *Witness to AIDS*, Cape Town: Tafelberg.

Dawson, A. (2005) 'Documenting the trauma of apartheid: Long night's journey into day and south Africa's truth and reconciliation commission', *Screen* 46 (4).

Freud, S. (1905a) *Three Essays on the Theory of Sexuality*, S.E. 7.

—— (1905b) 'Jokes and their relation to the unconscious', S.E. 8.

—— (1916) 'A mythological parallel to a visual obsession', S.E. 4.

—— (1917) 'Mourning and melancholia', in *On Murders, Mourning and Melancholia*, trans. S. Whiteside, Harmondsworth: Penguin, 2005.

—— (1933) 'Femininity', *The Essentials of Psychoanalysis: The Definitive Collection of Sigmund Freud's Writing*, selected by Anna Freud, trans. J. Strachey, Harmondsworth: Pelican, 1986.

Gilbert, P. and Andrews, B. (eds) (1998) *Shame: Interpersonal Behavior, Psychopathology, and Culture*, New York: Oxford University Press.

Gobodo-Madikizela, P. (2003) *A Human Being Died That Night: A Story of Forgiveness*, Cape Town: David Philip.

Jones, E. (1955) *Sigmund Freud: Life and Work*, Vol 2, London and New York: Basic Books.

Mollon, P. (2002) *Shame and Jealousy: The Hidden Turmoils*, London: Karnac.

Molnar, M. (1992) *The Diary of Sigmund Freud 1929–1939*, London: Hogarth Press.

Nussbaum, M. C. (2004) *Hiding From Humanity: Disgust, Shame, and the Law*, Princeton and Oxford: Princeton University Press.

Paton, A. (1953) *Too Late the Phalarope*, Cape Town: Frederick L. Cannon.

Posel, D. and Simpson, G. (eds) (2002) *Commissioning the Past: Understanding South Africa's Truth and Reconciliation Commission*, Johannesburg: Wits University Press.

Probyn, E. (2005) *Blush: Faces of Shame*, Minneapolis and London: University of Minnesota Press.

Rose, J. (2003) *On Not Being Able to Sleep: Psychoanalysis and the Modern World*, London: Chatto and Windus.

Rycroft, C. (1995) *A Critical Dictionary of Psychoanalysis*, Harmondsworth: Penguin Books.

Sachs, W. (1947) *Black Anger*, Boston: Little, Brown.

Singh, K. (2002) 'Guilt', in I. Ward (ed.) *On a Darkling Plain: Journeys into the Unconscious*, Duxford: Icon Books.

Spitz, E. H. (1991) *Image and Insight: Essays in Psychoanalysis and the Arts*, New York: Columbia.

Truth and Reconciliation Commission of South Africa (1998) 'Special investigation onto the Mandela United Football Club', in *Truth and Reconciliation Commission of South Africa Report*, Vol. 2, Cape Town: Truth and Reconciliation Commission.

Wicomb, Z. (1998) 'Shame and identity: the case of the coloured in South Africa', in D. Attridge and R. Jolly *Writing South Africa: Literature, Apartheid, and Democracy, 1970–1995*, Cambridge: Cambridge University Press.

Chapter 9

Fabric, skin, *honte*-ologie

Ranjana Khanna

It comes as no surprise, I'm sure, that in a discussion of shame (the *honte* of my title) the question of skin and fabric may arise, all the more in the psychoanalytic context. From the pre-psychoanalytic writings of Freud to the early psychoanalytic texts, the topic of shame arises in relation to nudity, frequently alongside concepts of disgust and morality. It is also linked to unpleasure, being still or anchored in one's body, or, at other times, to movement. At least some of these – nudity, stillness, or movement – are frequently understood in visual terms in the Freudian as well as in twentieth-century phenomenological texts, whether relating to being caught in one's own gaze, looking on at oneself anchored in one's own body in a relation of splitting, or being acknowledged or ignored in one's nudity by another. Each of these possibilities in turn poses a question concerning what is meant by affect. Is shame an affect, and, if so, does that assume that people are indeed affected by objects?[1]

Discerning the nature of shame for psychoanalysis, even if one were limiting an investigation to the early writings of Freud which, as Jacqueline Rose (2003: 1–14) has noted, are the most common texts in which a concern with shame can be found, proves challenging. In the absence of a theorization of the superego in the early writings (it does not come into existence until 1923; Freud 1923: especially 28–39), it is additionally difficult to discern exactly what shame is as verb or as noun. Is it always in response to a regulative ideal? Is it constituted through that regulation? Or is it organic? Is it a state in itself, or is it a dynamic entity even if not always public in the most literal sense? Whether verb (to shame) or noun (shame) one has to consider whether some kind of action is involved in both. Is it transitive or intransitive? Reflexive or not? Does its action pass over to an object or not? Is it a response to an object, or a function of being-in-the-world?[2]

If we shame someone, we 'call them out' on something, provoking a displacement, invoking therefore a social norm they have betrayed. In the case of children, this is often to instill a norm; in the case of adults, institutions, or states, it may involve moving a private or untold guilt into the public realm. Martha Nussbaum (2006) has suggested that such 'shaming' in the legal context always returns the receiver to the position of the child who is suddenly exposed with detrimental consequences. But Freud also states in the *Three Essays on the Theory of Sexuality* from 1905 that young children are 'essentially without shame and . . . show an unmistakable satisfaction exposing their bodies' (1905: 192) by which he seems to mean not only that they are rarely witnessed in a state of shame, but also that they are without the capacity for shame and do not have a sense of modesty. Shame quickly becomes its inverse, as it does in the accusation 'Do you have no shame?' which translates alternatively either as 'Do you have no modesty?' or as 'Aren't you ashamed of yourself?' to instrumentalize, if you will, an interpellation by shame.

This chapter addresses some of these questions through readings of passages from psychoanalysis (in particular Freud and Lacan) as well as some consideration of the Islamic veil, which has frequently been understood both in culturalist and in political terms as a signifier of shame, modesty, or defiance whether focusing on such diverse contexts as Iranian constitutionalism, the Iranian Revolution, decolonizing Algeria, or indeed contemporary France, Turkey, Afghanistan, and the UK.[3] I have argued extensively elsewhere that psychoanalysis is a colonial discipline. It is constituted alongside notions of self that were products of European nationalism and colonial power, drawing at the time of its inception on fields of exploration, archaeology and anthropology that were part of the apparatus of consolidation of nationalism and colonialism. I did not, however, draw the conclusion that someone like Fatima Mernissi has, that Freud's theories are of limited relevance outside of that context. Mernissi's comparison between Freud and Imam Ghazali are indeed quite fascinating and go some way to explaining the reasons for veiling and unveiling in a generalized Islamic context. She situated Freud through comparison suggesting that one was able to discern the marked difference between a notion of female sexuality as active in Islam and passive in the Judaeo-Christian world from which Freud emerged. Indeed Mernissi's (1985: 27–45) emphasis on context and historicity declined in favor of a culturalist distinction. I chose to emphasize the imbrications of psychoanalysis with colonial and postcolonial encounter to foreground the importance of psychoanalysis today in the study of coloniality's resistant melancholic hangover in the postcolonial context (see Khanna 2003). I hope to continue that same line of thinking here.

The juxtapositions I am considering here will hopefully also shed light on what kind of an affect shame is, and whether it should be considered an affect at all. But additionally it will force another set of questions: how we understand affect; whether affect is something that happens to a stable being or whether it begins to dissolve or divide that stable being; whether affect is or affects are translatable or whether they are the very state of displacement and movement that seems untranslatable; whether one has or is an affect for the duration of its existence; whether affect or affects are gendered; whether affect sets you aside from yourself; and how we understand the term affect more generally. It has often been said of Lacan that he had no theory of affect. This question will be addressed with reference to his discussion of shame in Seminar XVII, *The Other Side of Psychoanalysis*, which is one of Lacan's more political seminars referring as it does to the student struggles from 1968 that were continuing at the time of the lectures included in that volume (1969–70). It is in that context in which Lacan curiously proposes that it is one of the responsibilities of psychoanalysis to shame. Shame indeed is in many ways for him the other side of psychoanalysis.[4]

The susceptibility to shame

As Freud attempted to discern the distinctions between neurology and psychology at the end of 1895, he was also focused on the question of shame, and from where 'unpleasure' arose. It is in a letter to Fliess on 'The Neuroses of Defence' that he sketches the parameters of those who experience shame in developmental, gender, and class terms:

> We shall be plunged deep into psychological riddles if we enquire into the origin of the unpleasure which seems to be released by premature sexual stimulation and without which, after all, a repression cannot be explained. The most plausible answer will appeal to the fact that shame and morality are the repressing forces and that the neighborhood in which sexual organs are naturally placed must inevitably arouse disgust along with sexual experiences. Where there is no shame (as in a male person), or where no morality comes about (as in the lower classes of society), or where disgust is blunted by the conditions of life (as in the country), there too no repression and therefore no neurosis will result from sexual stimulation in infancy.
>
> (Freud 1896: 221–222)

Freud suggests that just as sexual stimulation comes from the outside, so the 'repressing forces' are also exterior. Prior to the knowledge of something being wrong, shameful, or disgusting, the 'unpleasure' which then inaugurates repression does not occur. Later, Freud understands shame as an anxiety affect (Freud 1926: 87–179) when anxiety seems to be a cause of repression rather than a result of it, something taken up by Lacan in his seminar on anxiety (Lacan, n.d.[b]) in which he theorizes anxiety as the affect par excellence. It should be said that Freud is not entirely convinced by his own elaboration here, but what remains nonetheless apparent is the uncertainty of the acquisition of shame, the fact that its associated terms (morality and disgust) have cultural and political parameters, and that it is indeed gendered. It also seems, as Freud adds, that shame – now as a repressive force as well as an affect – is easily lost, either by an excess of pleasure or by a perversion: '. . . (as, for instance, in cases of licking excrement or of intercourse with dead bodies) the sexual instinct goes to astonishing lengths in successfully overriding the resistances of shame, disgust, horror, or pain' (Freud 1905: 161). Here shame is both that which regulates against the threat of feeling shame (it is a resistance to it, or as he puts it elsewhere in the *Three Essays* 'a mental dam'; Freud 1905: 178 and passim) and also the shame itself. It is, then, something dynamic. In the terms Freud uses, its loss could lead to perversion as he focuses on the internal dynamics of repression. In the terms employed in the legal context to which Nussbaum alludes, its loss can lead to cruelty. So even though the experience of shame is undesirable, the loss of the capacity for shame is even worse. It reflects a return to an early stage of childhood in which neither shame nor pity (understood as linked in Freud) are fully developed (Freud 1905: 192). In fact, anxiety about the 'loss' of shame/modesty is at its core. It is, therefore, an affect associated with the loss of its self, or its own demise. But also, an excess of shame, as found among hysterics, may lead, Freud says, to both 'an instinctive aversion . . . to any intellectual consideration of sexual problems' and remaining 'in complete ignorance of sexual matters right into the period of sexual maturity' (Freud 1905: 164).

This shuttling forth between having and losing on the one hand, and having and being on the other as respectively the positives and negatives of shame also relates to the question of how it is acquired. And while Freud seems to suggest that phylogeny and ontogeny are reflected in each other as he begins to develop his own notion of sublimation, and that the forward movement of civilization is about the 'diversion of sexual instinctual forces from sexual aims and their direction to new ones' (Freud 1905: 178), he also claims that education is not the primary motivator of such a displacement. 'One gets an impression,' he writes, 'from civilized children that the construction of these dams is a product of education. . . . But in reality this development is organically determined and fixed by heredity' (Freud 1905: 177). It participates, therefore, in both a structure of norm on the one hand and normalization on the other. While ultimately I disagree with Michael Warner's (1999) desire to defend the category of the norm, his distinction, drawing from Foucault's *Discipline and Punish* (1977) and Canguilhem's *The Normal and the Pathological* (1989) is useful. Describing normalization as a process through which modern society is organized around distributional norms that are then understood as evaluative norms, we can see that through Warner's lens, this could be the product of the kind of education cited by Freud as occurring in civilization. But Freud also points to a more organic norm, which may, in Warner's terms be likened to norms we may not feel the need to question, and may be necessary to guarantee existence.

In his resistance to the cultural construction model, Freud seems to be more sympathetic to a Darwinian understanding of shame and blushing in his *Expression of Emotions in Man and Animals* in which there is something organic to the blushing: 'the most peculiar and the most human of all expressions' (Darwin 1979: 310). In Darwin, the subject-able-to-blush occupies a particular sort of interest, but there are people – like most natives of India – for whom blushing is not visible for whom, says Darwin, 'shame ... is expressed ... much more plainly by the head being averted or bent down, with the eyes wavering or turned askant, than by any change of colour in the skin' (Darwin 1979: 316). This is of course the basis for Silvan Tomkins' writings on shame, which, he writes, 'strikes deepest into the heart of man' making him feel 'naked, defeated, alienated, lacking in dignity or worth' (Kosofsky Sedgwick and Frank 1995: 133). Shame, then, seems to involve a loss of something, and is dependent on the idea that one thinks one should have dignity or worth. The ontological affect is thus reduced to the subject with dignity, although it is also about its potential loss and mourning of it. Shame for him too is a bodily affect signified by eyes cast down, the head bent or averted, or blushing, although it is a slightly later evolving of nine basic bodily affects to be distinguished from the muddier categories of emotions which are based on these clearer categories. It therefore brings together the physiological and the social through the psychological, but also through that liminal, porous entity, the skin. Tomkins draws an important distinction between affect and emotion here, which is less visible in Darwin's theories on which his work is based.

While the face is of primary interest to both Darwin and Tomkins, they both speculate on 'blushing' on other parts. Tomkins speculates that 'clothing originated in the generalization of shame to the whole body, and the consequent need to cover it from the stare of the other. In different cultures a cover may be worn over the genitals or the face or both, whichever are felt to be the most private parts of the body' (Kosofsky Sedgwick and Frank 1995: 134). He also suggested that Freud had an inadequate understanding of affect, and always confused it with drive rather than seeing them as primary motivations for all human behavior, although as we have seen in the *Three Essays*, shame seems to be a defense against drives. And in 'Inhibitions, Symptoms, and Anxiety' affect as anxiety seems to be a repressing force in and of itself. For Tomkins, Freud's lack of precision became a particular problem in his thinking of shame that too often became related to the anal drive for defecation control (Kosofsky Sedgwick and Frank 1995: 49–50). In neither the early writings nor the later, however, is shame so limited. If Tomkins's work highlighted the damaging effects of being shamed, it also implicitly revealed normative assumptions concerning dignity and worth as the internalized sense of what we have in a state of non-shame. Freud was keener to highlight shame's normalizing effects, which could not so easily be adopted into oppositions of shame and dignity, or indeed, shame and pride, to point toward its more political use.

For Freud, shame manifested in dreams is associated with the exposure of the private parts of the body with reference to the fairy tale 'The Emperor's

New Clothes' in which 'the Emperor walks out in this invisible garment, and all the spectators, intimidated by the fabric's power to act as a touchstone, pretend not to notice the Emperor's nakedness' as their own lack of virtue and loyalty would thus be revealed (Freud 1900: 243). However, in Freud's rendition of the dream of shame: 'The impostor is the dream and the Emperor is the dreamer himself' (Freud 1900: 244). While Freud does not go into the class implications of his example, he notes the fact that it is strangers, indifferent to the nakedness, who are in the presence of the naked figure rather than the old nurses of childhood who would have indifferently seen the child naked but also attempted to instill a sense of shame and were, for Freud, the source of some sexual interest. Freud's own dream consists of him running up stairs energetically when he saw a maid. He felt ashamed, and attempting to hide was glued to the spot. The naked Emperor derives his sense of shame from the possibility of being seen by the (no doubt indifferent) impostor. Both his dignity (to use Tomkins's Kantian term) and his shame are then derived partly from his aristocratic status, but they become affectively linked though they are the inverse of each other. And skin, with its liminal nature between inside and outside, also seems to mark the threat of porosity between classes. The strangers, who seem to have neither dignity nor shame (nor virtue or loyalty in the fairy tale) are inevitably indifferent and seem to have nothing to lose.

This linking between the Emperor that dreams and the naked Emperor demonstrates both a splitting of self and a fixity of self played out, if you will, by being stuck on the staircase – once again, there is a displacement in the moment of fixity. I take this to elaborate something similar to what Levinas means, 35 years later, in his early essay 'On Escape', when he writes:

> The necessity of fleeing, in order to hide oneself, is put in check by the impossibility of fleeing oneself. What appears in shame is thus precisely the fact of being riveted to oneself, the radical impossibility of fleeing oneself to hide from oneself, the unalterably binding presence of the I to itself. Nakedness is shameful when it is the sheer visibility of our being, of its ultimate intimacy. And the nakedness of our body is not that of a material thing, antithesis of spirit, but the nakedness of our total being in all its fullness and solidity, of its most brutal expression of which we could not fail to take note. . . . It is . . . our intimacy, that is, our presence to ourselves, that is shameful. It reveals not our nothingness but rather the totality of our existence. Nakedness is the need to excuse one's existence. Shame is, in the last analysis, an existence that seeks excuses. What shame discovers is the being who *uncovers* himself.
>
> (Levinas 2003: 64–65)

Shame in both the Freudian and the Levinasian script does not interrupt being as in the Sartrian context I will turn to in a moment, but rather fixes it in a technology as if one's own dream unravelled like a cinematic screen. It is not surprising that both Freud and Levinas will refer to psychic technologies in terms of the photographic or filmic apparatus in relation to such dreaming – the latter to Charlie Chaplin, the former famously to 'a compound microscope or a photographic apparatus'.[5] The process of splitting that takes place seems paradoxically then not to allow a dissociation from the experience of shame in which one could be a bystander like any other, but rather a binding in which he who has internalized the shamefulness of an actual or metaphorical shamefulness is the originator of his or her own shame. Here, there is a movement away from the self as subject, but simultaneously an excessive displaced response to it: a surplus indeed that can be suffered or enjoyed – or enjoyed because suffered – but precisely not transgressed. The displacement afforded by this splitting is not a doubling of self or a splitting into two subject positions, so much as a movement one could think of as a technology of seeing: one that sets us at odds with an excess of enjoyment within which we are caught.

Levinas ultimately moves to a less Heideggerian notion of Being in relation to shame in his later work, where shame, in a more Benjaminian vein, seems to be about the porosity of being, and a demand for responsibility that is definitely not seen in guilt for him. If for Lacan affect meant literally being affected by the Other and was in that sense quite distinct from the resulting feeling or emotion, in Levinas shame was something that occurred as a manifestation of unworthiness in relation to the Other. For Levinas, shame was not simply a feeling of guilty inadequacy in the face of symptomatic moral transgression. Rather, it became, in later work, exactly what gnaws away at the self. As such, as Ann Murphy (2004) has described it, shame becomes a 'symptom of sensibility' and an undoing of any identity category rather than an emotion that happens to a complete Being.[6] And for Derrida (2002), who was also interested in the workings of technologies of shame and seeing, shame could be initiated by a cat looking at one naked, in spite of the fact, or perhaps because of the fact, that one may realize the non-sensical nature of this response and the imposition and projection of ontology on to the non-ontological that goes along with it.[7]

Joan Copjec (2006) has suggested that Levinas, in the early essay *On Escape*, confuses shame with anxiety, and this is part of the reason that shame is associated with the suffocating nature of life under capitalism in which one is trapped by the capitalist mode of reducing being to identities that are not of one's choosing. Shame, in this context, rivets the ontic to the ontological and does therefore not allow for the possibilities (in the Heideggerian sense) involved in the seeing of Being as such. Shame seems like one of the few instances in which we cannot retain a position in which it is possible to see the self as shamed, and in that sense it is quite different from Heideggerian concepts of Being, or from Sartrian notions of nausea. Levinas seems rather to see shame as a moment in which one might be prompted to escape

Being without seeing it itself. Copjec pays particular attention to the editorial comments of Jacques Rolland who suggests a similarity between the language of being riveted in shame to that of being defined as a Jew in Levinas' 1935 writing.[8] Copjec shows effectively that this rigid anchoring to being that Levinas proffers is actually a symptom of capitalist racism and anti-Semitism itself, which transforms originary anxiety into moral anxiety, and with it shame into guilt. Following Lacan, she locates the sensation of inescapability with guilt (following an older Freudian distinction between guilt as a private introverted emotion and shame as a public one). This is an advance on Copjec's exquisite essay 'The Sartorial Superego' (1989) in which a resistance to utilitarianism and its colonial impulse is posited as the guilty pleasures found in Clérambault, whom Lacan called his only master, in his extreme fascination in the fabric of North African clothing which was in excess of useful bodily covering. There, the superego is characterized by its extraordinarily violent nature. As if mirroring the many folds of this fabric, Clérambault represented a guilty pleasure in excess himself, exemplified in the 20,000 photographs he took of men and women wrapped in such drapery.

Deleuze (1993: 94) suggested that North African drapery for Clérambault held its fascination because it had and concealed no object and manifested rather as an event.[9] One could read Clérambault, after Deleuze, as the photographer who calls attention to the different ways of seeing and the confusion of perspective in the fold that does not allow a knowledge of the object in isolation. Rather, the object is opened up to an infinite universe both dispersed and bound at the same time, denying the way in which the world has compressed fabric and folds into fixed pictures: 'In this way the psychiatrist Clérambault's taste for folds of Islamic origin and his extraordinary photographs of veiled women . . . amounts . . . to much more than a simple personal perversion' (Deleuze 1993: 38).

The veil and the technologies of shame

A book originating from an exhibition organized by inIVA (Institute of International Visual Arts) in London begins with the words: 'The veil is an item of clothing dramatically overburdened with competing symbolism' (Lewis 2003: 10). Many texts have been written on the relationship between the veil and shame in Islam from religious interpretation, to orientalist anthropological studies, to feminist scholarship.[10] Each, in turn, has criticized the former set of texts for various forms of prejudice – orientalism, culturalism, the conflation of different types of veil across vastly different cultural and political landscapes, and now there is a considerable body of scholarship by feminists on the problem of what has seemed like an obsession with the veil on the part of a significant body of feminist texts relating to women and Islam.[11] If Edward Said referred to orientalism not simply as negative stereotyping but also as a system of citation,[12] it does seem as if a repetitive tedium has settled on this need to keep returning to the veil, a fact noted also by Mieke Bal (1991) in her reading of Malek Alloula's *The Colonial Harem* (1986), a book which seeks to return postcards circulated by the French in Algeria of women in various stages of dress, veil, and fabric. Afsaneh Najmabadi (2005) has criticized Fatima Mernissi for her insistence on thinking of the veil – in all its varieties from a fashionable headscarf to the niqab and from Indonesia and India to Algeria and Egypt, and it seems for time immemorial – in Islam as having uniform significance. While acknowledging that Mernissi's argument is bold, she shows how it is ultimately contingent upon an understanding of heterosexuality and phallocentrism that does not necessarily describe some significant moments in the history of Islam in Iran. She shows how such work on the veil has disaffiliated work on gender from that on sexuality and has also made it a signifier of the modern that ignores entirely other significant signifiers like the size and shape of men's beards, hair, hats, and other such things that are crucial in understanding sexual and cultural difference and 'the (un)desirability of looking like the other' (Najmabadi 2005: 133).

Popular discussions of the veil frequently seem to reflect a total ignorance of the very complex political histories associated with it, seeing it as simply a signifier of women's oppression under Islam. Salman Rushdie, in one of his less than literary moments, has announced that 'veils suck' in the context of the recent rather frenzied controversy in the UK over a comment by Jack Straw, the Leader of the House of Commons and former foreign minister, who had objected to women in his constituency wearing the niqab – a veil that conceals all but the eyes – when they came to appointments with him (Butt 2006).

It is not my purpose in this section, however, to comment on the veil as a signifier of cultural and/or sexual shame or speculate on whether it is oppressive or not so much as to consider how it has been figured visually in ways that have cited shame in some configuration. Objections to Jack Straw's comments have mostly centred on liberal arguments around cultural difference and the need to hide from sight, to mark a border or threshold, and to introduce an idea of the forbidden, much in the terms that Mernissi (1991) suggests is the function of the veil. It also revealed something about levels of surveillance in the UK and the need for visual recognition. The average Briton is photographed about 300 times a day with approximately 4.2 million surveillance cameras in the country (Jones and Trevelyan 2006). Even as shame as cultural difference has been at the center of the conversation, it has also highlighted the nature of the police state that is quite familiar in the history of visual identification and surveillance under colonialism.

Malek Alloula (1986) suggested that the photographer was embarrassed by the enigma of the veil presenting an image of the photographer as intrusive violator caught up in his own fetishistic desire stimulated by the restrictions on seeing:

These veiled women are not only an embarrassing enigma to the photographer but an outright attack upon him. It must be believed that the feminine gaze that filters through the veil is a gaze of particular kind: concentrated by the tiny orifice for the eye, this womanly gaze is a little like the eye of a camera, like the photographic lens that takes aim at everything. . . . The photographer will respond to this in quiet and almost natural challenge by means of a double violation: he will unveil the veiled and give figural representation to the forbidden. . . . The photographer's studio will become . . . a pacified microcosm where his desire, his scopic instinct, can find satisfaction.

(Alloula 1986: 14)

But Alloula, like Fanon before him, also participates in a form of masculine identification where he projects the camera as weapon even as he claims to occupy the position of the figure who, in concealed fashion, casts her eye and shames the onlooker by forbidding him access to her modesty and becomes less than human herself as if a photographic lens. The feminine gaze becomes filter, aperture, or the eye of a camera. But the fabric too is more than the returned gaze itself, and opens up into a world in which the photographer, and indeed Alloula, may be seen from elsewhere.

Fanon's well-known essay 'Algeria Unveiled' is frequently discussed as a place in which the multiple political and cultural meanings of the veil are explained, not least because it was an important piece for Gillo Pontecorvo's film *The Battle of Algiers* (1966). But while this may be the case, there is nonetheless a moral psychology that runs through the essay. He writes:

The unveiled body seems to escape, to dissolve. She has an impression of being improperly dressed, even of being naked. She experiences a sense of incompleteness with great intensity. She has the feeling that something is unfinished, and along with this a frightful sensation of disintegrating. The absence of the veil distorts the Algerian woman's corporal pattern. She quickly has to invent new dimensions for her body, new means of muscular control. . . . The Algerian woman who walks stark naked into the European city relearns her body, re-establishes it in a totally revolutionary fashion.

(Fanon 1989: 59)

In spite of his own revolutionary desires for Algeria, Fanon's sympathies in the essay are famously with the Algerian man who feels ashamed that culture is turned to politics and that the women must unveil. The veil and its lack here become signifiers of male shame and female modesty. But more than skin, Fanon speaks of a bodily disintegration without shame as such – as if she were anyway dispossessed and had lost ideals for physical integrity without even knowing it before going out to fight. Pontecorvo famously staged the scene of physical transformation as if in a movie-set dressing room, as if to highlight the way in which the Algerian struggle was a war of spectacle and technologies of seeing as much as death.

If the postal system seemed in some ways complicitous with colonial rule in Algeria in Alloula's analysis, it is the postman who appears again in the creation of identification photographs in Algeria to aid in surveillance. The photographer Marc Garanger tells of how, when on his military service in 1960 in Algeria during the long war of independence, he was asked to photograph natives of the 'reassembled villages' – which were like refugee camps for two million internally displaced people in Algeria who were moved as part of de Gaulle's five-year 'Plan de Constantine' to increase Algerian production by 58 per cent.[13] The postmaster called up the villagers, and Garanger photographed 2000 people, mostly women, over ten days. He describes how they were forced to unveil and sit on a steel stool in front of a white wall. They would stare at him, he writes, at point-blank range as he witnessed their fierce protest to which he bore witness. His hope, in publishing the photographs, was to bear witness, in turn, to that very protest (Garanger 1982; see Figure 9.1). Garanger very briefly highlights the technology of colonial scopophilia as if to observe not any particular shame on the part of the unveiled women, but rather to instigate, in the absence of any possibility of legal consequences, some form of collective shame that can nonetheless have a surplus enjoyment. Here, shame shapes the social without loss of any sort, and without any form of liminality. In fact cultural difference is inscribed here as historical shame, kept vibrant affectively but having little distinction from collective guilt.

A world without shame

Lacan ends his seventeenth seminar in 1970 (June 17) with a session that begins:

> It has to be said: dying of shame is an effect rarely produced. Nevertheless, it is the only sign . . . whose genealogy we can be certain of, namely that it is descended from a signifier. . . . Dying of shame then. Here the degeneration of the signifier is certain – certain of being produced by a failure of the signifier, that is being for death, in so far as it concerns the subject – and who else could it concern? Being for death, that is, the visiting card by which a signifier represents a subject for another signifier. . . . This visiting card never reaches a safe haven, the reason being that since it bears the address of the dead person this card has to be torn up. *It's a shame (une honte)*, as they say, which should produce a hontology, to finally give it its correct spelling. . . . Meanwhile, to die of shame is the only affect of death that deserves – deserves what? Deserves *it*.
>
> (Lacan n.d.[a])

Figure 9.1 Marc Garanger, *Femme Algérienne*, 1960. Photograph. Courtesy the artist.

The seminar has been concerned with elaborating what Lacan calls the four discourses: that of the master, the hysteric, the analyst, and the university, each designated in a matheme by the same algebraic terms but in a different relation of quarter turns.[14] But this is in the context of relating Freud and Marx through Hegel to understand the nature of science and knowledge more generally, particularly the status of psychoanalysis in the university. A Department of Psychoanalysis had recently been established, which begged the question from two sides: the impact psychoanalysis could have on university discourse, and the impact university discourse may in turn have on psychoanalysis. Lacan spends time in the seminar commenting on the students' 'revolutionary' actions, especially in a session called an 'Analyticon'. (Lacan names it thus in order to reference the question of the spectacle developed in Debord's influence from Gracian's *Critikon*, which is mentioned, and possibly also Fellini's *Satyricon*.)

In the *Four Fundamental Concepts of Psychoanalysis*, Lacan commented on his difference with Sartre's attention to shame in *Being and Nothingness*. In Sartre's (1956: 386) text, the experience of shame occurs when being caught in the act while, for example, peeping through a keyhole. One is always seen by another at that moment. In Lacan (1981: 84) there is direct reference to Sartre but he takes his distance from it. In Sartre, consciousness is aroused in this shameful moment and forces a confrontation with the dialectic of being and nothingness, and in turn allows for a different relation to my world. But in Lacan, of course, there is no other person looking on initiating this turn of consciousness:

> The gaze in question is certainly the presence of others as such. But does this mean that originally it is in the relation of subject to subject, in the function of the existence of others as looking at me, that we apprehend what the gaze really is?
>
> (Lacan 1981: 84)

In Lacan, the gaze is the gaze of the Other and is therefore caught up in the desiring structure. There is nothing freeing then about this gaze, and it is never returned from the place from which one sees.

But in *The Other Side of Psychoanalysis* Lacan is not so focused on the gaze. He is more interested in showing why the student protests are participating in the Master's discourse rather than being the free revolutionary protests they imagine. While the students applaud themselves for defying the status quo and going from the university to the street to join with the workers, Lacan warns, in the session from 3 December 1969, that in fact they simply take the university with them, and search for a master there. He says:

> You are the products of the University. The surplus value is you and you are proving it. . . . You have all made yourself into credits. You leave here stamped with credits. . . . You play the role of serfs in this regime. . . . The regime is showing you off. It says, 'Look at them enjoying themselves!'
>
> (Lacan n.d.[a])

The role of psychoanalysis, by the end of the seminar, is not only to allow the analysts to work with the hysterics discourse which shows 'what Marx historically spelled out, namely, that there are historical events that can only be judged in terms of symptoms' (Lacan n.d.[a]). It is also to shame. Jacques-Alain Miller reminds us that Lacan (1966: 771) has suggested that 'The shamefulness of one forms the veil of shame of the other.'[15] But here Lacan bemoans the fact that we live in a world without shame, and that the kind of movement on to the streets represented by the students is indeed shame-worthy. They do not recognize themselves as symptoms of capitalist bourgeois logic, they do not see how their knowledge is being appropriated by the Master as regime, and their enjoyment is a combination of loss and surplus. It is only the hysteric who can point out that the Emperor is naked while also acknowledging his display of power: he is both naked and powerful and this is his enjoyment (why should he be so powerful when he is not?). If the students' university discourse was the inverse of the Master's, and was appropriated by the Master's turning enjoyment to surplus value, the analyst can respond to the hysteric's finding, and reintroduce shame in a world, he bemoans, which has lost it. And a focus on affect as anxiety is a place from which this can be done. Shame is a form of anxiety that guards against the outburst of the hysteric/impostor, but nonetheless provides some access to it.

Technologies of shaming and the return of the veil

As if to draw attention to the forms of violation in the colonial technology of shaming and the language of shame, some women artists have, I want to suggest, foregrounded the question of shame and the shaming mechanisms in their works. Mona Hatoum, Zineb Sedira, and Shirin Neshat are examples of such work. Playing with iconophobia, writing and calligraphy, and the etymologically related signifiers of shame and skin, they foreground the movement between analogical and digital that we can understand as the affect of shame. Many – including Negar Mottahedeh (2000), Laura Mulvey (1998), and Hamid Naficy (1994) – have written on the question of how the restrictions on unveiled women in Iranian cinema has gone into the production of different cinematic codes that both highlight the regime's technologies of spatial organization and confinement, as well as the notion of modesty, shame, and the forbidden that is referenced with it. The works of Kiarostami, but also Makhmalbaf, are frequently discussed for the different aesthetic that is produced, one, in fact, that we could call an aesthetic of shaming that works on at least two registers – the cinematic codes emerging from a politicized notion of shame, modesty, and the forbidden as spatial restriction on the one hand, and the cultural norms of shame modesty and the forbidden themselves – juggling between each.

But we can also see how this works in aesthetic production in both video art and photography. Shirin Neshat, from Iran, for example (see Figure 9.2, colour plate section) uses photography of the veiled woman with a gun in her 1994 'Women of Allah' series. She both references the threat of violence from the woman who holds the gun in defiant gesture, but also is inscribed with writing (including revolutionary poetry) that makes her both target and the face that is not quite a representation of a face. It is over-inscribed, but it also struggles with the prohibition against the representation of the face, as if it is not the face itself that is inscribed, but indeed photography and the dynamic of photography's technologies of shaming and response to it. Indeed the images are textured, folded if you will, so that the writing itself forms a layer over the image so skin, make-up, veil, and writing are folded into each other at the moment of seeing. This simultaneously foregrounds technologies of seeing and relegates them to a backdrop. As if to highlight another site of flesh not covered by the hijab, Neshat similarly inscribes an image of the feet, which are both assaulted and assaulting with the gun between them in an invagination. Calligraphy is referenced as the artistic tradition that develops in the place of figural representation, and its presence here seems to suggest that writing has always incorporated the trace of the face.

Playing with this idea of the hidden and the figurative, Zineb Sedira photographs herself in a series 'Don't do to her what you did to me II!' putting on a head scarf. The forceful accusatory, indeed shaming title opens on to photographs that depict various stages of the ritual. But rather than the plain white or black hijab common in Algeria, Sedira's headscarf is covered in digitalized passport photos of a woman. The fabric, then, is made up precisely of what is forbidden. Visual depiction and iconicity and the headscarf become simultaneously the inside and the outside. As if there were no originary site from which the face emerges, or indeed the admonitory note, each references technologies of travel and movement that give context to a discursive history and geography of the veil while releasing it from that history of confinement, and the confinement of geography. Sedira's video installation 'Silent Sight' (Figure 9.3) similarly invokes the question of inside and outside, perceiver and perceived, shamed and shaming. Ostensibly including a clear narrative voice of the artist's recollections of herself as a child, she relates a tale of anxiety – articulated as such in muffled sounds that have no obvious source – a kind of acousmatic noise that nonetheless diagnoses the narrative. And yet the sound of the narrative voice is also sourceless in some ways, it being unclear from where it emerges, and whether it is a voice emerging from a mouth hidden, and yet associated with the eyes that are visible on the screen.

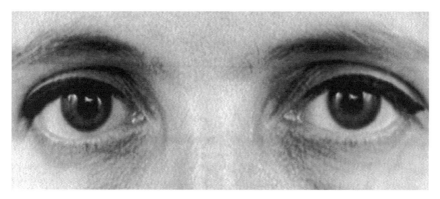

Figure 9.3 Zineb Sedira, *Silent Sight*, 2000. Video still. Courtesy the artist and Galerie Kamel Mennour, Paris.

The voice tells the story of a child seeing her mother veiling herself at the moment of arrival at a port. The response of the child is a series of questions she is nonetheless afraid to ask, culminating in the most poignant 'Will I recognise her?'

But the narrative is just one part of the video-installation. The visual consists of eyes (the artist's eyes) and eyebrows in the centre of the screen. There is no easy way to tell if the narrative is being read or is otherwise associated with the eyes, but it does not appear so. The image appears to resemble both a wide-angle shot in which the screen is divided into three with the centre bar showing the image, but it also references the subject matter of the narrative itself – the white veil that covers the body and the face with the exception of the eyes. The anxiety for the viewer is partly associated, then, with this lack of clarity, and which technology of viewing we are looking at. Ultimately, the narrative voice expresses comfort, saying that the body and the veil seem to be equivalent to home.

Hatoum's video piece, *Measures of Distance* (see Figure 9.4, colour plate section) similarly tells a story of belonging and not belonging, this time through the reading of letters between a mother and a daughter, one in Beirut, one in London. And yet the video also foregrounds the technology of the letter, of language, of voice, and of video itself as a technology of travel and migration. The video introduces voices before we understand them as the reading aloud of a letter. We are invited to listen to language itself and not just what it denotes as we switch from Arabic to English highlighting language as translation – as more than a transparent mechanism of communication. The letter also seems to have reached its destination with the daughter, but then it comes on to us, further highlighting postal mobility. And it becomes both intimate and singular to the situation, and part of a larger technology of belonging. In Hatoum's video, video itself is denaturalized as a technology of movement, and as, in a sense, a technology of diaspora. Video stills hold moments as if they were letters before the technology of mobility starts over.[16] And the letters form more than a spoken narrative. Drawing on the use of calligraphy and the veil, Hatoum uses Arabic script over the shower curtain that hides her mother's body, as if words too become the veil of modesty and function already as a concealing and restrictive fabric that nonetheless is simultaneously unconcealing and sensuous. The letters, then, are a fabric of desire and intimacy while simultaneously a resistance to the possibility of unmediated access to the words of another. The letter is literalized as handwriting, the veil is produced as a curtain of restricted access, the listening is already inscribed into a technology of belonging and unbelonging, and identity in this scenario becomes of secondary importance to the technologies of existence. For Heidegger as much as for Hatoum, the non-conceptual sound of language is where communication seems to occur, and it is this non-conceptual and sensual level in which the human as communicator paradoxically comes undone. If technology shows how we speak out of language as much as it makes us human, it also shows the way in which hearing functions to question the limit between human and animal.[17]

It is through technology, then, that the artwork performs itself a critical relation to its own technology, standing in a critical relation to the forms of exchange and communication that cannot encompass the affective resistance to these forms. The critical relation is in this sense priceless (to use a Derridean idea that further questions the metaphysics of presence) and unattached – in the realm of chrematistics rather than economics – as a byproduct of the economic, but also haunted by it in a critical relation.

These works do not only explore the internal dynamics of shame in the context of the Middle East or North Africa. Rather, they reintroduce, into a world without shame, the signifier of shame through the veil. The affect of shame thus moves beside itself. It begins to reveal the movement between the technology of clothing and unclothing in the Emperor fairy tale. Symptomatic and self-satisfied liberal responses fail, ultimately, to recognize shame as a technology and see it only as a lived oppression. In these works, shame becomes the affect, then, that moves the discourse of the hysteric a quarter turn, to one that allows us to glimpse an enjoyment that the analyst introducing the technology highlights. And the technology can therefore not be subsumed into the discourse of the master or the regime. Rather, shame is released from its dwelling in an object which in turn affects a person. It rather becomes the signifier for shame, a trace that reveals the very process of how shame is mobilized and circulates in the postcolonial encounter. As affect, it is therefore translatable even as the emotions associated with it seem intransigently opposed, hopelessly inadequate, and locked into an untranslated incompatibility, or a differend.

Notes

1 The question of whether objects can affect people, and what sort of relation there is between the thing-in-itself and the affective response to the appearance of the thing was, of course, a primary concern of Kant's, and has continued in post-Kantian literature. See in particular, Kant (2003). In turn, the critique of metaphysics has forced a questioning of the understanding of ontology implicit in a notion of the object that exists in a form that goes beyond what can be empirically verified.

2 Martin Heidegger's intervention into the Kantian notion of the affective response to the object is being referenced here with his particular turn to a phenomenological existentialism, and the particular kinds of temporality that are suggested by the relation of being and the relation to objects (see Heidegger 1927).

3 I am in no way suggesting that this manifestation of shame in the variety of geographical and historical contexts are the same, or even parallel, and am mindful of Afsaneh Najmabadhi's (2005) criticism of work that suggests this, as well, of course, as Edward Said's *Orientalism* (1978).

4 As the official translation of the official transcript of the seminar is yet to appear, I have worked with Cormac Gallagher's translation of the unofficial transcript, which includes additional materials.

5 Levinas (2003: 65) references the moment in Charlie Chaplin's *City Lights* when
he swallows the whistle. Freud's (1900: 536) reference to the psyche as akin to the
camera apparatus was famously discussed by Jean-Louis Baudry (1986a, 1986b).
For more recent discussions of both these moments to which I am indebted, see,
on Levinas, Copjec (2006: 90–114); and on Freud, Silverman (2000: 12–28) and
Doane (1987).

6 For Benjamin on temporal and spatial porosity in cities (in this instance, in
Naples), see, for example, Benjamin (1996: 414–421). For Levinas on shame as
gnawing being, see (Levinas 1981: 114). For a good commentary on the development of the idea of shame in Levinas, see Murphy (2004).

7 Derrida brings in this notion of following as if to depart from Heidegger's reading
of nature and Being. Heidegger discusses this extensively in *Being and Time* in
which grammatical connotation becomes a crucial factor in the understanding of
ontology. In German, 'Ich bin' (I am) suggests 'I reside,' 'I dwell alongside' which
thus also suggests that Being is a kind of dwelling. Derrida draws attention to the
different grammatical formulation of Being in French, in which 'je suis' (I am)
also means 'I follow', introducing motion and lack of stability into Being rather
than dwelling.

8 Jacques Rolland's annotations appear in Levinas (2003: 74–94). Rolland refers to
Levinas' essay 'Paix et Droit' (1991), originally published in 1935. For another
take on Levinas' essay in relation to Levinas' resistance to Heidegger, see Chaouat
(2005).

9 Meyda Yegenoglu (1998) has criticized Deleuze for his orientalism. This seems
incontrovertible but does not detract from the usefulness of his observation concerning the object and the event.

10 See Said (1978) and Graham-Brown (1987) for two examples of the work criticizing
such representation of Islam.

11 See, for example, Accad (1978); Makhlouf (1979); Fernea (1982); Mernissi (1985);
Abu-Lughod (1986); Wikan (1991); Zuhur (1992).

12 'Orientalism is after all a system for citing works and authors' (Said 1978: 23).

13 See Yacono (1969) and Sutton (1977).

14 For a helpful reading of the mathemes, see Zupancic (2006).

15 For a discussion of this, see Miller (2006: 12–13).

16 In this regard, work of the apparatus, technology, and desire seems profoundly
different for film and video. For more on this topic, see Doane (1983).

17 Tristan Moyle (2005: 73–82) writes of the Heideggerian *sensus communis* in terms
of language yet somewhat differently giving a reading that is more shaped by
Gadamer.

References

Abu-Lughod, L. (1986) *Veiled Sentiments: Honor and Poetry in a Bedouin Society*,
Berkeley, CA: University of California Press.

Accad, E. (1978) *Veil of Shame: The Role of Women in the Contemporary Fiction of
North Africa and the Arab World*, Sherbrooke, Québec: Naaman.

Alloula, M. (1981) *Le Harem Colonial: Images d'un sous-érotisme*, Geneva and Paris:
Editions Slatkine.

—— (1986) *The Colonial Harem*, trans. M. Godzich and W. Godzich, Minneapolis: University of Minnesota Press.

Bal, M. (1991) 'The politics of citation', *Diacritics* 21 (1): 25–45.

Baudry, J.-L. (1986a) 'Ideological effects of the basic cinematographic apparatus', in P. Rosen, *Narrative, Apparatus, Ideology*, New York: Columbia University Press.

—— (1986b) 'The apparatus: metapsychological approaches to the impression of reality in the cinema', in P. Rosen (1986) *Narrative, Apparatus, Ideology*, New York: Columbia University Press.

Benjamin, W. (1996) *Walter Benjamin: Selected Writings: Volume 1 1913–1926*, eds M. Bullock and M. W. Jennings, Cambridge, MA: Harvard University Press.

Butt, R. (2006) 'Rushdie backs Straw in row over muslim veils', *The Guardian*, 11 October, available HTTP <http://www.guardian.co.uk/religion/Story/0,,1892556,00.html> (accessed 30 November 2006).

Canguilhem, G. (1989) *The Normal and the Pathological*, trans. C. R. Fawcett, New York: Zone Books.

Chaouat, B. (2005) 'Being in France', *MLN* 120 (4): 790–806.

Copjec, J. (1989) 'The sartorial superego', *October* 50: 56–95. Reprinted in (1994) *Read My Desire: Lacan Against the Historicists*, Cambridge, MA: MIT Press.

—— (2006) 'May '68, The Emotional Month', in S. Zizek (ed.) *Lacan: The Silent Partners*, London: Verso.

Darwin, C. (1979) *Expression of Emotions in Man and Animals*, London: Julian Friedmann Publishers.

Deleuze, G. (1993) *The Fold: Leibniz and the Baroque*, trans. T. Conley, Minneapolis: University of Minnesota Press.

Derrida, J. (2002) 'The animal that therefore I am (more to follow)', *Critical Inquiry* 28 (2): 369–418.

Doane, M. (1983) 'The film's time and the spectator's space', in S. Heath and P. Mellencamp (eds) *Cinema and Language*, Los Angeles: American Film Institute.

—— (1987) 'Remembering women: Psychical and historical constructions in film theory', in *Continuum: The Australian Journal of Media and Culture* 1:2, available HTTP <http://wwwmcc.murdoch.edu.au/ReadingRoom/1.2/Doane.html> (accessed 30 November 2006).

Fanon, F. (1989) 'Algeria unveiled', in *Studies in a Dying Colonialism*, trans. H. Chevalier, London: Earthscan.

Fernea, E. (prod.) and Gaunt, M. (dir.) (1982) *A Veiled Revolution*, 26 min., First Run Icarus Films.

Foucault, M. (1977) *Discipline and Punish*, trans. A. Sheridan, Harmondsworth: Penguin.

Freud, S. (1896) 'Draft K – the neuroses of defence', S.E. 1.

—— (1900) *The Interpretation of Dreams*, S.E. 4, 5.

—— (1905) *Three Essays on the Theory of Sexuality*, S.E. 7.

—— (1923) 'The ego and the id', S.E. 19.

—— (1926) 'Inhibitions, symptoms, and anxiety', S.E. 20.

Garanger, M. (1982) *Femmes Algériennes 1960*, Paris: Contrejour.

Graham-Brown, S. (1987) *Images of Women, Portrayal of Women in Photography in the Middle East 1860–1950*, London: Quartet.

Heidegger, M. (1927) *Being and Time: A Translation of Sein und Zeit*, trans. J. Stambaugh, Albany: State University of New York Press, 1996.

Jones, M. and Trevelyan, M. (2006) 'Watchdog sounds alarm on U.K. "surveillance society" ', *New York Times*, 2 November, available HTTP <http://news.yahoo.com/s/nm/20061102/ts_nm/britain_privacy_dc> (accessed 30 November 2006).

Kant, I. (2003) *Critique of Pure Reason*, trans. N. Kemp Smith, 2nd edn, London: Macmillan.

Khanna, R. (2003) *Dark Continents: Psychoanalysis and Colonialism*, Durham: Duke University Press.

Kosofsky Sedgwick, E. and Frank, A. (1995) *Shame and its Sisters: A Silvan Tomkins Reader*, Durham and London: Duke University Press.

Lacan, J. (n.d. [a]) *The Seminar of Jacques Lacan: Psychoanalysis Upside Down; The Reverse Side of Psychoanalysis 1969–70 Book XVII*, trans. C. Gallagher, unpublished.

—— (n.d.[b]) *Seminar X: Anxiety 1962–1963*, trans. C. Gallagher, unpublished.

—— (1966) *Ecrits*, Paris: Seuil.

—— (1981) *The Four Fundamental Concepts of Psychoanalysis*, trans. A. Sheridan, New York: Norton.

Levinas, E. (1981) *Otherwise Than Being*, trans. A. Lingis, Pittsburgh, PA: Duquesne University Press.

—— (1991) 'Paix et droit', in *Cahier de l'Herne, no. 60: Emmanuel Levinas*, Paris: Editions de l'Herne.

—— (2003) *On Escape*, trans. B. Bergo, Stanford: Stanford University Press.

Lewis, R. (2003) 'Preface', in D. Bailey and G. Tawadros (eds) *Veil: Veiling, Representation, and Contemporary Art*, Cambridge, MA: MIT Press.

Makhlouf, C. (1979) *Changing Veils: Women and Modernization in North Yemen*, Austin: University of Texas Press.

Mernissi, F. (1985) *Beyond the Veil: Male–Female Dynamics in Modern Muslim Society*, London: Al Saqi Books.

—— (1991) *Women and Islam: An Historical and Theological Enquiry*, trans. M. J. Lakeland, Oxford: Blackwell.

Miller, J.-A. (2006) 'On shame', in J. Clemens and R. Grigg (eds) *Jacques Lacan and the Other Side of Psychoanalysis*, Durham: Duke University Press.

Mottahedeh, M. (2000) 'Bayram Bayzai's *Maybe . . . Some Other Time* The Un-present-able Iran', *Camera Obscura* 43 (15): 162–191.

Moyle, T. (2005) *Heidegger's Transcendental Aesthetic: An Interpretation of the 'Ereignis'*, Aldershot: Ashgate.

Mulvey, L. (1998) 'Kiarostami's uncertainty principle', *Sight and Sound* 8 (6): 24–27.

Murphy, A. (2004) 'The political significance of shame', *borderlands-e-journal* 3:1, available HTTP <http://www.borderlandsejournal.adelaide.edu.au/vol3no1_2004/murphy_shame.htm> (accessed 30 November 2006).

Naficy, H. (1994) 'Veiled vision/powerful presences: women in post-revolutionary Iranian cinema', in M. Afkhami and E. Friedl (eds) *In the Eye of the Storm: Women in Post-Revolutionary Iran*, Syracuse: Syracuse University Press.

Najmabadi, A. (2005) *Women with Mustaches and Men Without Beards: Gender and Sexual Anxieties of Iranian Modernity*, Berkeley, CA: University of California Press.

Nussbaum, M. (2006) *Hiding from Humanity: Disgust, Shame, and the Law*, Princeton: Princeton University Press.

Rose, J. (2003) 'Introduction: shame', in J. Rose *On Not Being Able to Sleep: Psychoanalysis and the Modern World*, Princeton: Princeton University Press.

Said, E. (1978) *Orientalism*, London: Routledge and Kegan Paul.

Sartre, J.-P. (1956) *Being and Nothingness*, trans. H. Barnes, New York: Washington Square Books.

Silverman, K. (2000) 'Apparatus for the production of an image', *Parallax* 6 (3): 12–28.

Sutton, K. (1977) 'Population resettlement: Traumatic upheavals and the Algerian experience', *Journal of Modern African Studies* 15 (2): 279–300.

Warner, M. (1999) *The Trouble with Normal: Sex, Politics, and the Ethics of Queer Life*, New York: Free Press.

Wikan, U. (1991) *Behind the Veil in Arabia: Women in Oman*, Chicago: University of Chicago Press.

Yacono, X. (1969) *Histoire de la colonisation française*, Paris: Presses Universitaires de France.

Yegenoglu, M. (1998) *Colonial Fantasies: Towards a Feminist Reading of Orientalism*, Cambridge: Cambridge University Press.

Zuhur, S. (1992) *Revealing Reveiling: Islamist Gender Ideology in Contemporary Egypt*, Albany: State University of New York Press.

Zupancic, A. (2006) 'The concrete universal and what comedy can tell us about it', in S. Zizek (ed.) *Lacan: The Silent Partners*, New York: Verso.

Chapter 10

Shame, disgust and idealization in Kara Walker's *Gone: A Historical Romance of a Civil War As It Occurred Between the Dusky Thighs Of One Young Negress and Her Heart* (1994)

Amna Malik

> I figured out that I was a milestone in people's sexual experience – to have made it with a black woman was one of those things to check off on your list of personal accomplishments. That already has a slightly masochistic effect: to have just been the body for someone's life story. I guess that's when I decided to offer up my side-long glances to be a slave just a little bit. . . . So I used a mythic, fictional kind of slave character to justify myself, to reinvent myself in some other situations.
>
> (Saltz 1996: 86)

> All black people in America want to be slaves just a little bit, because it entitles them to heaping teaspoons full of dignity and self-awareness.
>
> (Saltz 1996: 86)

Remarks like these by the African American artist Kara Walker have flamed the controversy over her work that broke out after she was awarded a MaCarthur prize in 1997. Protests from African American women artists Betye Saar and Howardina Pindell were based on her use of negative images that reiterated the racist stereotypes of African Americans as sambos, picaninnies or minstrels, in large-scale installations shown in numerous exhibitions throughout the US. The most sympathetic and astute of her critics, artist Thom Shaw, recognized that they are targeted at whites but insisted 'We're still looked at as sambos. So when you see them bigger than life, frozen in time, it does hurt' (cited in Bowles 1997: 13). The masochism that Walker referenced in knowing and being part of a relationship in which she has 'just been the body for someone's life story', and the similar sense of hurt that Shaw alerted us to, indicates the persistence of history experienced as a periodic traumatic confrontation. Returning to her experiences of interracial relationships when she was growing up in Atlanta Walker said:

> There are times when you're friends with somebody or you're having a
> relationship, and you're not thinking about race for a brief moment.
> Then suddenly the entire history of the whole United States of America
> or the American South or post-Reconstruction comes crashing down
> on you and you say to yourself 'Hmm, this reminds me of something.
> I'm not sure what it is, but it's vaguely familiar.'
>
> (Hannaham 1998: 116)

These remarks evoke the psychic structuring of the African American who
sees herself through someone else's phobic eyes; they appear to echo W.E.B
Dubois's definition of double consciousness as the condition of being split,
as neither 'Negro' nor American, in his seminal study *The Souls of Black Folk*
(1904). Robert Hobbs regards Dubois's approach to the 'Negro's' sense of
alienation as different to the existential battle with one's ego that he argues
marks Frantz Fanon's writings. For Hobbs this distinction is important
because he views Fanon's writings to be closer to Walker's practice (Corris
and Hobbs 2003: 436). Hobbs is correct in attributing to Walker's large-scale
installations a return to the primal scene of racism in the fantasized memory
of slavery that recasts Dubois's double consciousness as an ambivalent
encounter between master and slave. However, the tone, the register of this
battle is not the existential drama that marks Fanon's writings but satire and
irreverent humour and it is this aspect that makes them controversial and
misunderstood. Hobbs stresses that Walker's work is conscious of the danger
of spectators colluding with negative ideologies that 'often occurs through
humour, which cajoles people into laughing about situations that undermine
their own positions' (Corris and Hobbs 2003: 436). Yet, the trauma of the
encounter between 'black' and 'white' in Fanon's *Black Skin, White Masks*
(1986) is absent; instead pleasure, whether sadistic or jubilant, appears to be
dominant in her work.

In this chapter I want to examine psychoanalytic aspects of shame and
shamelessness as a condition of the relationship between spectator and object
in Kara Walker's silhouettes, and specifically in relation to her first set of
silhouettes *Gone: A Historical Romance of a Civil War As It Occurred
Between the Dusky Thighs Of One Young Negress and Her Heart* (1994), first
seen at the Drawing Center in New York in 1994 (Figure 10.1). In this set of
images as in many others, what is pronounced is the proximity between
'black' grotesque figures, half-naked and murderous and 'white' gentlemen
and women, noble, elegant, self-composed and controlled. Both groups
are caught out in acts of sexual depravation or violence; their shared fashion-
ing from the same black paper implies a pollution of 'whiteness' that transforms the silhouette's historical origin as a form of idealized portraiture
of the middle classes into an object of disgust. The uncomfortable associations between 'black' and 'white' deliberately courted by the artist evoke
cultural shame over a sexuality that is closely tied to the disgust prompted by

Figure 10.1 Kara Walker *Gone: A Historical Romance of a Civil War As It Occurred Between the Dusky Thighs Of One Young Negress and Her Heart* (detail, 1994) cut paper and adhesive on wall, 13 × 50 feet, image courtesy of Sikkema Jenkins & Co.

contact with parts of the body that also serve excretory functions like shitting, pissing and menstruating. Sexual pleasure requires the overcoming of these obstacles but so-called 'perverse' sexualities emerge when the object of the drive moves from the genitals to other parts of the body, hence the smell of dirty feet or faeces as forms of arousal. When we consider these aspects of Freud's writings on sexuality within the context of the history of slavery in the US then the activation of the 'black' woman as a freed slave in Walker's images can be understood as troubling the 'readymade' social space of inferiority through questions of sexuality. The desire for the black woman represents a lacuna in 'black' experiences of emancipation that were never addressed in the Civil Rights movement. They also remain a troubling aspect of Frantz Fanon's legacy, given his condemnation of homosexuality and black women's desire for white men as a betrayal of the race. This lacuna was addressed by a range of artists in the exhibition *Mirage, Enigmas of Race, Difference and Desire* at the ICA, London, in 1995. In his catalogue essay for the exhibition Kobena Mercer succinctly summed up the problems of this legacy:

Reading Fanon today, [-] a whole generation after 'external' decolonization began, there is a pervasive sense that the forward march of liberation

came to a halt precisely around the 'interior' spaces of sexuality. As if
sexual politics has been the Achilles heel of black liberation.

(Mercer 1995: 35)

The 'interior' space of sexuality is further spatialized and temporalized by
Walker as the 'inner plantation'. Walker has cited the figure of the mulatto
mistress in Thomas Dixon's novel *The Clansman: An Historical Romance of
the Klu Klux Klan* (1905) as an important starting point for her practice. A
figure she describes as a persistent stereotype but one that is 'all catlike trying
to influence the powers that be with her wily ways' (Golden 2002: 45). While
Mark Reinhardt views this and other allusions to the 'deep south' as an indication of the plantation's status as 'home' and hence as *unheimlich* in her
images (Reinhardt 2003: 117), Robert Hobbs views the spatializing of perverse
sexual couplings in various elaborate scenes as abject plays on Hieronymous
Bosch's *The Garden of Earthly Delights* (c. 1500; Corris and Hobbs 2003: 425).

These associations between sexuality and space as an interiority that is
made visible is relevant to my reading of *Gone* because they also indicate the
importance of space in the idea of liminality that is central to Julia Kristeva's
theorization of abjection. At the same moment that Fanon's legacy was being
debated, Kristeva's writings on abjection had become prominent in the contemporary art world, inflected by a fin-de-siècle preoccupation with death
and degeneration in the shadow of the AIDS epidemic. It reached its peak in
the Tate Gallery's *Rites of Passage* exhibition (1995) – the accompanying
exhibition catalogue featured an interview with her (Penwarden 1995: 21–27)
– but it had been present for some time in the work of North American
artists. The most prominent among them, Robert Gober, Cindy Sherman
and Kiki Smith, were discussed by Hal Foster in his seminal study *The Return
of the Real, The Avant-Garde At the End of The Twentieth Century* (1996).
Foster recognized that their preoccupation with the body's splitting, leaking
and decaying was a metaphor for the instability of identity, linked to the
disavowal of the maternal in Kristeva's writings, but without acknowledging
its racial dimensions as a traumatic effect of the legacy of slavery (Foster
1996: 153–168).

Equally the work of North American artists Paul McCarthy and Mike
Kelley has tended to be addressed in isolation from Walker's concern with
abject sexuality, although they are of the generation that turned to transgression as an artistic strategy. This transgressive turn was prompted to some
extent by the rise of the Christian right during the Reagan era and the admin-
istration's implementation of regressive social policies. Consequently, during
the so-called 'culture wars' of the late 1980s to early 1990s the Conservative
right's uncanny ability to focus on the power of images placed the emphasis
on images of sexuality and the representation of the body. The liberalism of
the 'white cube' became the contested terrain on which power and its limits
were tested, and over the rights of 'minoritarians' to have their culture valued

by being made public (Vance 1989). Unlike her contemporaries, Walker made the racial dimension of cultural disgust explicit. But the reaction to her work indicated the complex nature of abjection and artistic transgression that circulated around shame. Shame manifests itself in the breaking of a shared cultural code: Walker's satirical view of the 'black' race breaks the taboo of identity politics whereby attacks among members of a 'minority' are never to be exposed to a 'white' gaze. The form that the breaking of this taboo takes extends it further: the shame of being reduced to objects of disgust and seen as such within a sphere of idealization, the space of an art gallery, draws out the horror of *exposure* that is central to shame. In a recent monograph devoted to an art historical approach to Walker's sources, Gwendolyn Dubois Shaw argued that Walker's body of work 'reveals the general schism inherent in the work of a postmodern, post-Negritude, African American woman artist' (Dubois Shaw 2004: 9) and that her work challenges 'the middle-class African American culture in which she was raised and the liberal, white-dominated art world that currently supports her work' (Dubois Shaw 2004: 9). This challenge is arguably shared with other white artists of Walker's generation and circulates over ideas of abjection. However, for reasons best known to herself Dubois Shaw has ignored *Gone*, the first of Walker's installations. Addressing the subject of shame directly in 'Nigger Lover, Or Will There Be Any Black People In Utopia' (2000) Hamza Walker argued that these taboos do not apply to her images:

> If Walker's work is about anything, it is about shame or the lack thereof. In fact the work is shameless three times over, abandoning the historical shame surrounding slavery, the social shame surrounding stereotypes, and finally a bodily shame regarding sexual and excretory functions. Walker's characters are all too well aware that to speak of shame is to simultaneously speak of disgust, the overcoming of which is a prerequisite for sexual pleasure. The purposes of such illicit pleasure under the confines of slavery, however, become a rather dubious notion when the economy surrounding slavery is overlapped with that surrounding sex.
>
> (Walker 2000: 156)

Given that in the slave economy the masters' lusts made 'a gratification of their wicked desires profitable as well as pleasurable', as Frederick Douglas famously put it (Douglas 2000: 19), the eruption of libidinal interest that he noted in Walker's work renders sexual pleasure an erotic surplus beyond utilitarian ends. He linked this surplus specifically to Walker's tier of breast suckling women to the left of the scene in *The End of Uncle Tom and the Grand Allegorical Tableau of Eva in Heaven* (1995; Figure 10.2) with their implication of non-reproductive lesbian sexual pleasure that suggests similarities with a Bataillean or rather Sadean view of sexuality as a form of transgression.

Figure 10.2 Kara Walker *The End of Uncle Tom and the Grand Allegorical Tableau of Eva in Heaven* (1995) cut paper and adhesive on wall 15 × 35 feet, image courtesy of Sikemma Jenkins & Co.

However, Hamza Walker was also at pains to stress that pleasure as the locus of a certain bodily sovereignty does not in itself constitute power. One has to wonder then at the economy of visual pleasure that these tableaux convey, and the role of shame within that economy, given that they are depicted in a manner that encourages us to associate 'blackness' with defilement and disgust because of the contrast with whiteness that is part of the aesthetic form of the images.

When we look at Walker's installations the shimmering white walls place the symbolism of the 'white cube' at the forefront, although it is conventionally regarded as a neutral 'backdrop' bound up with a history of modernism that has emphasized the separation between art and the contingencies of everyday life. Brian O'Doherty has examined the way numerous artists in the twentieth century have disrupted this purity (O'Doherty 1986). The status of the walls as support makes explicit the contrast between the 'white' subjects of the silhouette and the white walls of the gallery; it implies that they are defiled by contact with 'blackness' and reiterate its associations with dirt, poverty, stupidity and savagery perpetuated in stereotypes. Thom Shaw's response to Walker's images came from an awareness that these historic associations between blackness and disgust are still operative. Attributing disgust to the 'black' slave body within the art world that prides itself on its liberal ideals might expose one to censure in the eyes of others. However, it is more likely to affect those who are already demonized because it exposes the degree to which they have internalized the legacy of slavery. Shame is reinforced by one's assigned position of 'lack' within an idealized symbolic order and the traumatic effects of being repeatedly reminded of that 'lack'. The shame that Walker's work generates is complex because it returns the spectator to a condition of abjection that reveals the inadequacies of a public rhetoric of racial pride. Its form seems to enact a shameful exposure of the historical romance and its popular dissemination in *Gone with the Wind* (1939) and other films and novels inspired by the antebellum South that are marked by a troubling nostalgia for the past.

Gone and the historical romance

In *Gone: A Historical Romance of a Civil War As It Occurred Between the Dusky Thighs Of One Young Negress and Her Heart* (1994) mass culture appears as a screen memory of slavery (Figures 10.3, 10.4, 10.5). The popularity of the film suggests the work of sublimation that screens over the historical facts of the Civil War and creates an idealized, illusory unity. The history of the US as a union of states lies in the abolition of slavery by the North and its resistance by the South. Abraham Lincoln's political will to make disparate states part of a unified whole might be understood to be subject to periodic traumatic events that return the nation-state to its earlier fragmentation. This trauma arguably lies behind the sublimation of hate into love in *Gone with the Wind*, drawn out in Walker's satirical references to the contemporary condition of the politics of race in the US. Joan Copjec adopts a similar reading of Walker's tableaux to account for their representation of a history in which the absence of the 'black' woman as a lacuna triumphantly returns as feminine jouissance (Copjec 2002: 82–107). This reading is compelling but as my study is concerned with the distance between reading the images as though they might be on a page and reading them as an oscillation between a phenomenological encounter with the object and a cognitive form of 'reading in' and 'reading as', I have adopted a different approach. Viewed from this perspective the 'black' slave body in *Gone* is turned into the 'objet petit a' – that for Lacan is 'the presence of a hollow, a void which can be occupied ... by any object' (Lacan 1994: 180) – as spectators attempt to assign categories of 'race' and 'gender' to what they see. Let us consider this further by examining competing interpretations of the tableau. Michelle Wallace offers the following:

> The scenario in *Gone* begins, as in nineteenth-century Southern melo-
> drama or an early silent film, with a nubile princess in hoop skirt under a
> mossy, moonlit tree. There is another set of legs, as though a youth were
> hiding under her skirts. She is leaning forward to kiss her gallant prince,

Figure 10.3 Kara Walker *Gone: A Historical Romance of a Civil War As It Occurred Between the Dusky Thighs Of One Young Negress and Her Heart* (detail, 1994) cut paper and adhesive on wall, 13 × 50 feet, image courtesy of Sikkema Jenkins & Co.

Figure 10.5 Kara Walker *Gone: A Historical Romance of a Civil War As It Occurred Between the Dusky Thighs Of One Young Negress and Her Heart* (detail, 1994) cut paper and adhesive on wall, 13 × 50 feet, image courtesy of Sikkema Jenkins & Co.

Figure 10.4 Kara Walker *Gone: A Historical Romance of a Civil War As It Occurred Between the Dusky Thighs Of One Young Negress and Her Heart* (detail, 1994) cut paper and adhesive on wall, 13 × 50 feet, image courtesy of Sikkema Jenkins & Co.

his sword pointed directly toward the derrière of an impish figure with devil's horns holding a swan by his broken neck on the bank of a body of water upon which floats a strange hybrid woman and boat. Behind her is an elegant, eighteenth century bust floating in the water.

We continue on to a mountain ridge with a little white boy whose hands reach skyward toward a little black male figure floating as the captive of a hugely inflated penis, while another little black boy kneels before him his mouth on the white boy's penis. Down the mountain ridge again, we find a Topsy figure with ragged braids whose legs are lifted to allow a series of foetuses to tumble from between them. Next comes a man in boots and spurs whose head is hidden under the ragged skirts of a slave woman with a broom. There are clouds, mountain ridges, and more trees. These are dreamscapes.

(Wallace 2003: 177–178)

The anxiety of fixing gendered and raced identities on to these figures appears in contested interpretations. For example, it was a surprise to me to read Wallace's description of the fellating figure (Figure 10.3) as a little black boy, where I had read it as a girl. Where Wallace described a gallant 'prince' I saw a confederate soldier, and so on. Similar differences in reading are evident when it comes to the image of Scarlett (Figure 10.4): Mark Reinhardt questioned her racial identity, though the 'sweep of her dress and the apparent gentility of her romantic encounter', he argued, might authorize her identity as a 'Southern belle'; when compared with the male she is 'studiedly ambiguous' – and might just as well be the Negress in the title (Reinhardt 2003: 113). Meaning becomes elusive and depends on a differential that remains internal to the scene; hence we assign identity by attempting to determine difference and similarity between 'Negro' and 'white'. Often it is clothing or the lack of it that is interpreted as indicative of the 'civilized' or 'brutish'. In his reflections on the scene's deployment of narrative convention Reinhardt began by reading it right to left but then corrected himself:

My conceit of panning rightwards was a response – conditioned by literary habit – to that absence or refusal. *Gone* is at once compellingly narrative and fundamentally disjointed: for all the microdramas one can construct among these images, and despite the title's promise of an overarching story, it is not certain whether the work enacts a sequence in which the same characters perform different scenes, or whether all that we see takes place in one spectacularly eventful moment.

(Reinhardt 2003: 112)

Space, identity, the order of events, all are left open to dispute and debate. There is no consensus on what one sees or how one makes meaning of it. The lure of reading race is so deeply embedded that it effectively directs most critical responses to narrative with its attendant emphasis on legibility. The outline of a silhouette seems to make explicit what we see, yet in Walker's hands it withholds knowledge, just as in the primal scene the child witnesses his parents having sex but does not understand what he sees. It is a kind of unknowing. It is at this point that Walker enters the history of slavery and makes its presence as a screen memory in mass culture evident – a point that Michelle Wallace seemed to recognize. She concluded her essay by pointing to the importance of seeing Walker's images in the gallery to gather 'the full impact of the environmental experience' because of the complexity of her images that, she stated, 'are far in advance of the narratives. The artist is outstripping the writer' (Wallace 2003: 179). The structures of narrative in the novel and cinema are sequential but here questions of scale and of positioning determine what immediately occupies our visual attention and what is relatively hidden. Likewise, the condition of being lured into the process of determining meaning when seeing the images in reproduction render the white spaces between them an absence so unremarkable because they are so ubiquitous. Examining these scenes in the space of the gallery is a different matter. Up close the position of the 'Prissy' figure comes down to the edge of the wall as it meets the floor (Figure 10.5), we become aware of the way that the framing of the scene is dramatically truncated by the side of the image, the far right-hand side seems to be abruptly cut off (Figure 10.1). The spectator has to negotiate the object-hood of these forms before the process of 'reading' a narrative can even begin. Our initial attempts at interpretation are confused by the conflation of sequence, events occurring one after another, with the simultaneity of seeing in a single glance, typical of paintings. The boundaries of the image that we strain to interpret as either 'white' or 'black' are marked by the contrasts of opaque black paper, dense and obdurate in its lack of reflections, texture or shading. The texture and layered surface of the image, the play between mark and surface as figure and ground that is commonplace in the 'expressive' forms of painting, figurative or abstract, is absent here. Instead the expanses of shimmering, hard, white surfaces bounce light off them and away from the black paper, catching the spectators' shadows in the spotlights. There is a splitting and doubling so that the lighting of the walls diverts our attention from the actual images, and the attempt to make meaning of them diverts us from their institutional frame. When we come up close and they refuse to yield themselves to our curiosity, we become aware of the deadness of their hard, black, inexpressive surface and our attention turns once again to the walls. The ceiling and floor become significant spaces that frame the wall and the work hanging on it, creating the sense of an 'inverted' world reflected in the highly polished surfaces of the floors. The cinematic aspects of the scene suggest a screen but the absence of perspective and realist space draw attention to the status of a surface that destroys any illusion of mimesis. In this respect it draws on the legacy of minimalism and particularly the way Frank Stella's early black paintings changed the nature of the white cube. Consider, for example, Brian O'Doherty's description of Frank Stella's canvases in New York, that 'powerfully activated the wall; the eye frequently went searching tangentially for the wall's limits' (O'Doherty 1986: 29):

> Flatness, edge, format, and wall had an unprecedented dialogue in that small, uptown Castelli space. As they were presented, the works hovered between an ensemble effect and independence. The hanging there was as revolutionary as the paintings; since the hanging was part of the esthetic, it evolved simultaneously with the pictures. The breaking of the rectangle formally confirmed the wall's autonomy, altering for good the concept of the gallery space. Some of the mystique of the shallow picture plane (one of the three major forces that altered the gallery space) had been transferred to the context of art.
>
> (O'Doherty 1986: 29)

The fracturing of the shallow picture plane and the shift between an ensemble effect and a sense of each element's independence seem to accord with Reinhardt's attention to the way the scene in *Gone* refuses any coherent sense of pictorial composition. The displacement of mystique from the image to the wall indicated in O'Doherty's description of Stella's work is continued in the splitting between the shining white walls and the monochromatic outlines in *Gone*. Unlike Stella who emphasized the literalness of the object and denied the desire to seek out expressive forms, the role of the unconscious in Walker's work suggests that she is concerned with how meaning emerges from what we don't see as much as from what we do see.

Abjection and the 'black' female body

The competing readings of *Gone* indicate the degree to which the empirical identification of 'race' is a lure for the categories 'black' and 'white', 'male' and 'female'. Spectators of Walker's work are seduced into an unconscious need to fix identity and inadvertently secure a hierarchy of difference within the realm of the symbolic. Walker's scene makes the antebellum South as the site of 'white' nostalgia evident in her attention to the landscape setting, the formation of trees, a mountain ridge, a moon/sun cut by a passing cloud, etc. The central position is taken up by the mountain ridge and the hyper-visible act of fellatio and the floating, monstrously testicled figure. The displacement of Scarlett to the side of the drama inaugurates a complex reading of similarity and difference in relation to 'whiteness' as idealized femininity, and 'blackness' as debased and yet also an object of desire and therefore a site of ambivalence.

Turning briefly to *Gone with the Wind* (1939) and its narrative structure one might argue that it functions as a screen memory which circulates between nostalgia and desire in which the figure of the 'mammy' signifies or embodies a form of restoration. Her potentially dangerous sexuality is neutralized and displaced on to the figure of Scarlett who is predatory, fiery and narcissistic. Much of the narrative that circulates over her girlish crush on Ashley and repulsion of Rhett's advances is directed by her inability to control the less gentle aspects of her womanhood. She is never quite as selfless, loving or modest as Melanie. Her shrewish manner and taming by Rhett Butler in a key scene when he picks her up and takes her to their bedroom was the focus for posters of the film and the one moment of the scene when an unbridled sexuality is on display. The cliché of the romantic couple is given a frisson by this display of masculine control of an untameable nature that sexualizes and genders the Civil War as a taming of the South by the North. The fantasy of masculine/Northern mastery over feminine/Southern savagery in *Gone with the Wind* could easily be altered to replace its preoccupation with white uncontrolled femininity with 'blackness' as savagery, were it not for the abject associations of black womanhood with disgust, defilement and pollution that perhaps explains, in Walker's interpretation of the film, why the silhouette of Scarlett is displaced from the centre of the narrative to its side.

This displacement foregrounds the pornography that marks the couple's contact, as though some truth is being exposed. One wonders if this is the only kind of intimacy that a collective consciousness can imagine between 'black' women and 'white' men: one that is pornographic and debases 'black' women. Pornography fragments the unity of the body into a series of part-objects, a splitting between and within the object of the drive and the love object. This splitting establishes a distinction between 'self' and 'other' but it is an illusory separation that abjection shatters. The conflation between people and objects is systematic throughout Walker's work; let's return, for example, to the figure fellating the 'upstanding' man on the mountain ridge. The formal play of the image encourages us to make associations between the open mouth fastened to the penis and the open-lipped vessel behind the male figure, the two bound by the echo of the handle and the kneeling figure's arm as if in symmetry. The monstrously testicled figure suspended in the upper parts of the tableau appears to be the object of the young man's imploring gesture. His grotesquely inflated testicles offering a sadistic pun on the hyper-masculinity attributed to the 'black' male is the only means of identifying his 'race'. The boat-woman bobbing along the water echoes the girl from whose skirts babies fall; these are all containers of one kind or another that can be sat in and rowed, poured into, or tipped to draw from. The figures to the extreme right recur again and again in Walker's images; men penetrating, hollowing out black women's bodies, as though to empty them but in a manner that negates the use of orifices for sexual pleasure. They become simply points of entry and exit.

In this work and in others, Walker is drawing on the obsessive depiction of the 'Negro' in numerous 'black face' objects. Many of them were in mass circulation as advertisements for products like maple syrup, flour, rice, coffee – in other words food to be ingested – and were obsessively preoccupied with 'mammies' and 'Aunt Jemimas'. A ceramic teapot fashioned to appear as the body of an 'Aunt Jemima', with a phallic spout positioned where her huge breasts might be; a tube of maple syrup fashioned to resemble her body that one squeezes to release the syrup; 'mammies' and 'Aunt Jemimas' fashioned to appear like biscuit tins that can be opened and used as containers. The African American Janette Faulkner amassed a collection of these objects at a time when they were no longer mass produced on the same scale and had become souvenirs. An analysis of these objects can be found in catalogue essays that accompanied an exhibition of the collection. In the Introduction Robbin Henderson remarked that although they 'represent' the 'Negro' they evoke the dominant consciousness that created them (Henderson 1982: 12). There is a sadomasochism latent in their forms that I have explored elsewhere (Malik 2006: 56–58) but the complexity of assigning to them a white or black consciousness does not entirely explain how they have been transformed from objects of use to souvenirs, nor why Faulkner, and Walker on a more modest scale, might wish to collect them (Corris and Hobbs 2003: 428). Susan Stewart has examined the importance of nostalgia in the habits of the collector and the appeal of souvenirs that appear to convey a certain 'exoticism' (Stewart 2003: 147). Extending this analysis to these objects one could argue that they indicate a desire for restoration, as a fantasy of oral plenitude that is latent in the nostalgia for the antebellum era of slavery and the plantation as the site of a picturesque America. It is this that establishes their appeal as souvenirs in which the potentially engulfing mother is domesticated as container. In Walker's images they appear to be displaced into pornographic and grotesque images that, through sexuality and humour, seem to be aimed at a defence against incorporation of the self into the other: a defence that is directed by an ongoing attempt to distance ourselves from a primary repression of the mother's body.

Kristeva's theorization of abjection relocates Lacan's 'objet petit a' from the symbolic to the prelinguistic movement of energies and affects that she terms the 'semiotic chora'. It is here that the abject pulverizes the subject and lures it back into the space where there appears to be no differentiation between self and other. The potency of abjection as a strategy for artistic transgression lies partly in the fragility and archaic nature of its sublimation. It is constantly under threat of dissolution; it cannot sustain the binding of the drives that constitutes an object, be it in a sign-system or the image, as it is always in a state of near disintegration and collapse because of its semantic and temporal proximity to the mother's body. There are two aspects in which the abject confronts us with its fragility and archaic form. First, the associations with animals, Kristeva argues, results in the separation between culture and nature, most visible in so-called 'primitive' societies that demarcate a space distancing man from animals and animalism, which are viewed as threatening in their status as representatives of sex and murder. The second of these is what she describes as 'a personal archaeology' that is the earliest attempts of the infant to release the hold of the maternal 'even before existing outside of her' (Kristeva 1982: 13). In this scenario the mother's absence within the symbolic realm and her problems with it does not enable or further the infant's reluctant departure from 'the natural mansion' (Kristeva 1982: 13). The close combat between mother and child results eventually in the pursuit of a reluctant struggle against what was earlier the mother but now becomes abject, because it must be repelled and rejected. However, this rejection of the mother is also a repelling and rejecting of the self because it predates the entry of the symbolic signified by the father. The importance of abjection lies then in its emphasis on a stage prior to that moment when the human subject is formed as an 'I'. Kristeva regarded this later moment as a mimesis whereby the 'I' is fashioned in accordance with the third element in the triadic structure and what was once the 'mother' is turned into the abject. Abjection threatens the illusion of the civilized 'I'. Later in her argument she turned to Freud's 'Analysis of a Phobia in a Five Year Old Boy' (1909); bringing together these two instances of abjection she indicated the presence of animalism in so-called 'civilized' society. Where Freud interpreted little Hans's phobia of horses as a disguised castration anxiety, because the child's witnessing of the primal scene had made his mother's lack of a penis evident, Kristeva saw a link between this fear and the semiotic. She argued that Hans's fear of horses was striking in its parallel with his ability to master language and concluded that the phobia was a hieroglyph that condensed all fears because it brought the nameable 'horse' into contact with 'that conglomerate of fear, deprivation, and nameless frustration, which properly speaking belongs to the unnameable' (Kristeva 1982: 35). Where Lacan might see the phobia of horses as the 'objet petit a' that signalled the presence of the real and the missed encounter with death, Kristeva drew attention to the normalization of phobia in the analytical situation that privileged the Oedipal stage in accordance with Freud's own subject position. For Kristeva then the metaphor of 'to be afraid of horses' was not indicative of castration anxiety but a *drive economy in want of an object*. It was symbolization that was missing:

Metaphor of want as such, phobia bears the marks of the frailty of the subject's signifying system. It must be perceived that such a metaphor is inscribed not in verbal rhetoric but in the heterogeneity of the psychic system that is made up of drive presentations *and* thing presentations linked to word presentations. The infancy of little Hans does not entirely explain the frailty of the signifying system that forces metaphor to turn into drive and conversely. One must also conclude, and phobic adults confirm this, that within the symbolic law accruing to the function of the father, something remains blurred in the Oedipal triangle constituting the subject. Does Hans's father not play a bit too much the role of the mother whom he thrusts into the shadows? Does he not overly seek surety of the professor? If phobia is a metaphor that has mistaken its place, forsaking language for drive and sight, it is because a father does not hold his own, be he the father of the subject or the father of its mother.

(Kristeva 1982: 35)

Abjection, idealization and rereading *Gone*

Kristeva's attention to the fragility of signifying subject marked by the phobia as a metaphor of want, allows us to understand how 'blackness' signifies as a void, or 'lack', a site of absence for 'whiteness' that also then desires it (Figure 10.6). The phenomenological encounter with Walker's silhouettes occupies a parallel vacillation in symbolization that is constantly under threat of dissolution, of becoming simply a blurring that exposes the presence of a drive economy, as things, surfaces, black holes. The outlines of the fellating couple on the mountain ridge depend on our 'filling in' what is essentially a single surface of black paper that brings together different components that our imaginations separate out from each other; the vessel, a standing figure and a young 'girl'. Placing a desire within the spectator to fashion meaning from absence, or materiality from what is in effect a void, is perhaps what links Walker's silhouettes most closely to a psychoanalytic framework. Leon Wurmser's writings on shame appear to be significant here. He has argued that one of the striking aspects of shame is that the subject who experiences it is often overcome by the desire to disappear, to be swallowed up by a hole in the ground (Wurmser 1987). Shame, then, activates a desire to erase the self that is felt to be an object of contempt by others. That erasure is not possible

Figure 10.6 Kara Walker *Gone: A Historical Romance of a Civil War As It Occurred Between the Dusky Thighs Of One Young Negress and Her Heart* (detail, 1994) cut paper and adhesive on wall, 13 × 50 feet, image courtesy of Sikkema Jenkins & Co.

when we look at Walker's images because of the scale of figures, some of them in the foreground, which are often larger than life size and at odds with the sources of these silhouettes in small portraits of nobility or a middle class aspiring to aristocratic good taste. Even the book illustrations that inspired Walker to use the silhouette bring to mind the act of private contemplation. We cannot, when faced with their scale and their location, shut them up, make them disappear. The shamelessness of these images comes from their refusal to be diminished in size and to occupy a private imagination in the book that has habitually been the locus for pornography and the silhouette as illustration.

The scale of the body when enlarged can take on either monumental or grotesque forms, the line of the silhouette defines either elegance or criminality, the slightest cut in paper can indicate nobility or savagery. The proximity between 'black' and 'white' requires a shared imaginary space that results in the enlargement of this grotesque body which is at odds with its psychical containment as an object of possession, that draws out the fantasy of penetration evident in the many spoons, teapots, cookie jars, ashtrays, salt cellars, etc. fashioned to resemble the 'coon', the mammy, the sambo, minstrel or tar baby. We can transform images of a small scale into imagined actions, attribute personalities and desire to them; but in large scale they become frozen and resist our attempts to internalize them in our fantasies. We have to enter into theirs, and in doing so we inhabit a paradoxical condition of passivity and aggression that enacts a sadomasochism in the act of viewing, propelled by the assumptions, desires, prejudices that Walker's spectators bring to the images. This animation is arrested when their forms loom over the spectator's body; at this point they assume a deadening quality. In other words, one can only see these images if one is already participating in the scenarios that energize dead matter into frenzied actions. There is, then, a participation of the African American subject in scenes of shameless excess that requires his or her own subjugation. This, arguably, is the truly scandalous nature of these images. Thom Shaw's response to the images as stereotypical and hurtful drew on their scale as a considerable factor in their shameful affect. Such associations rely on the history of these consumer and decorative objects that historically have naturalized the debasement of African Americans.

Kristeva's attention to the symbolic order as a form of semantic control goes some way to drawing out these aspects of Walker's practice. Little Hans's fear of being bitten by horses is an introjection of the desire to bite that allays the sense of a threat from some unnameable source outside the subject. The phobic, or rather counter-phobic, projections that created the collectible and unthreatening 'black face' objects, and particularly those of the 'mammy' or 'Aunt Jemima', indicate a fantasy of incorporation as an attempt to escape a corresponding fear – hence the many objects that are associated with the consumption of food. However, abjection lies in the persistence of fear even after this incorporation, of holding on to some aspect of

the 'black' mother's body, her breast, for example, because it comes at the
same moment as paternal prohibition. Consequently abjection is also constituted by a second defensive manoeuvre directed at this third, paternal agent,
who is imagined to be devouring the subject. One might conclude from this
that fear of the freed slave, despite the many phobic projections into objects
that can be contained, possessed, held or consumed, fails to be successfully
neutralized by the white subject. Kristeva views these as unsuccessful
attempts to circumvent anxiety, but never suggests (like Freud's view of the
Oedipus complex), that these fears are 'normal'. Fear remains irrational but it
comes to be associated with a liminal point whereby the subject lays just
inside the interior of the phobic other from which it sees itself; an impossible
position that threatens dissolution and disintegration of both subject and
object. One might call this process *projective disidentification*. Within the
fraught racial dynamics of the US this impossible position of liminality is
played out in the horror of miscegenation within the dominant consciousness. The 'blurring' that Kristeva identified in the Oedipal triangle might
equally lie in the child witness's suspicion that his birth lies in the transgression of racial purity: the 'black' slave woman is the mother to whom the slave
master 'daddy' seems to be doing strange things. The child witness's unknowing memory of the primal scene is saturated by the imaginary filling in of
what is not known, much like the viewer whose phobias fill up these silhouettes. Within the collective 'white' psyche it is the 'black' slave mother who
has been thrown into the shadows and it is she, more so than the father, that
cannot be assigned a form and who exists as an unnameable void behind her
phobic and counter-phobic projections. This is the condition of her ongoing
erasure from the symbolic law.

I would argue that the blurring of meaning does not take on an aesthetic
form in Walker's images but it is what happens to the spectator who is placed
within a vector of representation that draws on the tableau, narrative and
their cinematic associations. Her attention to a formal rhythm in the juxta-
position of different objects encourages debased associations but through
forms that are lyrical and rhythmic. In *Gone* Scarlett's 'blackness' is disguised
by her proximity to the 'prince'. Hence the gentility of the sweep of her skirt
or the flow of her hair encourages us to read her according to a template of
eighteenth-century silhouettes that linked civility with Graeco-Roman culture and by association with whiteness. The nobility of the 'prince' might
accord with a template of good character first set out in the eighteenth
century by Johann Casper Lavater in his *Physiognomy* (1775–8) and based on
the ideal of Graeco-Roman busts of emperors, which became the ego-ideal of
Euro-American masculinity. Hence the bust bobbing improbably along the
surface of the lake. The strange action of a child with horned plaits strangling
a swan may also have neoclassical associations (Figure 10.6). The swan
is part of Greek mythology as a disguised appearance of Zeus, famously
in the example of *Leda and the Swan*, and is also a symbol of monarchy,

while the child could easily be a reference to Pan. The devil appears in numerous African American folk tales as a trickster figure and God as the no-good slave master, while Brer Rabbit's wily tactics indicate that the metaphor of animalism is viewed as subversive and heroic rather than debased. The sense that there is a formal 'echo', a reverberation between the open-mouthed fellating figure and the vessel opposite it, also comes from a tradition of deploying classical motifs as markers of antiquity, such that the vessel becomes a classical urn, as in the example of Keat's famous ode:

> 'Beauty is truth, truth beauty', – that is all
> Ye know on earth, and all ye need to know.
>
> (Keats, 'Ode on a Grecian Urn', 1820: st. 5)

Yet what we see is entirely discomforting as a truth of beauty, either in art or in the human form, 'black' or 'white'. The force of abjection in art practice lies, I would argue, in this displacement of disgust from the culturally despised to the realm of the idealized.

The tendency to view abjection in contemporary art in images of the body as an object turned inside out, or that in other ways evokes fluids that signal the body's porousness, such as urine, blood or excrement, links Walker to McCarthy and Kelley. But this context is also problematic because it is based on an art historical methodology that privileges iconography rather than affect, on what can be seen rather than what happens between the object and different spectators. Perhaps for this reason psychoanalysis as a critical tool is best applied to excavating the conditions of spectatorship, and in this context the affective responses of spectators to images that provoke shame.

In the mid-1990s such subversions of neoclassical forms had considerable critical purchase given the rise of a conservative backlash reifying notions of quality that were seen to be under threat by minoritarian, i.e. gay, black and feminist issue-based art. The appeal to beauty as the terrain for this return to quality and a Kantian view of a shared humanist public sphere was played out in ambivalent ways in the art world. On the one hand it was directed by the celebration of the fashion industry in the museum, on the other it drew from the affective force of what seemed to be abject images. Dave Hickey's defence of Robert Mapplethorpe's photographs was on the grounds that otherwise explicitly sexual, even pornographic content was married to seductive gelatin silverprints that appealed to a conventional understanding of the aesthetic. It was this troubling double register, he argued, that made these photographs of gay sexuality so controversial (Hickey 1993: 21–22). Hickey's argument was to some extent drawn from the classical forms in which the 'black' body was posed in *The Black Book*, to resemble Graeco-Roman statues that, Kobena Mercer argued, constituted a form of elevation of its otherwise debased associations with savagery and licentious sexuality (Mercer 1994: 200). The figure of Scarlett indicates the concealment of one identity within another that changes the symbolic meaning of *Gone* so that what is at first a scene created by a pornographic imagination becomes a series of visual conceits that elevate the spectator but also draw out the libidinal aspects of a so-called disinterested aesthetic.

Conclusion

In conclusion we can argue that shame mobilizes an economy of visual pleasure whereby within the space of phantasy, economic and symbolic exchange collapse and return the spectator to the perverse nature of slavery as an institution. The endless reproduction of children is hinted at in the figure of a girl dropping babies from her skirts in *Gone*. In these scenes capitalist reproduction of objects of consumption are returned to their source in sexuality, ensuring a system that in effect reproduced its own labour power and depended economically on the disavowal of kinship. The construction of 'black face' objects allowed fantasies of penetration and ingestion of the 'black' captive body to continue in a domesticated symbolic form. Their large scale resist and complicate those fantasies and by tethering together 'black' and 'white' Walker's silhouettes bring together two orders of the simulacrum, the idealized portrait and the debased 'blackface' that have habitually been kept apart. In the process they activate prejudices and desires by cloaking what we see in a form that prompts projective identification, deploying the sadistic humour of satire as a means of shaming and exposing the liberal claims of the 'spectator'.

References

Bowles, J. (1997) 'Extreme times call for extreme heroes', *International Review of African American Art* 14 (3): 3–16.

Copjec, J. (2002) *Imagine There's No Woman: Ethics and Sublimation*, Cambridge, MA and London: MIT Press.

Corris, M. and Hobbs, R. (2003) 'Reading black through white in the work of Kara Walker', *Art History* 26 (3): 422–441.

Dixon, T. (1905) *Clansman: An Historical Romance of the Ku Klux Klan*, reprinted, edited, abridged and with introduction by C. D. Wintz, New York: Armonk/London: M. E. Sharpe, 2001.

Douglass, F. (2001) *Narrative of the Life of Frederick Douglass, An American Slave: Written by Himself*, Newhaven, CT: Yale University Press.

Dubois, W. E. B. (1904) *The Souls of Black Folk*, eds R. Gooding-Williams and D. Blight, New York: St Martins Press, 1997.

Dubois Shaw, G. (2004) *Speaking the Unspeakable: The Art of Kara Walker*, Durham and London: Duke University Press.

Fanon, F. (1986) *Black Skin, White Masks*, London: Pluto Press.

Foster, H. (1996) *The Return of the Real: The Avant-Garde At the End of The Twentieth Century*, Cambridge, MA and London: MIT Press.

Freud, S. (1909) 'Analysis of a phobia of a five year old boy', S.E. 10.

Golden, T. (2002) 'Thelma Golden/Kara Walker, a dialogue', in R. Reid-Pharr and K. Walker *Kara Walker: Pictures From Another Time*, Michigan: University of Michigan and Ann Arbor.

Hannaham, J. (1998) 'Pea, ball, bounce', *Interview* November: 114–119.

Henderson, R. (1982) 'Introduction', in R. Henderson, P. Fabry and D. Miller (eds) *Ethnic Notions, Black Images in the White Mind: An Exhibition of Afro-American Stereotype and Caricature from the Collection of Janette Faulkner*, Berkeley, CA: Berkeley Art Centre.

Hickey, D. (1993) *The Invisible Dragon: Four Essays on Beauty*, Los Angeles: Art Issues Press.

Keats, J. (1820) 'Ode on a Grecian Urn', in *The Poems of John Keats*, J. Stillinger ed., London: Heinemann, 1978.

Kristeva, J. (1982) *The Powers of Horror: An Essay on Abjection*, trans. L. S. Roudiez, New York: Columbia University Press.

Lacan, J. (1994) *The Four Fundamental Concepts of Psychoanalysis*, trans. J.-A. Miller, Harmondsworth: Penguin.

Malik, A. (2006) 'History in the present', in J. Connarty and J. Lanyon (eds) *Ghostings: The Role of the Archive within Contemporary Artists' Film and Video*, Bristol and Cardiff: Picture This and the Arts Council.

Mercer, K. (1995) 'Busy in the ruins of wretched phantasia', in F. Ragnar (ed.) *Mirage, Enigmas of Race, Difference and Desire*, London: ICA.

O'Doherty, B. (1986) *Inside The White Cube: The Ideology of the Gallery Space*, Santa Monica: Lapis Press.

Penwarden, C. (1995) 'Of word and flesh: An interview with Julia Kristeva', in S. Morgan and F. Morris (eds) *Rites of Passage: Art for the End of the Century*, London: Tate Gallery Publishing.

Reinhardt, M. (2003) 'The art of racial profiling', in I. Berry, D. English, V. Patterson and M. Reinhardt (eds) *Kara Walker: Narratives of A Negress*, Cambridge, MA and London: MIT Press.

Saltz, J. (1996) 'Ill-will and desire', *Flash Art* 191: 82–86.

Stewart, S. (2003) *On Longing, Narratives of the Miniature, The Gigantic, The Souvenir and the Collection*, Durham and London: Duke University Press.

Vance, C. (1999) 'The war on culture', in V. Wallis, M. Weems and P. Yenawine (eds) *Art Matters: How the Culture Wars Changed America*, New York: New York University Press.

Walker, H. (2000) 'Nigger lover, or will there be any black people in utopia', *Parkett* 59: 152–158.

Wallace, M. (2003) 'The enigma of the negress Kara Walker', in I. Berry, D. English, V. Patterson and M. Reinhardt (eds) *Kara Walker: Narratives of A Negress*, Cambridge, MA and London: MIT Press.

Wurmser, L. (1987) 'Shame: The veiled companion of narcissism', in D. L. Nathason (ed.) *The Many Faces of Shame*, London and New York: Guilford Press.

Chapter 11

Stain

Pennina Barnett

An ink stain on cloth is annoying, but not devastating. Others simply think you careless. A food stain embarrasses, a slippage to the infantile. But with blood or sweat – you blush with shame. It's curious that a stain causes such distress. (Why not simply turn away?) This chapter explores the relationship between cloth, body and stain through the works of three artists, Maria Chevska, Verdi Yahooda and Anne Wilson, who at different times and in different ways have taken stained cloth as their focus. What interests me is the intimate nature of cloth and its implication of the absent body. For if 'skin is where we find ourselves' (Porges 2001: 22) then cloth etymologically that which clings to the body (Kuryluk 1991: 179), becomes a second skin, a metaphor for the layer between ourselves and others.

The stain is commonplace, always there. Chevska, Yahooda and Wilson share a concern with the everyday, cloth as a material record of daily rhythm, gesture, habit, action and interaction. Questions of gender are referenced through the domestic: napkins, quilts, tablecloths – textiles of one sort or another. Returning art to its bare skin, revealing the naked substance of canvas – cloth stretched across wood – this has been the claim of Modernism. But it is also a feminine act. Cloth in the work of Chevska, Yahooda and Wilson doesn't fuss: it just *is*. Yet it becomes charged, urgent; its focus on detail: the edge, the surface, the fragment – the localized. In this their work reflects a postmodern approach, rather than totalising master narratives (Doy 2002: 8). The fragment is witness to a broken whole, a site of loss; yet also a place from which to start over. The edge is of boundary. And the surface? It too is boundary, always boundary. It returns us to skin, cloth and the double coded affect of the stain.

The absorption of liquid into a solid, into fabric, means that as the stain enters the texture of its support they become one (Didi-Huberman 1984: 69). If meaning rests on clarity, wrapping things up in discrete binary parcels – this is wet (liquid), but that is dry (solid); this is my blood, thick and reddy brown, but that is cloth, soft and porous; this comes from inside of me, but that lies outside of me – then the stain is indeterminate. Simultaneously both, its ambiguity confounds, disturbs, yet also fascinates.

In working towards an understanding of this affect, the concept of the abject, as formulated by psychoanalyst Julia Kristeva (1982) may offer some clues. Kristeva considers why body fluids, such as blood, mucous, saliva, semen, excreta, attract our attention and curiosity, yet elicit horror and disgust. These *abjects* leak, flow and dribble from the nose, mouth, genitals, anus, the orifices that mark inside and outside. 'Food, not yet the body is taken in through the mouth. Faeces, no longer the body, is expelled through the anus' (Oliver 1993: 57), neither part of our bodies, nor quite separate from them, from us. Blood, saliva, excreta. This is the precondition of material existence. The abject a composite, both border and in-between, marking the site of life itself.

Boundaries are what define us, give us identity, separate us from others: me from you, self from other. Without boundary, identity fails. Oliver (1993: 57) argues that the prototypal abject experience is that of birth itself: 'Before the umbilical chord is cut, who can decide whether there is one or two?' However, the formulation of the abject is focused on the mother–infant dyad, the state of symbiosis and dependence before the infant acquires language. Here, at one with the mother in an imaginary fullness, the infant is caught in a shifting field of libidinal forces and drives which lap across it,[1] and is governed by primary processes, predominantly oral and anal. It is in an abject relation to the maternal body, not yet able to separate from her, yet with a precarious and emerging grasp of its own identity and bodily boundaries; and the ever-present threat of being sucked back into the liquid, fleshy maternal body from which it came and of which it was part. The process of separation and individuation from the mother involves, in Kristeva's account, 'a mapping of the clean and proper body'[2] of the child; thus an expulsion of what is considered unclean and impure underlies the construction of subjectivity. In order to become autonomous, to make the break – to choose life – it rejects the maternal body, and turns it into an 'abject'. The abject then is less a quality or description, but a relationship of boundary, with the ever-present threat of dissolution. To make the break involves relinquishing the imaginary fullness of the mother–child dyad, and is thus accompanied by pain and loss. The affect of the stain – its pull–push, drawing yet repulsing – might in this context be conceptualized as an echo, or memory trace of that loss, of the psychic pain of separation.

Shame is the psychological process that reveals and hides the self in relation to the other. At the very moment we become the most vulnerable, we also become the most visible. We blush. The shame of it; our instinct to cover our faces. The artworks I discuss exploit the curious capacity of cloth and the stain to both hide and conceal. Ewa Kuryluk in this brief passage identifies the relationship between cloth, body and shame on the one hand, and subjectivity and identity on the other:

In Judaism, the original, embryonic condition of nakedness is likened to innocence in paradise, a heavenly womb, where Adam and Eve are united with divinity and thus do not perceive themselves as individuals. Clothing symbolizes the separation from God – the birth-exile into the world – and the beginning of reflection.

(Kuryluk 1991: 183)

Plucking fruit from the tree of knowledge, they knew they were naked, they knew shame. Covering symbolizes knowledge of the body, of sex, and of the self as a separate being. It also signals identity, independence and free will. So it is that individuation and separation permeate this text on the stained cloth. But it is boundary, above all, that is the recurrent theme.

Perpetua

In German, *das mal, malen*, and the Polish *malarz* share the same Latin root. The first designates a stain, mark, or sign; the second, to paint; the third, a painter – their shared derivation *macula*: a mark, stain or mole (Kuryluk 1991: 180). How apt this seems to Maria Chevska's series of paired mono-chrome paintings entitled *Books* (see Figure 11.1, colour plate section). These form part of *Perpetua* (1994), an installation of three parts that also includes *Cloaks* (eight latex sheets which hang from pegs on a wall), and *Blue Mono-chromes* (five large blue canvases). Square, minimal and seemingly abstract, *Books* appear at first little more than stained surfaces, some dribbled with paint. The right-hand panels, with their soft, uneven discoloration of fabric – some of them quilted – have a ghostly presence produced by dripping, soak-ing and pouring paint on to the back of the material, and letting it seep through to the front – 'a seepage that at times evokes both the bloodstained bandages of the dead Christ removed from the cross and the leakage of menstrual blood,'[3] an effect that emphasizes the very materiality of the cloth.

The paired down 'imagery' of these paintings produces an intensity – a case of less is more. The stain here, like a monochrome blush, suggests vulner-ability brought to the surface, a shameful exposure. Shame is experienced psychically and in our bodies. Blood rushes to the face, the neck. In order to see a stain or blush, we need to be close by, close up, sensitive to the other. Shame makes us want to look away, to hide from that proximity. But here, in *Perpetua*, vulnerability, humility, humanity look us in the face. Not proudly, but quietly, as if to say: that's how it is. 'Shame,' writes Elspeth Probyn, 'demands that big questions be asked in a modest way' (2005: xviii).

The corporeal qualities of these paintings are evoked in the title of the installation of which they are a part: Perpetua was a medieval martyr who prayed for the endurance of the flesh. It also refers to the name of a typeface designed by Eric Gill in the 1920s. This reference to writing is not accidental, just as the marks on some of the paintings are not as random as they might first appear. For these stains are written rather than painted – each canvas 'spelling out' three words beginning with the letter f: faithful, fickle, forget; flaunt, flirt, flinch; feckless, fake, fungal; fine, fatal, fondle. They contain an energy that disrupts, that oscillates between the verbal and the visual, permeating the very stuff, the material itself. Words have been a recurrent feature in Chevska's work, representing an urgency in the desire to communicate; yet she is aware that they can distort and fall short. Michael Archer[4] writes that Chevska refers, in her notes for these works, to the French writer Hélène Cixous, for whom the visual and verbal qualities of certain letters are significant:

> F is the letter that burns ('fait feu'), although its power is, of course, not a straightforward one. Each of Chevska's triads of f-words marks the inevitable gap between desire for connection between people and the compromised way in which that is played out, between eternal and absolute quantities of an ideal coupling and the partial, contingent and doomed nature of its realisation.

This has resonances with Probyn's notion of shame, as that which 'illuminates our intense attachment to the world, our desire to be connected with others, and the knowledge that, as merely human, we will sometimes fail in our attempts to maintain those connections' (2005: 14). Counterintuitive though it might seem, shame she argues, is positive. It is how the body registers interest; blushing its inscription, its way of calling out.

In one of Chevska's pale quilted panels, three rows of fine calligraphic marks float upon a grey anthropomorphic stain, which itself rests on or beneath a transparent 'water mark', its brown circular edges spreading to the very boundary of the painting. To suggest a likeness to Mary Kelly's *Post Partum Document*, where (in)famously the stained nappies of her infant son were displayed, might seem an affront to the haunting, poetic quality of Chevska's work. Yet Kelly's mapping of the phases of the child's development, from liquids to solids, sounds to words, home to nursery, as he moves into the world, remains in my mind. But while Kelly offers a direct commentary on maternal experience, with an excess of words, Chevska remains, if not silent, then reticent. Yet in her tonal marks and stains, with their blanks and absences, where the trace of words simultaneously offer yet close down meaning, we might perhaps detect traces of the semiotic, persistent, refusing to leave.

The *semiotic*, a term formulated by Kristeva,[5] is the raw material of language: its basic sounds, rhythms, inflections. It is associated with the mother–child dyad or union, which she calls the *semiotic chora*, and is likened to a receptacle or 'holding space'. Derived from the Greek, *semiotic* suggests a mark or trace, while *chora*, an enclosed space or womb. The semiotic is the register of the preverbal, where exchange between mother and infant is through sound – the rhythmic pattern of the voice, its texture and tone; and through gesture, smell and touch in all their complexities and variation. The semiotic is distinguished from the symbolic in Kristeva's writing,[6] that is from the sphere of 'law' (that which regulates), language and exchange or social relations. The symbolic takes the raw stuff of the semiotic, gives it form, order, solidity, and makes it 'mean'. She argues that in order to enter the symbolic, as we must, this 'other' of language is repressed. If we did not agree to lose the mother, Kristeva argues, we could neither name nor imagine her (1989: 41). For her to be represented, she must be relinquished, so that we may recover her in language. But the repression is only partial, for the semiotic seeps through, reverberating as a pulsational pressure, a liquidity within the symbolic. It is there in rhythm, repetition, alliteration; in that which disrupts language and sense: dissonance, fragmentation, contradiction, meaninglessness; in decomposition of form; and through gaps, silence and absence. Is this the melancholic imprint that Chevska presents? Her canvases minimal, paint and cloth barely disguised or mediated.

Cloth with Three Drops of Blood

The blood, you see, was not casually spilled. The mother took a knife to her finger and as the blood released, let three full drops fall on to a cloth, a white handkerchief. She handed it to her daughter. The girl was ready to leave, and what else could she do to protect her from what might lie ahead? The burden of parenthood.

There's an image by artist Verdi Yahooda that has stayed with me over time. It is called *Cloth with Three Drops of Blood* (1989; Figure 11.2) Its wide calico border is covered with dressmaking pins. Seen from a distance, they make an abstract almost decorative pattern. A wall piece, it measures nearly two metres high and a metre and a half wide. Big enough to envelop us. Inside the border hangs a large monochrome photograph. It has something of the uncanniness of the still life: *nature morte*, where everyday objects become a meditation on the fleeting nature of life. A crumpled, highly textured cloth forms both backdrop and foreground. Light falls diagonally, but unnaturally, unevenly upon it, bright here, murky there. Set out on its creased surface a thimble, a needle and some fragments of cloth. No more than that. But the lighting, the enlarged scale and long shadows create a sense of menace. The small swatch of material to the left, pieced by a needle, lacks the pull of gravity. Yet it is the larger fragment of white cloth that draws the eye, its edges rough with frayed cotton. Cloth on cloth. It resembles the open pages of a book, pristine, save for capitalized words inscribed upon it. And three dark stains.

The blood-stained handkerchief belongs of course to the tale of *The Goose Girl*. Recounted by the Brothers Grimm, it tells of a young princess betrothed to a prince in a far away land. When the time comes for her to leave – yes it was her mother that offered the three drops of blood – she is accompanied on

Figure 11.2 Verdi Yahooda *Cloth with Three Drops of Blood*, 1989. Silver Gelatin print, calico, pins. 182 × 152 cm.

her journey by her maid. Each has a horse, but Falada, the princess's horse, can talk. Twice on the journey the princess stops and bids her maid get her some water, but the maid refuses. As she bends over a stream to drink, the drops of blood witnessing the scene speak out, 'If this your mother knew, her heart would break in two.' It is this that is inscribed in the blood-stained cloth in Yahooda's work.

Predictably, the princess loses the handkerchief along the way, and with it her power and strength. The maid forces her to exchange horses and clothes, making her promise to tell no one at the royal court. On arrival the maid is hailed as the prospective bride, and the princess given the task of looking after the king's geese. As a further precaution, the maid ensures that Falada is slaughtered. The princess manages to procure his head and have it nailed up on a dark gateway that she passes each day with the geese. And as she goes through, Falada sighs, just like the drops of blood, 'If this your mother knew, her heart would break in two.' The princess keeps her promise not to tell, the imposter is found out and punished, and as we come to expect in such tales, all ends well.

It was while working on the piece that was to become *Cloth with Three Drops of Blood* that Yahooda came across the work of psychologist Bruno Bettelheim, and his analysis of fairy tales. Bettelheim argues that they help the children's development and inner growth: 'This growth begins with the resistance against the parents and fear of growing up, and ends when youth has truly found itself, achieving psychological independence and moral maturity' (1976/1988: 12). Their purpose, he suggests, can be likened to that of Freudian psychoanalysis in 'that only by struggling courageously against what seems like overwhelming odds can man succeed in wringing meaning out of his existence' (p. 8). Through simplification they lay out existential dilemmas, and offer role models that children may identify with; and because of this identification 'the child imagines that he suffers with the hero and his trials and tribulations, and triumphs with him as virtuous and victorious' (p. 9).

Crucially, they are 'future orientated' – it is only by going out into the world that the fairy-tale hero or heroine finds themselves, and in doing so finds others with whom they can live 'happily ever after' – by which he means never again having to experience separation anxiety. Bettelheim cites *The Goose Girl* as presenting this process of achieving autonomy.[7] The three drops of blood are also, of course, symbolic of her impending marriage and sexual maturity: of the knowledge of menstruation and fertility. As he points out, these represents a special bond, woman to woman, between mother and daughter. He also suggests that losing the protective cloth was something of a Freudian slip, avoiding as he puts it 'what she did not wish to be reminded of: the impending loss of her maidenhood' (p. 140). So she delays, and tragedy befalls, she is (temporarily) dethroned, and the magic horse killed. Warren Kinston argues that 'shame seems to belong to a theory of individuation', and that it 'implies that we realize we have the choice, the personal option to act destructively or creatively' (1983: 223). Is this what the tale cautions?

What I find most touching in the story of *The Goose Girl* is the gesture of the mother: the violence she does to her herself in order to try to protect her daughter. Perhaps she knows she is powerless. Knife to skin, her gift is her wound: the maternal/materiality of her own body. Blood, like tears, absorbs into cloth, as a mother absorbs emotions of her child. It is a gesture that needs no words: the stain, an external sign of the pain of separation, for mother as much as child. Perhaps that's why the girl 'accidentally' loses the maternal stains. It bears too heavily. My copy of the tale contains a single image: the head of Falada, nailed to the dark archway, still streaming with blood. The princess stands before him, dressed in her apron and surrounded by geese; head bowed, hand across her eyes. Shame personified. Shame is a reminder: it alerts us to be aware of what our actions might set in motion. Yet is also serves another purpose. The self-consciousness that accompanies feelings of shame maintains a sense of a separate identity protecting against the loss of boundaries. Losing the talisman, the stained cloth, was perhaps inevitable; autonomy needs to be achieved on our own terms.

But what of that other cloth that serves as both stage and backdrop in Yahooda's own *Cloth with Three Drops of Blood*? In middle-class Victorian homes furniture was draped and windows excessively curtained as if they were naked and in need of clothing.[8] Fabrics gave privacy, comfort, quiet. Here in Yahooda's dark interior little comfort is offered. The textured cloth that drapes across the image becomes undone, a fleshy surface, as skin beneath a lens.

Edges, no. 5

A fragment of a tablecloth has been washed and starched over and again, its border soft and frayed, with what remains of its owner's monogram a faint yellow mark. At a distance, this otherwise white and pristine cloth looks to be stained, a deep red bleed permeating its upper edge; it becomes bandage or menstrual cloth. On closer inspection this liquid flow reveals itself as long strands of auburn hair held in place by fine red thread. Its tiny stitches move along the edge, responding to the pattern of wear. Where it is most damaged, it is covered by the hair and stitched thread; where it is more finely worn the stitch responds, and also becomes fine. The wear, a result of years of handling, folding, of proximity to the body, speaks of time passing. Cloth registers, its surface a physical memory and record of the tactility of use.[9]

This haunting, yet beautiful piece, entitled *Edges, no. 5* (2001) is one of 11 works by Anne Wilson, from her *Edges* series, made by tearing the worn edges from found bed sheets and table linens (Figure 11.3; Figure 11.4 in colour plate section). These long horizontal strips, just four or five inches wide, are like physical drawings. They are the tail end of a large body of work in which Wilson explored themes of time, loss, gender, sexuality and the private and social rituals that organize our lives. Hair became her signature, stitched strand by strand to cover the torn, stained and worn areas of used cloth, sometimes covering whole stretches, exaggerating its already abject surface. Stain on stain you might say.

Figure 11.3 Anne Wilson *Edges, no. 5*, 2001. Cloth, hair, thread. 10.25 × 75.75 inches. Copyright 2001 Anne Wilson. Collection David and Bobbye Goldburg. Photo by George Bouret. Anne Wilson's artwork is represented by Rhona Hoffman Gallery, Chicago and Paul Kotula Projects, Detroit.

The tension in Wilson's work has something of the clean and proper body as it fights to maintain its boundaries against its own raw materiality, a matter of life and death. Although shame can be positive, self-evaluative, self-reflexive, it can also be misused as a tactic for punishment. In these and other works of Wilson's, linen, bleached and starched, comes to stand for repressive bourgeois propriety – the formality, decorum, and table manners of polite society, the well-kept home – and its tacit schema of permission, prohibition and proper social relations. Bed sheets, pillow cases, napkins, table linens, the found materials with which she works, reference the need to conceal the messy stuff of life as it is lived. They are the stuff of surface.

If the stain is careless, Wilson takes meticulous care to expose it, and hair, with its abject relation to the body becomes the means, 'a violation of the formal dining room by bodily function and animal instinct' (Yapelli 2002: 13). Detached from the body, hair not only loses its seduction, but also its identity. Out of place, it becomes dirt. As Mary Douglas points out in *Purity and Danger* (1966/1993), her classic analysis of the concepts of pollution and taboo, category is all:

> Shoes are not dirty in themselves, but it is dirty to place them on the dining-table; food is not dirty in itself, but it is dirty to leave cooking utensils in the bedroom, or food bespattered on clothing; similarly . . . upstairs things downstairs; under-clothing appearing where over-clothing should be, and so on. In short, our pollution behaviour is the reaction which condemns any object or idea likely to confuse or contradict cherished classifications.
>
> (Douglas 1996: 35–36)

Classification orders our world, tries to make sense of it. In this, certain things, objects, people are assigned as positive, while others rejected to become negative. What these are will vary from culture to culture, but Douglas perceives a fundamental dichotomy in the social structuring of different societies: order as purity, and disorder as pollution. That which is rejected has no place, is *out of place*; a threat to order, it must be brushed away.

In considering this process, Douglas identifies two stages in our attitude to the rejected 'bits and pieces'. They can be rendered 'harmless' through pulverizing, dissolving and rotting away, so that all identity is gone. However, before that, and while they are still *recognisably* out of place, they remain a threat because:

> at this stage they have some identity: they can be seen to be unwanted bits of whatever it was they came from, hair or food or wrappings. This is the stage at which they are dangerous; their half-identity still clings to them.
>
> (Douglas 1966/1993: 160)

This 'half-identity' is the indeterminacy of the stain, of the abject, of the margin – not quite this, but not quite that; disturbing the need for classification and precise meaning: 'All margins are dangerous,' warns Douglas, and '. . . any structure of ideas is vulnerable at its margins' (p. 121). Our attitudes to our bodies and emotions fuse with social experience. The edge is where body meets world. Fine hair covers all but our soles and palms, protecting vulnerable boundaries, proliferating where we are most fragile. In an earlier series of work, *Mendings*, Wilson took fragments of collars and cuffs, the very edge of garments, and 'worried' their damaged surfaces, tears and holes, making reference to bodily orifices; while in *Edges, No. 5*, the hair remains, literally, at the edge.

Yet Douglas also argues that there is energy at the margins (p. 114), and in the as-yet-unstructured. It is this double-coded energy that Wilson harnesses, embracing the contradiction. The linen cloths in her work hold out for cleanliness and purity, the intrusion of hair improper, unsettling, like the unruly and disruptive force of the semiotic. In systems of purity and pollution, one sex is usually seen to be endangered by the other through contact and bodily fluids. More often it is women whose bodies take on the burden of shame through the 'difference' of menstruation and childbirth. Rather than hiding this shame, or indeed the shame induced by any repressive sanction on behaviour, *Edges, no. 5* unashamedly draws attention to it: a rebellious act of exposure, and celebration of the historically and culturally unwanted.

It is ironic that the white cube, the modernist gallery, has become the condition for the presentation of art. Its white walls, scrubbed wooden floors and sparce interior give it the appearance of a clinic. Yet, art can be a form of disturbance, exploring what lies at the margins, falls through the gaps, disturbs equilibrium (Kingston 1994). *Perpetua, Cloth with Three Drops of Blood* and *Edges, no. 5* focus on detail, the domestic, the ordinary. What could be more inconsequential than a small fragment of stained cloth? But the stain is multivalent, and in this lies its power. It is a memory trace of the abjects that must be expelled to maintain the clean and proper body, yet are essential to its material existence, to life itself; and of the plenitude and loss that accompany the emergence of the self. If cloth is surface, boundary, edge, where body meets world, then the stain is a reminder of the fragile liminality of that boundary, a site where meaning becomes, yet also dissolves. Embarrassing, shaming, abject. Systems of order and purity may try to expel it, but such attempts are in vain. For as Douglas cautions: 'that which is negated is not thereby removed. The rest of life, which does not tidily fit the accepted categories, is still there and demands attention' (1966/1993: 163).

Notes

1 Eagleton (1993: 164) points out that 'infant' means speechless.
2 Kristeva, cited in F. Carson, 'Feminism and the body', in S. Gamble, *The Icon Critical Dictionary of Feminism and Postmodernism* (Cambridge: Icon Books, 1999: 123).
3 S. Hubbard, 'Maria Chevska', in *Chora*, exhibition catalogue, London, Underwood St. Gallery; Bath, Hotbath Gallery; Bracknell, South Hill Park; Kendal, Abbot Hall, 1999, p. 14. Bizarrely, as Kuryluk points out, menstrual blood and the blood of Christ are often conflated in the writings of Medieval male mystics describing dreams of wounds, stigmata and blood, some even believing themselves to be 'menstruating' in imitation of the feminine and maternal physicality of Christ, see Kuryluk (1991: 133).
4 M. Archer (1994) 'Perpetua', in *Maria Chevska, Perpetua*, Nottingham: Angel Row Gallery (unpaginated).
5 J. Kristeva (1986) '*Revolution in Poetic Language*', in T. Moi (ed.) *The Kristeva Reader*, Oxford: Blackwell. The semiotic in Kristeva is distinct from what we have come to call semiotics, that is the study of signs.
6 Oliver (1993: 10) argues that the semiotic is not strictly opposed to the symbolic. Given that we cannot talk about anything outside of the symbolic, the semiotic is a part of it; or rather that it moves both inside and beyond the symbolic.
7 He also sees it as a cautionary tale against a pretender (the maid) usurping the place of the hero, (the princess), offering an Oedipal reading: that it is better to accept one's place as a child, than to take the place of a parent.
8 Doy (2002: 11) draws this from the work of Penny Sparke.
9 This discussion on Wilson's work draws on email correspondence with the artist, August 2006.

References

Anne Wilson, Portfolio Collection (exhibition catalogue), Winchester: Telos Art Publishing, 2001.
Anne Wilson: Unfoldings (exhibition catalogue), Boston: Massachusetts College of Art, 2002.
Bettelheim, B. (1976/1988) *The Uses of Enchantment: The Meaning and Importance of Fairy Tales*, Harmondsworth: Penguin.
Chora (exhibition catalogue), London: Underwood Street Gallery; Bath: Hotbath Gallery; Bracknell: South Hill Park; Kendal: Abbot Hall, 1999.
Didi-Huberman, G. (1984) 'The index of the absent wound (monograph on a stain)', *October* 29: 63–81.
Douglas, M. (1966/1993) *Purity and Danger: An Analysis of the Concepts of Pollution and Taboo*, London and New York: Routledge.
Doy, G. (2002) *Drapery: Classicism and Barbarism in Visual Culture*, London and New York: I.B. Tauris.
Eagleton, T. (1993) *Literary Theory*, Oxford and Cambridge, MA: Blackwell.
Gamble, S. (1999) *The Icon Critical Dictionary of Feminism and Postmodernism*, Cambridge: Icon Books.
Kingston, A. (1994) 'Art and dirt', in *Hygiene: Writers and Artists Come Clean and Talk Dirty*, Birmingham: Ikon Gallery.

Kinston, W. (1983) 'A theoretical context for shame', *International Journal of Psycho-Analysis*, 64: 213–226.

Kristeva, J. (1982) *Powers of Horror, An Essay on Abjection*, trans. L. S. Roudiez, New York: Columbia University Press.

—— (1989) *Black Sun, Depression and Melancholia*, trans. L. S. Roudiez, New York: Columbia University Press.

Kuryluk, E. (1991) *Veronica and her Cloth: History, Symbolism, and Structure of a 'True' Image*, Cambridge, MA and Oxford: Blackwell.

Maria Chevska, Perpetua (exhibition catalogue), Nottingham: Angel Row Gallery, 1994.

Moi, T. (ed.) (1986) *The Kristeva Reader*, Oxford: Blackwell.

Oliver, K. (1993) *Reading Kristeva: Unveiling the Double-Bind*, Bloomington and Indiana: Indiana University Press.

Porges, T. (2001) 'Postminimal and after', in A. Wilson *Portfolio Collection*, Winchester: Telos Art Publishing, p. 22.

Probyn, E. (2005) *Blush, Faces of Shame*, Minnesota and London: University of Minnesota Press.

Yapelli, T. (2002) 'Over time', in *Anne Wilson: Unfoldings* (exhibition catalogue), Boston: Massachusetts College of Art.

Chapter 12

Shame, disgust and the historiography of war

Suzannah Biernoff

This chapter approaches the phenomenology of disgust and shame obliquely, through a particular historiographical aversion in the literature on the Great War. Facial disfigurement is rarely discussed outside the objective aims and contexts of clinical medicine and medical history.[1] I would like to take a more speculative approach to this historical subject by drawing material from contemporary journalistic representations of facial injury, personal reflections and photographic archives. One of the first things to be said about these very different sources is that they helped to render their subject invisible to all but a professional minority – to the extent that *not looking* defines the public response to facial disfigurement in wartime Britain. This paradoxical invisibility takes multiple forms: the absence of mirrors on facial wards; the physical and psychological isolation of patients with severe facial injuries; the eventual self-censorship afforded by developments in prosthetic 'masks'; and an unofficial censorship of facially disfigured veterans in the British press and propaganda (Figure 12.1). Unlike amputees, these men were never celebrated as wounded heroes. The wounded face, I will argue, is not equivalent to the wounded body; it presents the trauma of mechanized warfare as a potentially contaminating – and shameful – loss of identity and humanity.

The historian Joanna Bourke claims that the absent limbs of amputees 'came to exert a special patriotic power' during the Great War (1996: 59). Those who were designated 'sick' (physically or mentally) had to live with suspicions of malingering. The 'wounded', however, bore a visible sign of their sacrifice and valour, and the accoutrements of death and injury took on a talismanic quality, like the relics of a saint. This aura can be detected not only in the personal effects of the deceased, but in the prosthetic legs and arms manufactured for amputees, which are presented as objects of fascination and beauty in the illustrated press.[2] This visible 'transfiguration' of the maimed male body was achieved, in part, through a Christianized iconography of redemptive sacrifice, enabling the wounded male body – even, in some circumstances, the recently dead body – to be imbued with heroic as well as tragic-erotic connotations (Figure 12.2). This tradition does not so much *overcome* the disgust and shame of corporeal violation as frame and

Figure 12.1 Photograph by Horace Nicholls of a patient examining the mould of his face. Imperial War Museum, Q.30.455. Reproduced by permission of the Trustees of the Imperial War Museum.

sublimate it in the interests of personal salvation or patriotic duty. You will find positively angelic faces on wounded or dying soldiers; the clearest complexions fairly glowing with moral incorruptibility. The face signifies a transcendent wholeness that compensates for the loss of limb or life. Even in death – at least, death imagined as peaceful repose – the face denotes the incorporeal self: inside or outside the mortal body, but emphatically other than the body.

Facial mutilation was evidently harder to reconcile with the rhetoric of patriotic self-sacrifice and heroism reserved for those with other kinds of injury. In one of the few discussions of the patients' experience of facial surgery, Andrew Bamji remarks that the 'horror of facial disfigurement is universal and enduring . . .' (1996: 500). As Curator of the Gillies Archive at Queen Mary's Hospital in Sidcup, Bamji is more familiar than most with the visual evidence of facial injury in World War I. The images in some 2500 case files – documenting the corporeal effects of the 'war of munitions' on British soldiers and corresponding developments in facial reconstructive surgery – are, he admits, 'both disturbing and fascinating; suddenly one is transported from the calm realms of death to the indignity of disfigurement' (1996: 495–496). The fantasy of a calm death underscores the anxiety surrounding this kind of injury. Death lends itself to narrative and iconographic sublimation.

THE MESSAGE FROM THE TRENCHES.

Drawn for this Magazine by H. H. FLERE.

Figure 12.2 A 'Message from the Trenches' from *Young England*, a popular boys' paper published by the Sunday School Union, 1916. Reproduced with thanks to Michael Paris.

Disfigurement – *facial* disfigurement – is altogether more difficult to romanticize. 'Indignity' in its various guises will be a recurring undercurrent in this chapter, as I attempt to make sense of the abiding horror of disfigurement as well as its particular cultural and historical associations in Britain during the Great War. To this end, we will concentrate here on the psychological terrain of disfigurement, with particular attention to disgust and shame – socializing emotions that interact with and modulate our sense of self.

I

The most detailed popular account of facial injury and its treatment is to be found in Ward Muir's *The Happy Hospital*, which was published in 1918. A corporal in the Royal Army Medical Corps, Muir had some success as a novelist[3] and contributor to periodicals including *The Spectator, The Nineteenth Century, Country Life, The Daily News* and *The New Statesman.* He also edited 'Happy-Though Wounded', a fundraising publication with contributions from staff and patients at the Third London General Hospital in Wandsworth, drawn from the hospital's *Gazette. The Happy Hospital* relates Muir's experiences as a medical orderly at the Third London General Hospital. The facial ward lends an ironic, and ultimately tragic note to Muir's otherwise 'Happy Hospital'. It is 'something of an ordeal', he writes:

> to talk to a lad who, six months ago, was probably a wholesome and pleasing specimen of English youth, and is now a gargoyle, and a broken gargoyle at that, – the only decent features remaining being perhaps one eye, one ear, and a shock of boyish hair. . . . You know very well that he has examined himself in a mirror. That one eye of his has contemplated the mangled mess which is his face – all the more hopeless because 'healed'. He has seen himself without a nose. Skilled skin-grafting has reconstructed a something which owns two small orifices that are his nostrils; but the something is emphatically not a nose. He is aware of just what he looks like: therefore you feel intensely that he is aware that you are aware, and that some unguarded glance of yours may cause him hurt. This, then, is the patient at whom you are afraid to gaze unflinchingly: not afraid for yourself, but for *him*.
>
> (Muir 1918: 144)

Muir is clearly disturbed by what he encounters on the facial ward (a sight his readers can only imagine), but at the same time he is fascinated, imagining how this man or that must see himself, how it must feel to be horrified by one's own reflection. Empathy alternates with disgust, an emotional conflict that manifests as visual discomfort. It seems to me that Muir *is* afraid for himself: these patients are different; Muir says he has never experienced such acute embarrassment with another patient, 'however deplorable his state, however humiliating his dependence on my services, until I came into contact with certain wounds of the face' (p. 143). It is not hard to identify with his dilemma – few people would not be haunted by the sight of such appalling injuries, especially as the Third London General was plainly unable to cope with the numbers of facial casualties arriving from the front. John Glubb spent three months at the hospital towards the end of 1917, during which time, he says, 'No doctor ever looked at our wounds or removed the bandages.'

He was finally transferred to the new hospital for facial injuries at Sidcup in Kent, where he was treated by Harold Gillies (Glubb 1978: 193).

Nobody had anticipated the number of facial casualties, or the kind of injuries machine guns and shells could inflict on the human body. Around 5000 servicemen received treatment at Sidcup alone, amounting to over 11,000 operations between 1917 and 1925 (Bamji 1996: 495). The introduction of the steel helmet in 1915 increased a soldier's chances of survival, but exposed his face to shrapnel and shell fragments; while innovations in weapons technology resulted in larger, more complex wounds than those caused by ordinary rifle fire (Bosanquet 1996: 456). At the Cambridge Military Hospital in Aldershot following the Somme offensive of 1 July 1916, 200 extra beds were set aside for facial casualties. Two thousand patients arrived. 'Men without half their faces; men burned and maimed to the condition of animals,' wrote Gillies. 'Day after day, the tragic, grotesque procession disembarked from the hospital ships and made its way towards us' (quoted in Bamji 1996: 495).

Drawing on recent literature on the psychology of emotion (Lewis 2000; Rozin *et al.* 2000) I want to offer a speculative theory of disgust that may begin to elucidate the interaction of this seemingly universal and distinctively human response with the vicissitudes of cultural history. Muir's semantically, emotionally and visually complex reaction to the patients in his care is a good place to start, but it is not the whole story: he only hints at the significance of gender in the visual culture of disfigurement, for the spouse or carer (wife, mother, nurse) as well as the patient. 'Could any woman come near that gargoyle without repugnance?' he asks rhetorically of one of the patients (p. 145). Yet the figures of the saintly wife, the devoted fiancée or attentive (and very attractive) nurse were well-established tabloid fare. An article in the *Sunday Chronicle* (previously published in the *Daily Mail*) describes a wife's first visit to her maimed husband. He has not had the courage to tell her the extent of his injuries, and when she arrives at the hospital, matron takes her aside to prepare her for the worst:

> 'He told you of his wound?'
> 'He said he was hit by shrapnel, ma'am, but not bad.'
> Matron motioned her to sit down, and then, with an infinite pity in her face ... told the little woman before her in a few words what Sergeant Bates in his agony of mind could not write.
> 'So you see, Mrs. Bates,' she ended gently, 'you must be brave when you see him, because – he dreads this meeting – for your sake.'

Ushered to her husband's bed, around which the sister has hastily drawn a screen:

> She took one searching glance as involuntarily he turned his 'good' side to her and then, deliberately choosing the other, she went right up to the

bed, and with a hand on each shoulder kissed him – ever so lightly – on the worst scar of all.

(Sunday Chronicle, June 1918)

Reports like this rely on a shared shudder of revulsion; without it, the wife's gesture would be unremarkable. Disfigurement turns conjugal love into a parable of patriotic devotion, in which the wounds of war are salved – and the horror of war erased – by the reinstatement of domestic bonds. The *Sunday Chronicle* anecdote exploits the stereotypical image of the nurturing, self-sacrificing wife (or mother, or nurse) whose empathic gaze and touch overcome the memory and physical trauma of combat. The gendering of emotions like empathy, pity and sympathy – but also disgust and shame – has received very little attention. This is not an omission that I have set out to rectify here, partly because almost all of my examples assume a male gaze at a male body. As a result, I can only offer a limited and oblique account of the relationship between gender and affect in wartime Britain, while stressing the need for further research.

II

Rozin *et al.* (2000: 649) argue that 'disgust is in many respects the emotion of civilization'. Contrary to Darwin's belief, it is not found in nonhumans (or in feral humans, see Malson 1972), and seems to develop some time between the ages of four and eight, playing a powerful role in children's socialisation (Rozin *et al.* 1986). They distinguish between four levels of disgust: *core disgust* (initially focused on food and oral ingestion, but extending to secondary modes of physical and symbolic incorporation); *animal-nature disgust* (provoked by anything that reminds us of our mortality and animal nature); *interpersonal disgust* (which usually serves to reinforce social hierarchies via notions of contamination); and *moral disgust* (where immoral acts are condemned as 'disgusting'). The aim of Rozin's article is to synthesize developmental and cross-cultural research.[4] The category of core disgust incorporates Darwin's classic formulation in *The Expression of the Emotions in Man and Animals*: disgust 'refers to something revolting, primarily in relation to the sense of taste, as actually perceived or vividly imagined; and secondarily to anything which causes a similar feeling, through the sense of smell, touch and even of eyesight' (1872/1965: 253). What starts out as a defence of the body against real or imagined contamination becomes a defence of the soul (Rozin *et al.* 2000: 637) as disgust 'expands through animal-nature disgust, interpersonal disgust, and moral disgust' (p. 639). While interpersonal and moral disgust vary from culture to culture, comparative studies show very little variation in the elicitors of core disgust and animal-nature disgust.[5] Different foods are disgusting in different cultures, but there seems to be a 'preparedness' (Seligman 1971) to find certain kinds of things disgusting and not others.

Muir's *Happy Hospital* contains two of the most common elicitors of disgust: 'violations of the ideal body "envelope" or exterior form' (Rozin *et al.* 2000: 641) and death – not necessarily in the literal sense that we are confronted with 'living corpses', but because the men Muir describes have *seen* death, anticipated it, hallucinated it, in many cases longed for it; and because the odour of death literally clings to them. Nurse Catherine Black, who was in Gillies' team at Aldershot, recalled that the hardest task of all was 'trying to rekindle the desire to live in men condemned to lie week after week smothered in bandages, unable to talk, unable to taste, unable even to sleep, and all the while knowing themselves to be appallingly disfigured . . .' (quoted in Bamji 1996: 497). With no antibiotics, infection was endemic. The fertile, manure-rich soil of the battlefields on the Western Front harboured an ' "invisible enemy" of microbes' (Bosanquet 1996: 452). John Glubb remembers noticing 'a very evil decaying smell, which I attributed to some foul drains which must be near by, but when my wound was dressed the stench suddenly became so overpowering that I realised that it came from myself . . .' (Glubb 1978: 191). The smell of decay is not innately revolting – small children don't hold their noses – but for Rozin this is the 'prototypical odor of disgust' precisely because it confronts us with our own mortality (2000: 642). Muir does not use the word disgust, but its presence is unmistakable in passages like this:

> Hideous is the only word for these smashed faces: the socket with some twisted, moist slit, with a lash or two adhering feebly, which is all that is traceable of the forfeited eye; the skewed mouth which sometimes – in spite of brilliant dentistry contrivances – results from the loss of a segment of jaw; and, far the worst, the incredibly brutalising effects which are the consequence of wounds in the nose, and which reach a climax of mournful grotesquerie when the nose is missing altogether.
>
> (Muir 1918: 143–144)

Muir's own revulsion is betrayed when he imagines the 'repugnance' with which a woman would view such a 'gargoyle' (p. 145). The gargoyle is a recurrent figure in his account, and calls up a long history of corporeal deviations or 'grotesques', from Pliny's monstrous races, to the hybrid creatures that crouch on the edges of medieval cathedrals and manuscripts; the narrative deformations of Gothic horror, and the grotesquely disfigured and hybridized creations of Max Beckmann or Otto Dix.[6] One would not want to conflate such a disparate range of objects and fantasies, but they do have something in common. Geoffrey Harpham proposes a structural definition of the grotesque, rather than attempting to trace a continuous iconographic or literary tradition. The grotesque, he argues, is 'a species of confusion' (1982: xv). The word itself serves as 'a storage-place for the outcasts of language, entities for which there is no appropriate noun; and this accords

with the sense of formal disorder we perceive in grotesqueries, in which ontological, generic, or logical categories are illegitimately jumbled together'
(1982: xxi). Disgust, too, is a response to perceived transgressions of 'natural'
order; a visceral (and frequently moral, social or political) 'casting out' of
things that we find unbearable precisely because they confuse the categories
by which we live and think. Like Harpham's 'grotesqueries', the things that
disgust us are often characterized by their indeterminacy, and they share this
peculiar quality with the phenomenon of abjection, as described by Julia
Kristeva in *Powers of Horror*. In fact disgust, for Kristeva, is a primary
symptom of abjection. It is not 'lack of cleanliness or health that causes
abjection [and disgust] but what disturbs identity, system, order. What does
not respect borders, positions, rules, the in-between, the ambiguous, the
composite' (1982: 4).

Disgusting things and sensations remind us that we are porous, transient
beings; that our material and psychological boundaries are not the reliable
containers – or fortifications – that we imagine them to be. In *The Anatomy
of Disgust*, William Miller attempts to map the 'domain of the disgusting'
through the following set of oppositions:

> inorganic vs. organic
> plant vs. animal
> human vs. animal
> us vs. them
> me vs. you
> the outside of me vs. the inside of me
> dry vs. wet
> fluid vs. viscid
> firm vs. squishy (compare hard vs. soft and rough vs. silky)
> non-adhering vs. sticky
> still vs. wiggly
> uncurdled vs. curdled
> life vs. death or decay
> health vs. disease
> beauty vs. ugliness
> up vs. down
> right vs. left
> ice-cold/hot vs. clammy/lukewarm
> tight vs. loose
> moderation vs. surfeit
> one vs. many (as in one cockroach vs. ten million)

(Miller 1997: 38)

While this list has an encyclopaedic appeal, its tidiness belies the 'species
of confusion' that Harpham observes in the grotesque, and which I would

suggest is one of the defining features (and motivations) of disgust. Indeed, one could go further and define disgust as a species of contamination, for – unlike the grotesque – the disgusting thing implicates us, threatening the imagined boundaries of the individual body, the social body and indeed the body politic. Harpham notes that grotesques tend to be marked by the 'co-presence of the normative, fully-formed, "high" or ideal, and the abnormal, unformed, degenerate, "low" or material' (1982: 9). Muir's gargoyles are not, in fact, disfigured beyond recognition; their humanity is not completely erased or negated by their injuries. He is haunted by what remains: a 'shock of boyish hair' and a perfectly formed ear become metonyms of youthful, wholesome, English masculinity. It is the inconceivable, illegitimate conjunction of these things that is so grotesque: this is not simply a story of lost or ruined youth; the faces that Muir describes present something akin to vandalism: a defaced ideal. This helps to explain Muir's inability to refer to the patients in his care as 'men': they are at best 'patients', at worst 'gargoyles' or 'victims'. Their reconstructed features fall short of anything resembling a human face: that 'something which owns two small orifices' is 'emphatically not a nose'; in another case (this time a civilian who had undergone reconstructive surgery after the removal of a facial ulcer), the 'before' photograph leaves him speechless. There are 'some things,' he says, 'which, quite literally and in every sense, cannot be described' (1918: 146).

Disgust, as Rozin *et al.* define it, originates in and repeats the processes of socialization: it may feel like a 'gut reaction', but disgust is a cognitively sophisticated means of differentiating (and separating) the familiar from the unfamiliar, the 'safe' from the 'dangerous', self from other, human from animal. There may be levels of metaphorical abstraction, but even 'core disgust' requires enculturation (2000: 646). This observation alone would lead one to expect some historical as well as cultural variation in the articulation of disgust and other uniquely human emotions, like shame, guilt, and pride and embarrassment, which also appear later in childhood (Rozin *et al.* 2000: 647). These are sometimes referred to as 'self-conscious emotions' because they rely on and interact with a notion of self. Disgust seems to be fixated on the disgusting *object* (rather than involving any *self*-reflection), but the self – body, soul or social collective – is constituted, policed and maintained in the act of repulsion or exclusion.[7]

Rozin *et al.* propose a 'course of biological and cultural evolution' by which disgust acquires social and moral dimensions; however, they admit that very little is known about the history of disgust (2000: 650) and the question remains unanswered as to how – through what social, institutional and discursive mechanisms – 'primitive' disgust is metaphorically extended into the social and cultural realms. They have simply mapped cultural difference on to the more familiar and observable axis of developmental psychology. The very notion of cultural 'evolution' is, in other words, entirely speculative. We can, in any case, do without it if we accept the coexistence (in any culture, at any time) of multiple genealogies of disgust – rather than a continuous, linear history in which 'primitive' forms evolve into more sophisticated ones. This certainly seems to be the case with facial injury and disfigurement. Ward Muir's disgust has a 'deep' cultural history (of the monstrous, the abject and grotesque) and also a constellation of more immediate associations to do with masculinity and corporeal containment; militarism; a redemptive ideology of work; and the contradictory images of the disabled soldier as hero and victim.

III

The face is our most visible attribute; a privileged signifier of subjectivity (Figure 12.3). Joanna Bourke notes that 60,500 men suffered head or eye injuries during the war compared to 41,000 who had one or more limbs

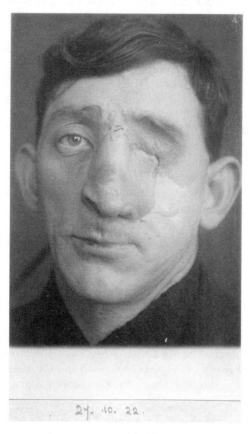

Figure 12.3 Photograph of patient after facial reconstructive surgery. Cholmondley case file, Gillies Archives, Queen Mary's Hospital, Sidcup. Reproduced with permission.

amputated (Bourke 1996: 33). The Ministry of Pensions included 'very severe facial disfigurement' in the list of injuries for which the full pension would be paid (also included in this category were: 'the loss of two or more limbs, loss of an arm and an eye, loss of a leg and an eye, loss of both hands or all fingers and thumbs, loss of both feet, loss of a hand or a foot, total loss of sight, total paralysis, lunacy, wounds or disease resulting in a man being permanently bedridden, wounds to internal organs or head involving total permanent disability' (Ministry of Pensions leaflet, c.1920, in Bourke 1996: 66). As Bourke points out, from 1917 the calculation was made not on the basis of a loss of function or earning capacity, but in relation to a normative concept of masculinity. 'Each part of men's bodies was allocated a moral weighting based on the degree to which it incapacitated a man from "being" a man, rather than "acting" as one' (1996: 65). This distinction is exemplified by facial disfigurement, where disability was defined aesthetically rather than functionally (although in practice severe facial injury usually resulted in loss of function as well).

There are reasons to suspect that facial injuries were both shameful and shaming, but the evidence is behavioural rather than verbal. Whereas disgust, in its most literal form, is a fear of oral contamination, shame is often linked to sight: from Adam and Eve's dawning awareness of their nakedness in the Garden of Eden to Darwin's description of shame as a response to another's (or the Other's) gaze.[8] Faces have received very little attention in discussions of the body and embodiment. Perhaps this is because faces (and heads in their totality) have appeared to speak for themselves, without the need for scholarly interpretation or translation. Bodies, on the other hand, have fascinated many theorists and historians precisely because, in their mute materiality, they have seemed a final frontier; a place of unwritten, unspoken, perhaps even unimagined truths.

When faces are discussed – in relation to portraiture, for example, or physiognomy – the body is usually absent. Portraiture has, until recently, been concerned with the idealization of the individual, while the study of physiognomy was supposed to reveal psychological, racial, sexual and social deviations from an imagined ideal. Both practices rely on the face as a visible index of character. Neither conventional portraiture nor the pseudo-science of physiognomy could accommodate the wartime reality of facial disfigurement, which often rendered the face inscrutable, disrupting its communicative and symbolic functions. The medical archives documenting facial injuries present a kind of anti-portraiture, in which the materiality of the wound eclipses the remaining signifiers of individuality and interiority. For a surgeon like Harold Gillies, the mutilated face was not, of course, illegible; on the contrary, Gillies' case files and wax models (Figure 12.4) suggest the emergence of a new physiognomic lexicon, in which the wounded face presents a kind of autobiography of injury and its surgical repair (or prosthetic concealment). But to someone without this specialist knowledge – even someone

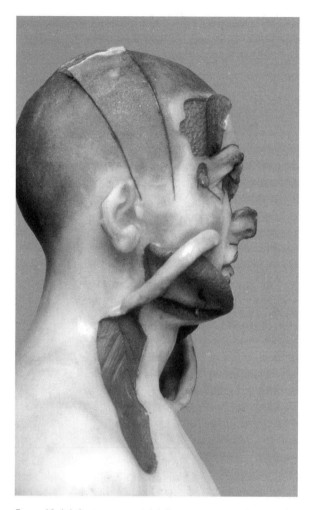

Figure 12.4 Life-size wax model illustrating surgical techniques. From the Gillies Archives, Queen Mary's Hospital, Sidcup. Reproduced with permission.

like Muir familiar with combat injuries – facial mutilation was horrific
(and embarrassing, disgusting or shameful) because it rendered the face
carnal. We think of the face as the least fleshly part of the body: it is associated with visual and auditory perception (the 'higher' senses) as well as
taste (and, by extension, refinement, discrimination, civilization) and of
course communication – speech and facial expression. Facial patients were a
special case because their wounds were symbolic and semantic as well as
physical.

Both traditional portraiture and physiognomy rely on, and help to reinforce, a visual logic according to which an individual's character, intellect and

emotional life can be read from the external appearance of the face. This is by no means a recent idea,[9] but it does have specifically modern permutations. Richard Twine (2002) contends that the 'representationalism' of physiognomy (and the related practice of phrenology, which focused on cranial topography rather than facial features) is indicative of a broader epistemological shift in eighteenth- and nineteenth-century science and culture. The emphasis on observation and visual classification in modern medicine – as in the new disciplines of anthropology, ethnography, criminology and psychiatry – has its literary equivalent in the nineteenth-century novel. Just as doctors were becoming adept at reading the physical body symptomatically, novelists were exploiting the literary – and often comic – potential of physical appearance rather than relying on action as a signifier of character (Shortland 1985: 283–284).

Physiognomy itself went in and out of fashion, and was certainly discredited as a science by the end of the nineteenth century. As a set of pseudo-scientific principles, physiognomy is 'not difficult to critique', says Twine; but 'shaking off its perceptual agenda is more problematic' (2002: 85). This is why physiognomic assumptions have had such an enduring cultural currency, and continue to inform perceptions of race, class and gender today. Twine attributes the popularization of physiognomic and phrenological ideas (and, more importantly, their underlying 'perceptual agenda') to the social uncertainty produced by the industrial revolution and its demographic effects. As people became more mobile and cities more populous, contact with strangers – and with 'difference' in all its guises – became more common; especially with the advent of illustrated papers and other mass media. Physiognomy and other methods of reading the body helped to ameliorate the 'uncomfortable emotional experience of rapid sociocultural change' (Twine 2002: 73). One could make a similar point about the experience of war – particularly the 1914–18 war, with its mass mobilization of women and adolescents on the home front. The speed and extent of sociocultural change during the First World War was unprecedented, as was the civilian population's exposure to the corporeal effects of mechanized warfare: from the mass spectacles of uniformed recruits and the unifying discipline of military drill, to the infinite variability of the mutilated body.

'Representationalism', to use Twine's terminology, took many forms, including the physiognomic differentiation (and dehumanization) of the enemy and, closer to home, the visible transformation of men's bodies into munitions of war. One of the mechanisms – or 'inspection effects'[10] – of the war economy was the classification of recruits into categories according to their suitability for combat (Figure 12.5). Medical inspectors paid particular attention to the shape of men's bodies; their weight, chest measurement and height. While the photographs reproduced here were not intended for the general public – they were published in the *British Parliamentary Papers* – the military language of physical classification became part of popular culture as

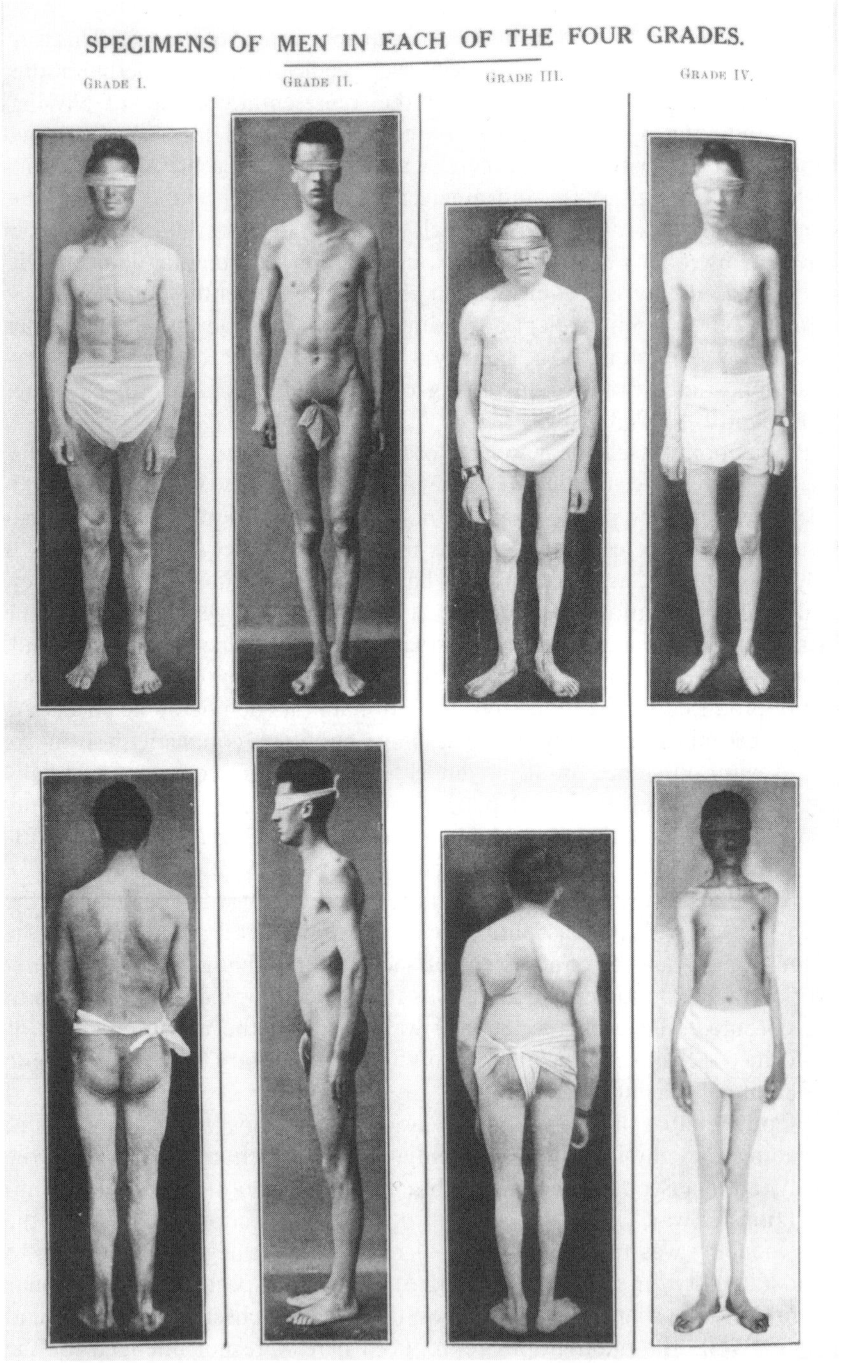

SPECIMENS OF MEN IN EACH OF THE FOUR GRADES.

GRADE I.   GRADE II.   GRADE III.   GRADE IV.

Figure 12.5 'Specimens of Men in each of the Four Grades', *British Parliamentary Papers* 1919 xxvi, 308. By permission of the British Library.

well as political rhetoric (Bourke 1996: 175–176). The state, in this instance, was concerned less with character or intelligence (or with 'manliness' as defined by the Ministry of Pensions) than with the military functionality of the body: Grade Two men should be able to walk six miles 'with ease', while Grade Three men were not considered suitable for combat, and Grade Four men were 'utterly unfit' (Bourke 1996: 172). The men shown here – as the caption makes clear – are no more than specimens illustrating these functional categories; hence the rather bizarre addition of the blindfold – with its connotations of privation and incarceration – and the diaper-like loincloth or fig leaf.

The wounded male body was also subject to professional scrutiny. Harold Gillies' surgical case files contain a wealth of visual material, including extensive photographic documentation, x-rays, and more traditional methods of medical illustration. Photography itself has often been seen as emblematic of (and instrumental to) the perceptual, disciplinary and institutional 'regimes' of western modernity, from new technologies of surveillance to visual (often explicitly physiognomic) stereotypes of national identity, gender, class and race.[11] In the case of medical archives, however, the notion of a unified visual culture (or 'surveillance society') is unhelpful because it so often presumes an undifferentiated gaze on one side, and set of equally visible images or artefacts on the other. The wife visiting her maimed husband in hospital does not 'see' the same thing as the surgeon; and the surgeon's gaze is different again from that of the medical orderly, or the general public, or indeed the historian. The patient might not have seen his wounds at all. One regular hospital visitor, writing in the *Daily Sketch* in June 1918, often takes a little pocket mirror as a gift when visiting the war wounded:

> They say it's 'company' to see their own faces now and again. But there is one particular hospital where the least tactful visitor wouldn't take a mirror, and where it wouldn't be 'company' for the wounded to see their faces, because those faces are so scarred or bandaged that they no longer seem familiar, even to their owners.
>
> ('Unfamiliar Faces,' *Daily Sketch*, June 1918)

The visibility of veterans with facial disfigurement was carefully managed and framed. As far as Muir was concerned, artifice provided the only hope of long-term recovery. His comments on the psychological and social benefits of prosthetic masks are illuminating:

> The mask is so light that it needs little support; with some of the smaller ones, spirit-gum suffices. . . . It is difficult to convey a fair impression of the extraordinary, thousandth-of-an-inch sort of correctitude with which these membrane-like but strong metal masks adhere to the face and cover the grisly gap beneath them. At a slight distance, so harmonious are both the moulding and the tinting, it is impossible to detect the join where the

live skin of cheek or nose leaves off and the imitation complexion of the mask begins. Figure what this means to the patient! Instead of being a gargoyle, ashamed to show himself on the streets, he is almost a normal human being and can go anywhere unafraid – unafraid (a happy release!) of seeing others afraid. Self-respect returns to him. His depression departs.[12]

(Muir 1918: 152)

When the specialist hospital for facial injuries opened in Sidcup in July 1917, the new facility and its patients received considerable media attention. The physical and psychological isolation of the men was a recurring theme, as were the marvels of modern surgery. Most of the articles in the hospital's collection of news cuttings are not illustrated, and those that are rarely show the patients' injuries.[13] Occasionally one sees bandaged men engaged in boyish pursuits of leapfrog or bowls, or making toys in the workshop (hardly a 'manly' activity by contemporary standards). One photograph shows patients feeding chickens on the hospital farm; another carries the caption 'Petting before potting – the men take much interest in the rabbits'. Views of the impressive house and grounds were favoured, either emphasizing the estate's seclusion (Figure 12.6), or using it as a picturesque backdrop for photographs of visiting patrons.

Figure 12.6 View of the estate at Frognal, Queen Mary's Hospital album. From the Gillies Archives, Queen Mary's Hospital, Sidcup. Reproduced with permission.

Shame involves a totalizing attack on the self; it annihilates self-respect. The overwhelming desire is to hide, to disappear, even to die. While published photographs of Queen Mary's Hospital disavow the psychological and physical trauma of facial injury, written accounts are more explicit. Depression seems to have been common (although there was no clinical record of the patients' psychological trauma).[14] Disfigurement is described in the popular press as a 'dreadful abyss';[15] the 'worst loss of all' because it deprives a man of the 'visible proof' of his identity:

> The torturing knowledge of that loss, while it lasts, infects the man mentally. He knows that he can turn on to grieving relatives or to wondering, inquisitive strangers only a more or less repulsive mask where there was once a handsome or welcome face.
>
> (*Manchester Evening Chronicle*, May–June 1918)

Lewis notes that shame is typically accompanied by confusion, which disrupts speech and ongoing behaviour (2000: 629): a clinical observation with methodological implications for anyone interested in the phenomenology of war. Experience is a slippery category for historians at the best of times, but traumatic experience is especially difficult to write about (*as* experience) because of its resistance to memory. As Cathy Caruth points out: 'traumatic recall or reenactment is defined, in part, by the very way that it pushes memory away' (1995: viii). For Caruth, the traumatized 'become themselves the symptom of a history that they cannot entirely possess' (1995: 5). The horror of disfigurement, then, is not going to be easily historicized. Trauma, we could say, is inherently dehistoricizing. The trauma of facial injury and disfigurement was part of the physical but also imaginary legacy of mechanized warfare; subject to surgical and prosthetic intervention, but also mediated by aesthetic and discursive conventions. Moreover, the fear of disfigurement, the 'worst loss of all', was fundamentally a fear of visibility, or perhaps that should be invisibility, for it was precisely that 'loss' of visible identity that provoked a collective aversion of the gaze.

Notes

1 An exception is Sander Gilman's *Making the Body Beautiful: A Cultural History of Aesthetic Surgery*. See in particular Chapter 5, 'Noses at war: fixing shattered faces' (1999: 157–185).

2 Guyatt (2001) provides a detailed account of developments in prosthetic limb technology during and after World War I, while Bourke examines the social, economic and political significance of the mutilated body (1996: 31–75).

3 Muir's pre-war publications include the following titles: *The Amazing Mutes* (1910); *When We Are Rich* (1911); *Cupid's Caterers* (1914).

4 The psychoanalytic literature is treated only briefly. Freud is summarily dismissed along with any intrinsic link between disgust and sexuality.

5 The Hindu caste system, for example, relies on a particularly complex elaboration of interpersonal contagion, often mediated by food, while North Americans show an 'interpersonal aversion to contact with possessions, silverware, clothing, cars, and rooms used by strange or otherwise undesirable persons' (Rozin *et al.* 2000: 643).

6 One could pursue this affinity through discussions of the grotesque (and related concepts) in Camille (1992), Friedman (1981), Mishra (1994) and Lubbock (1999).

7 To quote Kristeva (1982: 2): 'abject and abjection are my safeguards. The primers of my culture.'

8 'The habit, so general with every one who feels ashamed, of turning away, or lowering his eyes, or restlessly moving them from side to side, probably follows from each glance directed towards those present, bringing home the conviction that he is intently regarded; and he endeavours, by not looking at those present, and especially not at their eyes, momentarily to escape from this painful conviction' (Darwin 1872/1965: 328–329)

9 Johann Caspar Lavater's four-volume work, *Essays on Physiognomy* (1775–8), was largely responsible for the resurgence of interest in physiognomy in western Europe. Lavater's sources included Aristotle, Plato and Della Porta's *De Humana Physiongnomia* (1586).

10 Bourke (1996: 171) borrows the term 'inspection effect' from Peacock and Wiseman (1961: xxiv).

11 See for example, Tagg (1988), Crary (1991), Amirault (1993–4), Cartwright (1995) and Hamilton (2001).

12 Journalists' accounts of advances in facial prosthetics were just as awestruck. One article in *The Times* reported that 'magical results are being achieved . . . by the provision of masks perfectly counterfeiting the lost section of the physiognomy' ('Mending the Broken Soldier', 12 August 1916: 9). On the contribution of artists and sculptors to these developments, see Romm and Zacher (1982) and Crellin (2001).

13 The file is held at the London Metropolitan Archives (HO2/QM/Y01/05) and covers the period from January 1917 to December 1930.

14 Depression is mentioned or alluded to in most of the articles on the Queen's Hospital. The *Evening Standard* claims: 'Not every one of the sailors and soldiers who have been severely wounded in the face or jaw at Frognal suffer from acute depression: but most of them do so . . .' ('Music in the Wards . . .', June 1918).

15 'Men shattered in the war', *Evening Standard*, June 1918.

References

Amirault, C. (1993–94) 'Posing the subject of early medical photography', *Discourse* 16 (2): 51–76.

Bamji, A. (1996) 'Facial surgery: The patients experience', in H. Cecil and P. H. Liddle (eds) *Facing Armageddon*, London: Leo Cooper.

Bosanquet, N. (1996) 'Health systems in khaki: The British and American medical experience', in H. Cecil and P. H. Liddle (eds) *Facing Armageddon*, London: Leo Cooper.

Bourke, J. (1996) *Dismembering the Male: Men's Bodies, Britain and the Great War*, London: Reaktion.

Camille, M. (1992) *Image on the Edge: The Margins of Medieval Art*, London: Reaktion.

Cartwright, L. (1995) *Screening the Body: Tracing Medicine's Visual Culture*, Minneapolis: University of Minnesota Press.

Caruth, C. (ed.) (1995) *Trauma: Explorations in Memory*, Baltimore: Johns Hopkins University Press.

Crary, J. (1991) *Techniques of the Observer: On Vision and Modernity in the Nineteenth Century*, Cambridge, MA: MIT Press.

Crellin, S. (2001) 'Hollow men: Francis Derwent Wood's masks and memorials, 1915–1925', *Sculpture Journal* 6: 75–88.

Darwin, C. R. (1872/1965) *The Expression of the Emotions in Man and Animals*, Chicago: University of Chicago Press.

Friedman, J. B. (1981) *The Monstrous Races in Medieval Art and Thought*, Cambridge, MA: Harvard University Press.

Gilman, S. L. (1999) *Making the Body Beautiful: A Cultural History of Aesthetic Surgery*, Princeton: Princeton University Press.

Glubb, J. (1978) *Into Battle: A Soldier's Diary of the Great War*. London: Cassell.

Guyatt, M. (2001) 'Better legs: Artificial limbs for British veterans of the First World War', *Journal of Design History* 14 (4): 307–355.

Hamilton, P. and Hargreaves, R. (2001) *The Beautiful and the Damned: The Creation of Identity in Nineteenth-Century Photography*, London: Lund Humphries in association with The National Portrait Gallery.

Harpham, G. G. (1982) *On the Grotesque: Strategies of Contradiction in Art and Literature*, Princeton, NJ: Princeton University Press.

Kristeva, J. (1982) *Powers of Horror: An Essay on Abjection*, New York: Columbia University Press.

Lewis, M. (2000) 'Self-conscious emotions: Embarrassment, pride, shame, and guilt', in M. Lewis and J. M. Haviland-Jones (eds) *Handbook of Emotions*, London and New York: Guilford Press.

Lubbock, T. (1999) 'Doing damage', *Modern Painters* 12 (1): 58–61.

Paris, M. (2000) *Warrior Nation: Images of War in British Popular Culture, 1850–2000*, London: Reaktion.

Malson, L. (1972) *Wolf Children*, New York: Monthly Review Press.

'Mending the broken soldier', *The Times*, 12 August 1916.

'Men shattered in the war', *Evening Standard*, June 1918, London Metropolitan Archives, HO2/QM/Y01/05.

Miller, W. I. (1997) *The Anatomy of Disgust*, Cambridge, MA: Harvard University Press.

Mishra, V. (1994) *The Gothic Sublime*, New York: SUNY Press.

Muir, W. (1918) *The Happy Hospital*, London: Simpkin, Marshall, Hamilton, Kent.

'Music in the wards . . . fund for Queen's Hospital mounting up', *Evening Standard*, June 1918, London Metropolitan Archives, HO2/QM/Y01/05.

Peacock, A. T. and Wiseman, J. (1961) *The Growth of Public Expenditure in the United Kingdom*, Oxford: Oxford University Press.

Romm, S. and Zacher, J. (1982) 'Anna Colemann Ladd: Maker of masks for the facially mutilated', *Plastic and Reconstructive Surgery* 70: 104–111.

Rozin, P., Fallon, A.E. and Augustoni-Ziskind, M. (1986) 'The child's conception of food: The development of contamination sensitivity to "disgusting" substances', *Developmental Psychology* 21: 1075–1079.

Rozin, P., Haidt, J. and McCauley, C. R. (2000) 'Disgust', in M. Lewis and J. M.

Haviland-Jones (eds) *Handbook of Emotions*, New York and London: Guilford Press.

Seligman, M. E. P. (1971) 'Phobias and preparedness', *Behavior Therapy* 2: 307–320.

Shortland, M. (1985) 'Skin deep: Barthes, Lavater and the legible body', *Economy and Society* 14 (3): 273–312.

'Surgical marvels. Restoring the men who went over the top. A national appeal', *Sunday Chronicle*, June 1918, London Metropolitan Archives, HO2/QM/Y01/05.

Tagg, J. (1988) *The Burden of Representation: Essays on Photographies and Histories*, Amherst: University of Massachusetts Press.

Twine, R. (2002) 'Physiognomy, phrenology and the temporality of the body', *Body and Society* 8 (1): 67–88.

'Unfamiliar faces', *Daily Sketch*, June 1918, London Metropolitan Archives, HO2/QM/Y01/05.

Index

Abel, L. G. G. 75
abjection 3–5, 135, 184–5, 192–200, 204, 213, 224
Abraham, K. 38
Abu Ghraib prison 16
Adam and Eve 30, 130, 132–4, 135, 136–7, 139, 227
adolescent sexual offender: differential diagnosis of 80–2; and treatment/management programmes 87–9
advertisements 12, 30, 194
affects 50, 57–8, 96, 159, 160–1, 163; theory of 16, 93, 165; *see also* emotions
Agenda 153, 154
Ajootian, Aileen 144
Alexander, F. 101
Algeria 168–9
Alloula, Malek 167–8, 169
amputees 217, 226
Amsterdam, B. 26
anal organization 38–41, 50, 80
Anna Freud Centre 36
Anthony, J. 99
anti-Semitism 14, 94, 110, 114, 166
anxiety 26, 44, 54, 78, 110, 113, 161–2, 165–6, 172
apartheid 15, 148, 149–50, 151, 154
Archer, Michael 206
Arlow, J. A. 55
Arnobius 145
Augustine, Saint 12–13
autonomy 10, 25, 26, 32, 138, 152, 209, 210

Baartman, Sarah 152–3
Bal, Mieke 167
Bamji, Andrew 217

Barthes, Roland 130
Baubo 144–7, 152, 154, 157
Becker, J. V. 75
Berger, John 12
Bettelheim, Bruno 6, 209
Black, Catherine 223
Blackledge, Catherine 144–7
blackness, and disgust 186–7, 192, 193
blushing 1, 26, 138–9, 162–3, 204, 205
body ego 38, 41, 102
Bosch, Hieronymous 184
boundaries 3–4, 7, 17, 38, 41, 130, 191, 203–5, 225; loss of 4, 100, 210; *see also* *Edges, no. 5*
Bourke, Joanna 217, 226
Bowlby, John 12
British Parliamentary Papers, classification of bodies of recruits 229–31
Broucek,F. J. 86, 98
Burgner, M. 41
Bursten, R. 85–6, 99

calligraphy 173, 174, 205–6
Cameron, Edwin 149
Canguilhem, G. 162
Cantlie, Audrey 132
Caruth, Cathy 233
castration anxiety 10, 13, 41, 46, 67, 78, 100, 102, 195
Charcot, Jean-Martin 147, 153
Chasseguet-Smirgel, J. 80, 101, 102–3
Chevska, Maria 203, 205–7
child sexual abuse 30, 75–89; and betrayal 87–8; case study 82–7; and development of sexual body image 79–80; differential diagnosis of adolescent offender 80–2; and shame